John Buchan Telfer

The Crimea and Transcaucasia

Vol. I

John Buchan Telfer

The Crimea and Transcaucasia
Vol. I

ISBN/EAN: 9783744754309

Printed in Europe, USA, Canada, Australia, Japan

Cover: Foto ©ninafisch / pixelio.de

More available books at **www.hansebooks.com**

MOUNT ARARAT.

THE CRIMEA AND TRANSCAUCASIA

BEING THE NARRATIVE OF

A JOURNEY IN THE KOUBAN, IN GOURIA,
GEORGIA, ARMENIA, OSSETY, IMERITIA, SWANNETY, AND
MINGRELIA, AND IN THE TAURIC RANGE

BY

COMMANDER J. BUCHAN TELFER, R.N., F.R.G.S.

'Scribitur ad narrandum non ad probandum'—QUINTILIANUS

WITH TWO MAPS AND NUMEROUS ILLUSTRATIONS

IN TWO VOLUMES
VOL. I.

HENRY S. KING & CO., LONDON
1876

TO

MY WIFE

WHO APPEARS IN THESE PAGES AS K.

AND TO WHOM I AM MATERIALLY INDEBTED

IN THE COMPILATION OF THIS WORK

THIS RECORD

OF A PORTION OF OUR WANDERINGS

IS AFFECTIONATELY INSCRIBED

PREFACE.

A THREE YEARS' residence in the South of Russia, afforded the author the opportunity of visiting the Crimea and Transcaucasia upon two occasions. In the compilation of this work, he has condensed his experiences by uniting the two journeys and making of them one tour to extend over a period of ninety-two busy days, the point of departure and of ultimate arrival being the commercial and important city of Odessa, a place that may now be reached from London *via* Cracow and Lemberg in four days and a half.

In his description of places and people, the author confines himself to what passed under his own personal observation, admitting in a few instances only the accounts of eye-witnesses upon whose statements he believes he can implicitly rely; however numerous, therefore, the imperfections of his work, he hopes it may lay claim at least to fidelity of description. In priding himself upon this excellence, he does not by any means pretend to having made any fresh discoveries; indeed, he unhesitatingly professes his anxiety to escape any such severe criticism as that once pronounced by a well-known and uncompromising moralist on the offering of one, young in letters—criticism, which, if his memory serves him well, was in such words as these: 'In diesem Buche findet man viel Wahres und Neues; nur schade dass das Neue nicht wahr und das Wahre nicht neu ist.' The author's narrative is a simple statement of facts, in the relation of which he abstains from adding comments, or offering any decided opinion on the character of the people through whose country he passed, from a feeling that his intercourse with them was of too short duration.

In his account, the author seeks to excite interest in the localities visited, by inserting such brief historical and archæological notices as could be gleaned in a limited space of time, and to demonstrate the feasibility of travelling with safety and tolerable comfort in regions rarely visited, yet second to none in their fascination, in their antiquarian and ethnological attractions, where also the botanist, the geologist, artist, mountaineer, and sportsman will find scope and every incentive in the pursuit of their avocations and pleasure.

The works of Professor Brosset of St. Petersburg, of

Professor Ph. Bruun of Odessa, and of Dubois de Montpéreux, have been more especially largely consulted, and the author takes this opportunity of expressing his gratitude for the facilities afforded him by Professor Bruun, when desiring to consult the books in the University Library at Odessa.

The Emperor of Russia is mentioned more than once in terms to command respect; however absolute his power, his autocracy has a limit, for circumstances render him impotent to carry out many a scheme for reform; and in Alexander II. we see a sovereign whose personal efforts for the advancement of his people are paralysed by an ancient and subtle system.

A knowledge, however slight, of Turkish, Greek, French or German, is a matter of necessity in the Crimea and Transcaucasia (see Appendix XVI. for a vocabulary of Russian terms); and the cost of travelling scarcely exceeds two-thirds of the expenses incurred on the continent of Europe. Luggage should be restricted in quantity, but include an oval bath in lieu of a portmanteau, fitted with a strong lock and stout straps.

The more suitable dress in countries where journeys are performed in carts, on horseback, and on foot, streams having frequently to be forded, is certainly a short jacket and knickerbockers, with top-boots or gaiters, it being advisable to include a black coat in which to make calls on Russian officials, who are most particular in the etiquette of dress; and some kind of uniform cap, if worn out of towns, will ensure almost as much respect and attention as the exhibition of a document that bears the stamp of the black double-headed eagle.

If the idea of a tour in the mountains is entertained, a tent, cushions, saddles, and revolvers are indispensable articles; and a sketch-book, barometer, thermometer, compass, glasses, and such simple medicaments as quinine, seidlitz-powders, chlorodyne, sticking-plaster, lint, &c., are under any circumstances most desirable possessions. A few clasp-knives, scissors, and one or two pocket-revolvers will prove a good investment, because the natives, who disdain to take money, will unhesitatingly accept such trifles in acknowledgment of the services they render, which at times are really invaluable.

Necessaries, such as Liebig's extract, preserved milk, tea, brandy, biscuits, &c., are obtainable in most towns.

The preferable time of year for starting on a tour in the Crimea and Transcaucasia would be April and at the end of August, the latter month and September being objectionable in the lowlands of Transcaucasia, though a most enjoyable season in the mountains. Guides are not easily secured, but Englishmen will meet with every attention and assistance, whether at the hands of Russians, whose hospitality knows no bounds, or of the natives in both territories, also particularly well-disposed towards the English. The author is under a heavy debt of gratitude to many Russian officials, and especially to General Count Levaschoff, General N. N. Karmaline, the Conseiller d'Etat Actuel Talyzyn at Tiflis, General Loris Melikoff, and Colonel Theodore Hrinewsky, whose names he takes the liberty of recording here.

Difficulty having been experienced in the orthography of Russian and native names, the author attempts to imitate their sounds by giving a phonetic value to certain letters, which, with the aid of accentuation, may possibly offer some facility in their correct pronunciation, the almost absolute rule being, that every letter should be aspirated.

The acute and grave accents are employed in polysyllables, the grave accent on the last syllable only, as—Akstafà, basklỳk, zournà ; but when a stress is laid on the final syllable, the last letter of the word is repeated, as—Aiann, doukann (Turk : doúkkèn), Djevatt.

The acute accent on a penultimate syllable, has the effect of shortening the word, as—Feódorovitch, Hassánskaya, pamóshtchnyk.

The apostrophe ' denotes an independent but rather soft breathing of a letter, as—Mysh'orr, which, without the apostrophe would read as My-shorr.

When the letter *o* has combined with it the pronunciation of *a*, the latter letter has been invariably employed:—

>Mountain, spelt in Russian *gorà*, appears as *garà*.
>Water   „   „ *vodà*   „ *vadà*.

a, broad, as in Italian—*amava*.
c, usually hard—*Cossack, Crim, Ctenous*.
ch is employed in well-known words, such as *Chersonesus, Chosroes*.
e, broad, as in Italian—*mentre*.
g, usually hard, if the first letter of a word—*Goudaour, Gourzouff*; otherwise it assimilates *j*, in French—*Japon, jardin*.
gh, guttural, the sound of *h* completing that of *g*.
i, like the English *e*, a special stress however being on the letter.
j, as in French—*Japon, jardin*.
k, hard, as in—*king*.
kh, guttural, the sound of *h* completing that of *k*.
o, as in Italian—*coltello, omaggio*.
ou, as *u* in Italian—*futuro, muro*.
tch, like *ch* in—*charter*.
u, as in English—*mute*.
w, is adopted as the last sound of the Georgian *v*.
y, like *e* in English, and sometimes *y*—*me, pity, easy*.

All dates having reference to the Russians are according to the Julian Calendar; by adding twelve days, the date in the Gregorian Calendar is obtained.

CONTENTS
OF
THE FIRST VOLUME.

CHAPTER I.
FIRST AND SECOND DAY.

Nearing the Russian shores—Loss of the 'Tiger'—As viewed by the Russians—Odessa—Its foundation—Public buildings—Destruction of the batteries in 1854—The Virgin of Kásparoff—A miracle in 1872—The Prison—Jewish influence—Obsequies of the dead—The sign of the Cross—Departure for the Crimea . . . . PAGE 1

CHAPTER II.
THIRD DAY.

Eskyforos Lighthouse—The British fleet—Saky Salt-lakes—Post-horses—The *perecledudya*—Eupatoria—Its history—Cape Chersonese—Sevastópol and the fortifications—The Tchórnaya-retchka—St. Clement's monastery—Fortress of Calamita—Inkerman—The field of battle—The Sapouun ridge—British head-quarters—Cathcart's hill 16

CHAPTER III.
FOURTH DAY.

Monastery of St. George—Miss Nightingale—The Criumetopon—The Tauri—The Chersonese—A Black Sea fog—Allied camps—Balaclava—Ancient history—The Greek battalion Ulysses—British occupation—Genoese castle—The Sutherland hillock—Scarlett's brigade—Lord Cardigan's cavalry charge . . 28

CHAPTER IV.
FIFTH DAY.

The Malakoff Redan—French cemetery—The ancient Chersonese—The defence of Diophantes—Ctenous—Free institutions of the Chersonians—Their wars

Treachery of the Bosporians—Ingratitude of the Chersonians—Vladimir the Grand Prince—His conversion—Decadence of Chersonesus—Its destruction—Ruins of the city—Christian churches—The Alma . . . . . . PAGE 42

CHAPTER V.

SIXTH DAY.

Departure from Sevastopol—Valley of Baidar—The betrothed Tatars—A Tatar cottage—The Pass of Phoros—The Chaos—Aloupka—The late Prince Woronzoff—'Trois femmes célèbres'—Dolmens—Cyclopean remains—Imperial residences—The Bay of Yalta—Gourzouff—Ayou-dagh—Lambad—Aloushta—The ancient Chabum—Athenaon 56

CHAPTER VI.

SEVENTH DAY.

Arrival at Theodosia—Earliest history—The Genoese—The Turks—Our passengers—The Karavy rocks—Ancient Kimmericum—Grecian colonies—Pavlovsky fortress—Port of Kertch—Panticapæum—Kingdom of the Pontus; of the Bosphorus—The Alans—Huns—Goths—Kyertcheff—The Museum—Mount Mithridates—Catacombs—The Bashlȳk—Excavations—Scythian burial 71

CHAPTER VII.

EIGHTH AND NINTH DAY.

Yeny-Kalch—Tzarsky-kourgan—Mud volcanoes—Byzantine church—Antiquities—Embarkation for Taman—Cimmeria—The Bosphorus—The Cymri—Tmoutorakan—Mstislaff—Matracha—Taman—Ancient remains—Sennaya 87

CHAPTER VIII.

TENTH DAY.

Jewish tombstones—The Khozars—Their conversion—Their disappearance—Phanagoria—Its Necropolis—The Corocondamitis—Exploration of Tumuli—The 'Great Twins' Tumuli—Their antiquity 97

CHAPTER IX.

ELEVENTH AND TWELFTH DAY.

Ak-tanysh-liman—Tytorovko—Black Sea Cossacks—The sect of the Shalapoutts—River Kouban—Its navigation—Commerce—Michelthal—The farmer's curse—Anapa—Ancient inhabitants—Prince Mentchikoff—Raïeffsky—Saints and Sinners 105

CHAPTER X.

THIRTEENTH AND FOURTEENTH DAY.

The sect of the Douhobortsy—Their doctrines—Sacraments—Sanctity of churches—Persecution and exile—Morality—Arrival at Novorossisk—A market day—The inhabitants—Ancient localities—The ship 'Vixen' . . . . PAGE 112

CHAPTER XI.

FIFTEENTH AND SIXTEENTH DAY.

Departure from Novorossisk—Ghelendjyk—River Pshad—Dolmens and barrows—Touapse—Camara and Katcherma—The coast of Abhase—Pytzounda—Soukhoum Kaleh—Its prospects—The *Eucalyptus globulus*—Climate—Dioscurias and Sevastopolis—Superb vegetation—Elbrouz—Grotto of Gounasky . . . 117

CHAPTER XII.

SEVENTEENTH AND EIGHTEENTH DAY.

Arrival at Poti—The great mountain range—The river Rion—Lake Paleostom—The Phasis—Ancient and modern fortresses—A breakfast party—Preparation for Gouria—Journey along the coast—Noblemen Cossacks—Evil practices—Swampy country—Nicolaya—Russo-Turkish frontier—Gouria labourers—The ancient Petra—Arrival at Ozourghety—Sovereignty of Gouria—Population—Costume—The (Prince) Gouriel—Monastery of Tchemokmedy—Travelling in the Caucasus—Coinage . . . 125

CHAPTER XIII.

NINETEENTH DAY.

Early departure—The fair of Gouria—The *Diospyrus lotus*—Women of Gouria—The wine country—Fair at Orpyry—Railway at Samtredy—Pass of Byelagory—Numerous ruined churches—Their supposed origin—The Poti-Tiflis railroad—Souram—King Vakhtang—Arrival at Tiflis 138

CHAPTER XIV.

TWENTIETH DAY.

Foundation of Tiflis—Population—Climate—River Kour—Its fish—Water supply—Public buildings—Monastery of St. David—Gryboiedoff—His popularity—Fortifications at Tiflis—Botanic Gardens—Cemeteries—An exciting scene—The bazaars—Character of Georgians—A ball—Georgian ladies—National dance . . . 143

CHAPTER XV.

TWENTY-FIRST DAY.

Reception by the Grand Duke Michael—Poor petitioners—The Grand Duchess Olga—Persian bazaars—The Bourka—The Great Prison Nationalities of the inmates—Cathedral of Zion - St. Nina's Cross—Catholicos of Georgia The Georgian and Russian Churches The Exarch—Prince Tzytzyanoff—A miraculous image—Sacred edifices—Nuns of St. Stephen—Evening concert—Purification . . PAGE 157

CHAPTER XVI.

TWENTY-SECOND DAY.

A merry officer—The Bagration-Moukhranskys—A Georgian tradition—Town of Gori—Its defences—Churches—Clubs—A native saddle—Rock of Ouplytz-tzykhè—Excavated chambers and crypts—Their distribution—Origin—Crypts at Vardagh—Royal sepulchres—Arrival at M'zhett 166

CHAPTER XVII.

TWENTY-THIRD DAY.

An Imperial hand-basin—Russian Ablutions—Mtzkhetha, the capital of Karthly—Kings of ancient Georgia—Georgian alphabets—Conversion of the Karthlosides—The Cathedral at M'zhett—Relics and miracles—Tombs of Kings—Annexation of Georgia to Russia—Chapel of St. Nina—Disturbed graves—Lermontoff the poet—The Iron Castle—The Orbeliani family—Presbyter John 175

CHAPTER XVIII.

TWENTY-FOURTH AND TWENTY-FIFTH DAY.

Departure for Armenia—Comfortable travelling—Armed shepherds—Droves of camels—Abdoullah—The *Tchapars*—Their organisation and duties—The telegraph—Tatar noble and suite—Supply of horses—Human warrens—Novo Akstafa—Post-stations—Russian soldiers—Delyjam—A heavy supper—The sect of the Malakany—A copper mine—Endurance of camels—The Goktcha lake—Ancient monastery—Armenian mountaineers—Abdoullah again—Feats of horsemanship—Mount Ararat—Obsidian—Arrival at Erivan—Accommodation for travellers 187

CHAPTER XIX.

TWENTY-SIXTH DAY.

Foundation of Erivan—The fortress - Sardar's palace—Mosque—The 'Blue Mosque'—A strange custom—A passion play—The bazaars—Armenian churches—Rites - The Persian quarter—Persian women—Education of Christian children . . . 203

CHAPTER XX.

TWENTY-SEVENTH AND TWENTY-EIGHTH DAY.

Rough road to Ghergarr—Fierce dogs—Reception at the monastery—Its history—The 'holy lance'—The church and rock-cut sanctuaries—Inscriptions—Legend of Rousoukna—Bash-Gharny—Magnificent ruins—Throne of Tiridates—Basalt—Artaxata—Coins and antiquities—Return to Erivan . . . PAGE 210

CHAPTER XXI.

TWENTY-NINTH DAY.

Vision of St. Gregory—Road to Edchmiadzin—Wines of the district—The monastery—Reception by the Patriarch—The library—Printing office—The patriarchal church—Consecration of bishops—The treasury—Relics—Letter to the Saviour—His reply—The three churches—The college—Conversion of Tiridates—A present from the Patriarch 225

CHAPTER XXII.

THIRTIETH AND THIRTY-FIRST DAY.

Excursion to the plains—Church of St. George—Burial in Armenia—Mourning—Poplar plantations—Armenian cottages—Murder—Civic government in the Caucasus—A patient—Monastery of Khorvyrab—Martyrdom of St. Gregory—A wedding procession—Armenian nuptials—Seclusion of Armenian women—Turcoman gipsies—The River Araxes—Aralyk—A Mahomedan colonel—The Kabardines—Ride to Ararat—The Kurds—Arkhoury—St. James, *Myzpynsk*—A piece of the Ark—Ascensions of Mount Ararat—Cossack dances—A pleasant evening 238

CHAPTER XXIII.

THIRTY-SECOND DAY.

Lesser Ararat—The Persian frontier—A break-down—The Araxes—Its supposed ancient course—Return to Erivan—The Armenians—Their good qualities—Characteristics—Population—Religion—Patriotism—Sufferings—Road to Nahitchevan—Cosmetic waters there—Routes to Tiflis—Situation of Ani 253

CHAPTER XXIV.

THIRTY-THIRD TO THIRTY-FIFTH DAY.

The Sardar's summer residence—Yousouf and Mariam—The last of Abdoullah—The Lesghians—Departure from Erivan—*Essdatyn*—Intractable *tchapars*—Insects—The Marie Canals—The Karayass steppe—Arrival at Tiflis—The 'Merchant of Venice'—The Armenians enthusiastic—Defaulters in high places . . . 262

CHAPTER XXV.

THIRTY-SIXTH AND THIRTY-SEVENTH DAY.

Arrangements for crossing the great range—Outskirts of Tiflis—The 'Devil's Knee—First-class post-stations—Time service—A bad night—Ananour—Broad-tailed sheep—Siberian exiles—The Emperor's solicitude—Pasanaour—The Hefsours—The Ph'tchavy Osset villages—M'lety Ascent of the great range—Goudaour—The mountain spirit—Limits of vegetation—Tinted snow—Koby—Crystals and Pyrites—A speculative *storoj*—Kasbeck . . . . PAGE 268

CHAPTER XXVI.

THIRTY-EIGHTH DAY.

Legends of Kasbeck—The Cross—Superstition—The Capra ibex—Osset respect for the dead—The Kysty—Their pagan altar—The river Terek—Pass of Darial—Russian fort—Queen Dary'ya—Dar-i-alan described by authors—Lars—Tribes of the Ossets—Balta—Arrival at Vladykavkaz—Visit to the Governor—The Club—Emancipation of Russian ladies—Bridal Gifts—Inns and private houses—Russian character—District of Ossety—The Ossets—Their history—The Ossets and the Alains . . . 281

LIST OF ILLUSTRATIONS

TO

THE FIRST VOLUME.

*Mount Ararat, from the Window of the Sardar's Chamber, Fortress of Erivan . . . . *Frontispiece*

    PAGE

Jews of Odessa 15

*Castle of Calamita, and Crypt Monastery of St. Clement   27

Arms of the Emperors of Trebizond . . 32

*Genoese Castle, Balaclava . 41

Russian Monk   55

*A Tatar Interior . 58

*Dolmens at Aïtodor   70

Terra-cotta Mask from a Tomb of Panticapæum .   86

Entrance to the Tomb, Tzarsky-Kourgan   96

*Tombstones Disinterred at Sennaya   *to face* 98

*The Perecloodnáya . . . 104

*Armorial Bearing over a Stable-yard Door, Anapa . 111

*Marble Statues Disinterred at Anapa . *to face* 115

*Circassian Cart . . 116

Coin of Dioscurias . . . 124

*Delta of the Kion . 126

*Monastery of Tchemokmedy . 135

Those marked * are from original sketches by the author.

ILLUSTRATIONS TO THE FIRST VOLUME.

	PAGE
*Throne of the Metropolitan, Tchemokmedy. Eighteenth Century	. 137
*Cart of Gouria	. . 142
The Lezghynka (Music of a National Dance) .	to face 154
A Touloun'tchve	. . 156
View of Tiflis .	to face 160
Georgian Female Wearing the Tchadra	. . 165
*Vaulted Chamber, Ouplytz-tzykhé	. . 170
*Rectangular Chamber, Ouplytz-tzykhé	. . 171
*Canopy over the Throne of the Kings of Georgia at Mtzkhetha. Seventeenth Century	. 174
Macrocephalous Skull, M'zhett	. to face 182
*Throne of the Catholicos at Mtzkhetha. Thirteenth Century	. 186
*Shyhylou .	. . 193
*Tchapar Station on the Steppe	. 202
*Persian Woman	. . 209
*The Rousoukna Sanctuary, Keghart	. 216
*Wall Sculptures over Arched Recesses, Keghart	. . 219
*Ornamental Sculpture at Bash-Gharny .	to face 222
Ancient King of Armenia	. . 224
Armenian Monk . .	. 237
*Monastery of Khorvyrab	. . 243
A Musical Party	. 252
Arms of the Christian Kings of Armenia .	. . 261
*The Red Bridge	. 265
Georgian Noble	. . 267
Ananour	to face 271
*A Doukann	. . 280
*Kasbeck from the Post-Station	. 282
Women of Ossety	. . 297

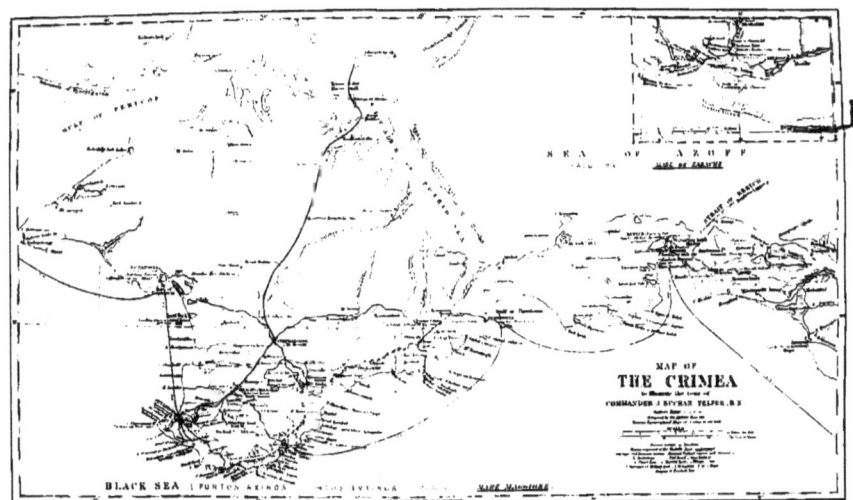

THE
CRIMEA AND TRANSCAUCASIA.

CHAPTER I.

FIRST AND SECOND DAY.

Nearing the Russian shores—Loss of the 'Tiger'—As viewed by the Russians—Odessa—Its foundation—Public buildings—Destruction of the batteries in 1854—The Virgin of Kásparoff—A miracle in 1872—The Prison—Jewish influence—Obsequies of the dead—The sign of the cross—Departure for the Crimea.

THE Russian steamer 'Taurida,' on board of which we embarked at Galatz, was a comfortable vessel, and an agreeable change from the unpleasantly crowded Austrian river-boats in which we performed the voyage from Basiash to Galatz. We entered the Black Sea at 5.20 P.M. the previous evening on passing the Soulinà Lighthouse, and at 2 A.M. the fixed light at Cape Fontana showed that we were approaching the shores of Russia. The coast thence trends to the north, and four or five miles beyond the Cape stands a conspicuous white villa, the property of Mr. Cortazzi a British subject, situated above that part of the shore which was the scene of the disaster that befel H.M.S. 'Tiger,' when that vessel stranded during a dense fog at 150 yards from the cliff on the morning of May 12, 1854, three weeks after the destruction of the batteries at Odessa. Every exertion was being made to save the ship, when a body of Russian infantry and a battery of eight 24-pounders took up a position in front of the villa, and, the weather having partly cleared, kept up a heavy raking fire for the space of nearly an hour, which it was found impossible to return with any effect owing to the extreme elevation required. The enemy's red-hot shot was doing its work, and a shell having disabled four men and carried away Captain Giffard's right leg and wounded him in the left foot, that officer, from a desire to avoid unnecessary loss of life, hoisted the Russian colours in token of surrender.[1]

After the disembarkation of the officers and men as prisoners of war had taken place at about 11 A.M., H.M. ships Niger and Vesuvius appeared off the coast and opened fire; but the Russians ceased hostilities, and the force, now increased to a battalion of infantry with some lancers, besides artillery, numbering in all about 3,000 troops, retired with its captives, and the British ships steamed away to report the catastrophe to the Commander-in-chief.

Aide-de-camp General Count d'Osten Sacken, who was in military command at Odessa in the years 1853-54, has quite lately given his relation of the 'attack on that city' and loss of the 'Tiger,' when endorsing an appeal that was made to the public for contributions in behalf of an asylum for orphans and the infirm, which it was proposed to found near Odessa, 'en commémoration de la prise du Tigre, vapeur Anglais, et des artilleurs victimes de la canonnade de 1854.'[2]

At 6 A.M. we entered the quarantine port of Odessa, and upon landing went through some mild customhouse formalities; but the passport regulations are vexatious, and entail serious inconvenience and loss of time. The passport is a document without which it is

[1] *Personal Narrative of the First Lieutenant of H.M.S. Tiger.* Alfred Royer, Lieut. R.N. 1854.
[2] See Appendix I.

impossible to travel in any part of the empire, it being demanded at most inns and hotels for the information of the police, and it must also be produced to travel on post-roads.

Numerous vehicles, called *droshkys*,[1] with which the city is well supplied, were at the landing quays; they are quaint conveyances, capable of containing three persons comfortably. One horse is harnessed to the shafts, the second with loose traces prances playfully on the off-side, seeming scarcely to be under the control of the *ysvostchyck*[2] in the national *armyak*,[3] who drives rapidly through the streets, and is one of the few men in the empire who, appreciating the value of time, does his work off-hand.

Odessa is situated on a cliff at the end of the steppe in the province of Kherson, at an altitude of 120 feet above the bay, and presents a handsome appearance from the sea. The broad streets, planted with the acacia, look bright and cheerful in spring; and the pavement, laid by British contractors, is fast remedying the inconvenience that was experienced by clouds of dust in dry, and deep mud in wet, weather.[4] The houses make a creditable show, and are built of shell concrete (for bricks are unaccountably dear) obtained from tunnelled quarries that extend beneath the city itself, and have become the resort and refuge of vagrants and malefactors, upon whom the police occasionally make a raid. The shops are good, but the necessaries of life imported from other countries are of inferior quality, especially if they are British, and the high prices are readily accounted for, when tradesmen consider a profit of 30 per cent. 'a bad business.' As a city of considerable commercial

---

[1] A small two-seated vehicle.   [2] The driver of a hired carriage.
[3] A wadded garment reaching to the ankles.
[4] The fearful condition of the streets of Odessa in Poushkin's time, induced the great poet to compare the city to an ink-bottle in winter, and a sand-box in summer.

importance, Odessa has Consular officers of all foreign powers, Great Britain being represented by a Consul-General.

The site of Odessa, where antiquities, chiefly in pottery, have been found at various times, was anciently known as Ysiakonlimen, or Yako,[1] and afterwards by the names of Ginestra, Zinestra, and Langistra, as seen on the Italian charts of the fourteenth and fifteenth centuries. When possessed by the Turks, Hadgy bey was a fortress and the residence of a pasha; it was carried by assault in 1788 by General De Ribas,[2] during the Russo-Turkish war; and the treaty of Jassy, December 29, 1791, secured to Russia the territory from the Boug to the Dniester. The first stone of a new military and commercial port was laid by De Ribas in 1795, by command of the Empress Catherine II., and a twelvemonth later the Turkish name of Hadgy bey was changed to Odessa, in remembrance of the ancient port of Ordesus on the same coast.

When the Duke de Richelieu[3] was appointed governor in 1803, the population of Odessa numbered 9,000, and the revenue amounted to 40,675 roubles assignat;[4] in 1874 the inhabitants amounted to 180,922, and the value of exports and imports reached the sum of 93,153,136 Rs. To the solicitude of the Duke and of his able successors, Count Langeron and the late Prince (then Count) Woronzoff, was due the rise and steady development of the new town. Count Woronzoff was the founder of numerous institutions; he gave an impulse and encouragement to trade and commerce, and as an eminent administrator was successful in checking

---

[1] Arrian, *perip.* and Anon: *perip: Ponti Euxini*, &c., from which works are quoted the ancient names on the Russian sea-board in the Black Sea. The Italian charts consulted, include those of P. Vesconti, 1318; the Portolano Mediceo, 1351; of the Brothers Pizzigani, 1367; A. Bianco, 1436, &c.

[2] See notes to Cantos vii. and xvi. of 'Don Juan.'

[3] See preface and notes to Cantos vi., vii., viii. of 'Don Juan.'

[4] The rouble assignat was of the value of one-fourth the present rouble.

fraud among the servants of the Crown; while at the same time the Countess imparted to the newly-formed society a tone that has declined with her influence. The construction of the harbours commenced in 1794, was only completed in 1850, and the works for their extension and improvement after the designs of Sir Charles Hartley, that are being progressed with at a cost of 600,000*l.*, will afford, when completed, 180 acres of secure anchorage.

Among the public buildings of interest is the Museum, where are Scythian and Greek antiquities from the south of Russia, including the Crimea; objects from the Danubian principalities, Egypt, and Magna Græcia; *babas*, the hewn stone figures from tumuli in the Government of Kharkoff and Yekaterynadar; a numismatic collection of upwards of 20,000 specimens from the old Greek colonies on the Black Sea shores—Tyra, Olbia, Chersonesus, Theodosia, Nymphæum, Panticapæum, Phanagoria, Dioscurias, &c.; coins of the kings of the Bosphorus and of the Pontus, of the Byzantines and of the Genoese; and there are many old MSS. and engravings of interest. A relic of special concern to Englishmen is a flat candlestick that was once the property of John Howard the great philanthropist, who died at Kherson in 1790.

The building opposite to the Museum is the English club-house; and the edifice to the right is the Exchange, in front of which stretches away the boulevard, a fashionable promenade overlooking the busy ports. In the centre of it is a statue in bronze of the Duke de Richelieu; a shot that hit the basement during the attack made on the batteries in 1854 has been fixed where it struck, a memorial of the 'bombardment of Odessa,' as the Russians are pleased to term that insignificant event in the war. The facts were simply as follows.

From a British squadron of four ships that appeared off the

town, soon after the declaration of war, a boat was sent with a flag of truce to bring away H.M.'s Consular officer ; the answer returned being that the British Consul had already vacated his post, the boat left the shore, and when half-way off to the ships, was fired upon from a battery. The British Admiral immediately demanded reparation for this breach of the laws of war, by requiring that all Russian vessels in port should be surrendered, and that neutral vessels should be permitted to quit. The only reply made to these demands being the liberation of the neutral ships, the destruction of the batteries and shipping was decided upon and effected ; a few shot fell wide of their mark into the town, the result of accident due to a sea swell and the long range of 2,000 yards at which the batteries were engaged. The British loss amounted to one killed and four wounded, and no sooner were the batteries silenced and hostilities at an end, than the squadron was reinforced by four other ships.

Within the Nicolaïeffsky sanctuary in the Cathedral, an edifice destitute of architectural pretensions dedicated to the Preobrajényye, 'Transfiguration,' is annually placed for a term and worshipped, a wonder-working image,[1] known as the Virgin of Kásparoff, to whose intervention is attributed the safety of the city, and *the defeat of the hostile squadron* at the bombardment of Odessa. An episode in the career of this miraculous picture illustrates how prince and people amuse themselves in Russia, in this the nineteenth century.

It is the custom for the precious Kásparoffskaya Virgin to be brought in the month of October of every year from Kherson to Odessa, where it is retained until the fourth day of Easter, and then embarked with great pomp upon its return journey to

---

[1] By *images* in Russia should be understood painted pictures, for graven and sculptured figures are not tolerated.

Kherson, the procession that accompanies it from the Cathedral to the quay being attended by the Metropolitan and clergy, and the highest military and civil authorities; a temporary chapel on board the steamer receives the idol, and the national flag is at the same moment hoisted at the main.

Upon a late occasion of its sojourn at Odessa, the Kásparoffskaya was suddenly missed (February 17, 1872) from the Cathedral, to the horror of all true believers. The lower classes, and many not of the lower class, unhesitatingly laid the crime of robbery to the Jews; the agitation of the public was extreme, and the police were exhibiting their wonted zeal in an unremitting search after the lost treasure, when a miracle, great at least as any that had yet been wrought by the blessed image, led to its recovery; for when the Emperor arrived at Odessa from the north, on March 20, 1872, the report reached His Majesty that while preparations were being made for his reception, the Kásparoffskaya was found by a soldier named Smoyansk in a pit within the grounds of the Villa Donati, near the Convent of St. Michael; and the merry peals that went forth from the churches to greet the sovereign, at the same time hailed the advent of the saint. There were great demonstrations of joy, crowds of people parading the streets for days together, making common festival! And the Press explained how the soldier, having received directions from his superior officer, the colonel in command of the quarantine force, to procure loose earth for filling some flower-pots, had been told *by the merest chance in the world* to fetch it from a particular pit in the garden of the villa, and there he found, first to his consternation, then to his infinite joy (when he fainted), the missing image wrapped in a clean white napkin; but, alas! the jewels to the value of 20,000 roubles, that had adorned the virgin, had disappeared. Smoyansk was promised a reward of

500 roubles for finding the saint, of which sum, after long and patient waiting, he received the tenth part. It was afterwards whispered about by some wicked infidels, that when found the napkin was short of one of its corners.

The Roman Catholic church at Odessa will be recognised by the square bell tower. It is related that when the design for this church was submitted to the Emperor Nicholas for his approval, he observed that, if it was carried out, the projected steeple would be loftier than those of the Holy Orthodox churches, and therefore commanded that it should not be constructed.

Near the railway terminus is the City Jail. I wish I could pass over it in silence! But prisons are stern realities, and after visiting a Russian prison one becomes the more firmly convinced that the cellular system possesses important advantages, and whatever Russia may determine upon doing, after the deliberations of the International Congress that met in London in July 1872, she cannot too quickly come to the relief of the unfortunate creatures who fill her prisons, to deliver them from the misery and degradation of their existence. Russia, however, repudiates the oppression practised on prisoners by aimless and unremunerative toil at the treadmill, the crank, shot-drill, and similar torments, for when convicts are employed it is at lucrative hard labour.

The jail stands within and is partly masked by a high quadrangular wall. At the entrance are the governor's quarters, the offices, waiting and guard rooms; near at hand is a dreary underground dungeon, eclipsed in its horrors by the dark cells only, where are confined vagrants and those arrested by the police for being without passports. No boards even are supplied to these unhappy beings, but they have to lie on the bare ground, being detained sometimes for months, until satisfactory information with reference to their antecedents entitles them to be set at liberty. It is calculated that upwards of 100,000 individuals are thus arrested in Russia annually, of which number many are detained frequently for years before their cases are decided.[1]

In each ward on the first floor are confined from fifteen to twenty-five adults of all ages, an arrangement that must tend towards vitiating and brutalising youthful offenders and older delinquents, who meet and pass their days and nights together, with seldom any occupation, as one day so the next, and thus these guilty ones are left to themselves, to exchange thoughts that lead to the exposition of new crimes and fresh wickedness. Nobles, that is to say, men of birth or in the service of the State, are allowed the privilege of separate bed places, bed linen, and a liberal diet, unless under condemnation to hard labour.

Boys under nineteen were in charge of an instructor, who taught them to read and write; they had been convicted chiefly of petty thefts, their countenances betraying brutishness rather than cunning; neglected lads probably, more sinned against than sinning. They are liable to corporal punishment, which, however, is seldom inflicted.

One of the late inmates was a criminal of some celebrity, named Tchoumak, who had effected his escape upon three different occasions from the hard-labour mines in Siberia; he was a septuagenarian, a fine tall man of commanding appearance, who stood convicted of seventeen murders. When asked upon one occasion why he had so cruelly shed such an amount of blood, he piously turned his eyes upwards, and folding his hands together replied: 'I thank God, I have never shed any person's blood; I only strangled people!'

---

[1] When visiting the great prison at Kieff, in September 1874, I was informed by an official that one of the inmates had been awaiting his trial five years.

In another cell was a young soldier under sentence of death for insubordination and attempt to murder a superior; he had appealed to the Emperor, but his appeal was considered a hopeless one. The penalty of death is not included in the civil code in Russia, but when a case arises in which the authorities are of opinion that the accused, being a civilian, should suffer capital punishment, he is arraigned before a military tribunal which is empowered to condemn, and the criminal is shot.

The prison suit consists of a long 'dressing-gown,' trousers and cap, of coarse grey cloth, and a cotton shirt; each man is supplied with a felt blanket, and sleeps on boards raised above the ground. The daily meal, which is washed down with a liberal allowance of *kvass*,[1] is brown bread and *shtchy*,[2] here a greasy compound of insufficiently cooked herbs and barley, the desideratum evidently being quantity and not quality; meat is only given upon occasions of great festivals. The limited use of water everywhere tells its own tale. The sick wards, though deficient in ventilation, were cleanly; but all else—the cells, passages, kitchens, clothing, and persons of the prisoners, indeed everything—was in the highest degree nasty. A fair proportion of the prisoners were Jews, who are kept quite apart from the Christians.

There are 65,000 Jews in the city of Odessa,[3] whose prosperity excites the envy, but scarcely the emulation, of the Russians, who have only themselves to thank for being behind in the race. The influence exerted by the Jewish element, due to its energy and wealth, is enormous, and to Odessa may literally be applied the words of Sidonia, 'that the world is governed by very different per-

---

[1] A fermented liquor made from barley malt, wheat, rye, wheat flour and buckwheat.
[2] An excellent vegetable soup.
[3] The Jewish population in the province of Kherson amounts to 128,000.

sonages to what is imagined by those who are not behind the scenes.' As in Poland, the Jews of Odessa are at once recognised by the *talarr*, a greasy, long-skirted coat, and the *pejés*, short curls that adorn the temples. These Jews are Talmudists, not observers of the law of Moses, but followers of the sainted Juda, the great rabbi who was 'above the kings and princes of the earth'; who conceived the idea of collecting the traditions, interpretations, and commentaries of the rabbins, and founding that Hebraic jurisprudence named the Mishna, the text and precept of the Talmud that has usurped the place of the law of Moses, and on which the Ghemara or disputations of the Jewish doctors is a commentary.

The feeling against the Jew is outrageously exhibited at Odessa, where the simple mention of him is odious to the Orthodox Christian; but his success is easily accounted for.

A large proportion of the Jews are included amongst that class whose principal and most remunerative labour is in the corn trade. Petty agents, sorters, sifters, packers and carriers earn from two roubles to five roubles daily. The Russian is bound to keep at the least forty-four holy-days, besides Sundays, during the year; on Saturdays and feast-days he expends at the *vodka*[1] counter of the Jew—for Jews keep nearly all the public-houses—his week's wages, and during a season of lengthened festival he runs up a score which has to be squared off upon the next receipt of wages—so that the Russian labourer is invariably in drink or in debt. He either finds an early grave, or ekes out his existence as a labourer. The Jew observes the Sabbath and fifteen feast-days in the twelve months; he is an abstemious man, living with his wife and family on bread, vegetables, and *krass*; at the close of each week he lays by a fair proportion of roubles, takes his family to the synagogue three times

[1] Spirits.

on the Sabbath, clad in their best, and looking as clean and respectable as earnest Talmudists are ever likely to, and on Sunday morning he returns to his working suit and his toil. In a few years he is a small capitalist, owning some hundreds of roubles, when he immediately commences business on his own account, often as a usurer, his earliest clients being too frequently his Christian fellow-labourers. Ever thrifty and parsimonious, his capital accumulates, and if endowed with some ability, he eventually becomes a man of substance. The Russian, still a labourer, looks with envy on the rising man, whom he does not cease to vituperate for being a scoundrel, and a man who has robbed his employers.

So with the shopman. While the Russian is carousing at the café, restaurant, or billiard-room—for Russians are the most improvident of people—the Jew is hoarding, and living on *kvass* and esculent herbs. The Jews, and it should be added, the Greeks —they are the bone and sinew of trade at Odessa—are more than a match for the less wily, good-natured, and procrastinating Russ.

The obsequies of the dead in Russia are a very distressing sight; but at Odessa they are revolting.

On the morning of the interment, the door of the house in which the deceased lies is thrown open, and the family privacy becomes invaded, for every passer-by has the right to walk in and kiss the face and hands of the corpse laid on a catafalque; the friends of the afflicted relatives enter the house at an early hour, being rarely dressed in mourning, and take their places on seats ranged around the mortuary chamber, where they remain chatting until the heart-rending scene of leave-taking, which is the signal for the funeral.

When the procession is formed, it moves away at a smart pace, headed by a cross borne aloft, banners and lighted lanterns being carried at the sides. A friend of the deceased follows with a large dish, on which is a rice cake,[1] frosted and liberally ornamented with sugar-plums (at the funeral of a pauper, a brown loaf replaces the cake); then comes the coffin-lid borne by four persons, and after it the coffin furnished in violet, rose-coloured, white or black cloth or velvet, ornamented with tawdry lace and silver braid; it is laid on a bier, the face and hands of the corpse being exposed; the rear is brought up by mourners on foot and in vehicles, with whom a crowd of idlers mix and hurry. When the procession reaches the cemetery, a short service takes place in the church, and a paper band, upon which is inscribed the name, age, and date of death, is secured around the brow of the deceased. The coffin is then hastened to the grave, where the mourners are awaiting it and a large number of paupers of both sexes are assiduously mumbling their prayers and crossing themselves. Another short service, and a wailing and hysterical sobbing is set up, much of it doubtless from the fulness of the heart, the rest from some kind of sympathy; then, all of a sudden, the competition for kissing the exposed parts of the dead body becomes great, and is zealously continued until the priest makes a sign, and the coffin is lowered into the grave, a sprinkling of holy water concluding the ceremony. But scarcely has the priest turned to move away, after receiving his fee and tasting the cake, than the mendicants, losing all sense of decency and forgetting their devotion, make a rush at the unfortunate creature who holds the dish, and a sad scramble takes place, even before the earth has closed over the poor remains. Then comes the last scene, and handfuls of coppers are distributed, with the object of securing prayers for the souls of the dead:[2]

---

[1] Emblematic of the resurrection, 1 Cor. xv. 37.
[2] There is a strange festival called the *pomynky*, 'the day of remembrance.' The

> . . . some are hung to bleach upon the wind,
> Some plung'd in waters, others purg'd in fires,
> Till all the dregs are drain'd, and all the rust expires.
> All have their manes, and their manes bear:
> The few, so cleans'd, to these abodes repair,
> And breathe, in ample fields, the soft Elysian air.
> Then are they happy, when by length of time
> The scurf is worn away, of each committed crime ;
> No speck is left of their habitual stains,
> But the pure ether of the soul remains.—ÆNEIS, vi. 1003.

The devotion of the lower classes in Russia is excessively demonstrative, especially during the recital of prayers and in churches, or whilst their sense of sight is sanctified by the presence of an image or cross; it is devotion nevertheless that does not impede a current of low conversation, nods of recognition and other signs of greeting, whilst in churches locomotion is rendered easy by reason of the absence of chairs and forms. These people bow and cross themselves at the sight of a church, no matter at what distance, also on passing a corpse ; they cross themselves when waking or lying down to sleep, before commencing a meal, upon sneezing or yawning ; when sorrowful to tears, or in merry laughter ; on commencing the day's work, when starting upon a journey, before bathing, when using their powers of persuasion, when experiencing disappointment, when swearing and employing blasphemous language. Upon all such occasions the sign of the cross is made once, twice, and oftener, for there is no rule ; it is simply a mechanical action, with scarcely a thought of the All-seeing eye, of the Omnipresence of the All-

relatives of the dead repair to the cemeteries on May 6, and following day ; the former, which is the greatest day, is commenced in prayer ; food and drink is spread at the side of each grave, and the abundance of good cheer is blessed by the priests who go about reciting orisons and sprinkling holy water. At noon the people dine and drink, and drink again ; not men only, for I have seen women also, stretched helplessly intoxicated on the turf !

mighty Power. Tertullian attached so great importance to the sign of the cross, that he wrote: 'In all our actions, upon rising, when dressing, when at meals, whatever the nature of our occupations, let us scare away Satan by signing the cross on the forehead.' St. Cyril of Jerusalem taught similarly in his catechisms for the young.

It is no rare circumstance on the voyage between Odessa and the Crimea, to see the saloon tables and sofas on board the crowded steamers occupied at night as bed places; it therefore behoves the traveller to make the earliest possible application for a cabin, and embark in ample time to secure it.[1]

[1] For tables of departures and arrivals, to and from the Crimea and Transcaucasia, see Appendix II.

JEWS OF ODESSA

CHAPTER II.

THIRD DAY.

Eskyforos Lighthouse—The British fleet—Saky Salt-lakes—Post-horses—The *perv-clodnaïya*—Eupatoria—Its history—Cape Chersonese—Sevastopol and the fortifications—The Tchórnaya-retchka—St. Clement's monastery—Fortress of Calamita—Inkerman—The field of battle—The Sapounn ridge—British head-quarters—Cathcart's hill.

THE first Crimean land is made at Cape Tarhankoutt or Eskyforos Lighthouse; it was at a rendezvous forty miles west of this point that the British fleet anchored for the first time off the coast, September 9, 1854, and waited until Lord Lyons and Lord Raglan had fixed upon a suitable spot for disembarking the allied troops. On November 3, the fleet drew near to the port of Eupatoria, and the place being defenceless, officers were despatched to summon it. The governor was an official personage in a high state of discipline, but he had nothing wherewith to oppose except the forms of office. But to him the forms of office seemed all-sufficing, and on these he still calmly relied; so, when the summons was delivered, he insisted upon fumigating it according to the health regulations of the little port. When he understood that the Western Powers intended to land he said that decidedly they might do so, but he explained that it would be necessary for them to land at the lazaretto and consider themselves in strict quarantine. The following day the place was occupied by a small body of English troops.[1]

The stay of the steamer at Eupatoria [2] is too short to enable passengers to see the place, but should the traveller desire to land, he will find a rough conveyance to take him over a dreary and uninteresting steppe to Sympherópol, or along the shore of the bay erroneously called Calamita to Sevastópol, passing through Saky, celebrated for mud-baths and salt-lakes, and crossing the rivers Boulganack, Alma (close to the field of battle), the Katcha and Belbeck; but this also is a cheerless road, and at any rate it is more prudent to make Sevastópol the *point de départ*.

The bay of Eupatoria offers an undesirable anchorage, but small vessels are sheltered from the south-west if they anchor close in shore. In the early autumn the roadstead is crowded with shipping waiting to load with salt from Saky and other lakes. The late Prince Woronzoff, recognising the medicinal properties of the mud at Saky, long appreciated by the Tatars, erected quarters for the reception of patients suffering from skin diseases, rheumatism, paralysis, &c.; and it is now sufficiently held in estimation to induce the Government to keep an establishment for naval and military patients. The mud is perfectly black, and has a disagreeable ammoniacal smell.

Beyond Saky is Kyzyl-yar lake, separated from the sea by a strip of sandy beach whereon the allied forces landed, September 14, 1854.[3] The subsequent skirmish on the Boulganack and the battle of the Alma, were the opening of the campaign.

---

[1] *The Invasion of the Crimea*, by Alex. Wm. Kinglake; chap. xxxviii.
[2] Pronounced Evpatoria by the Russians.
[3] British force . . . which included 1,200 cavalry; 26,000 and 60 guns.
French force . . ,, 200 spahis; 25,000 and 66 guns.
Turkish force . . . 7,000
Total 58,000   126 guns.

Post-horses are obtained in the Crimea upon application at the stations, the charge being at the rate of 3 copecks per *verst*[1], for each horse, and a gratuity of 15 or 20 copecks is given to the *yemstchyck*[2] at the end of each stage. The regulations permit post-horses to travel at 10 *versts* per hour over a good road in dry weather; a courier in the service of the State is conveyed at 12 *versts* per hour, and upon special service for His Majesty, the feld-jäger is driven *ventre-à-terre*. Should a horse become exhausted by the way, the traces are cut and the animal is left to perish. During the late reigns, before the extension of railroads and telegraph wires, this was an event of frequent occurrence.

The vehicle supplied at post stations in Russia is a four-wheeled *teléga*, a quadrangular box firmly fixed to shafts without any springs; across its rear-half, a rope is passed to and fro crossways in lieu of a seat, upon this network are piled the traveller's bed and cushions, and thus he sits throughout his journey, having to endure fearful jolting in an exquisitely uncomfortable position; there is never much luggage among the busy classes, a change of linen being considered a cumbersome luxury when on the road, but bedding is a paramount necessity. An abundance of hay and a *padoúshka*[3] is an excellent substitute, and far preferable, I conceive, to the rope seat. The driver of the *teléga* sits in front, between the box and the horse's tail, it is difficult to say where, but he is always very clever and sure, and will race up or down hill with the greatest safety and apparently with little enough exertion. The *teléga* is more commonly called a *pereclodnáya*;[4] in a country sparsely populated as is Russia, the *pereclodnáya* is an expedient

---

[1] One verst = ⅔ mile.   [2] The driver of a travelling carriage.
[3] Cushion—sometimes supplied at stations, when it is stuffed with hay.
[4] From the verb *perecladyvatte*, to transport, remove, &c.

conveyance in which to traverse the great spaces that intervene from town to village; should an accident occur, a rough spar and the axe, or a piece of rope, readily repairs the damage.

Eupatoria was formerly called Kozloff by the Russians, after the Turkish Khezlevè; it was named Eupatoria in remembrance of the fortress Eupatorium, built in the time of Mithridates (Eupator) 123–63 B.C. Frequent topographical errors appear to have been committed in reviving old names in the wrong places, as in the case of Odessa; Sevastópol after Sebastopolis, a seaport of the Eastern empire, now known as Soukhoum-Kaleh; Kherson on the Dneiper, after the Heracleotic Chersonese, and others.

Khezlevè was the principal port during the dominion in the Crimea of the Sultans of Turkey, but the place was devastated by General Count Münich in 1736, one monument only escaping destruction—the elegant mosque of Jum'à Jámy, or Ghyoúnu Jámy, 'Friday's mosque,' built in 1552 by the Khan Dyvlett Ghyrey on the model of St. Sophia at Stamboul. The Karaïm Jews are in great force at Eupatoria, where they number 300 families, and have a 'Spiritual Institution' under the direction of their *Gahan*.

On approaching Sevastópol, with the reddish cliffs to the south of Cape Ouloukoll on the port beam, Tchadyr-dagh, 'tent mountain,' the highest point of land in the Crimea, appears to the east; Cape Chersonese (lighthouse), the extreme south-west headland of the peninsula, is right ahead, and as the vessel approaches its destination the several bays and inlets to the west of Sevastópol become more distinct. Soon Fort Constantine, pierced for 104 guns, is seen as if suddenly risen out of the water, looking as grand and solid as if it had been completed but yesterday, although numerous indentations and its splintered masonry are evidence of past rough usage. Away to the right and rear of this fort on an advanced height is Telegraph battery, and the remains of the Wasp battery are beyond. Of the numerous havens inside the lighthouse, the first is Dvoynáya, 'double bay,' or Kazátskaya, 'Cossack bay'; the next, Kamiesh, or more correctly Kamyshóvaya, 'reed' bay, where the French disembarked their reinforcements and stores during the war; Kroúglaya, 'round bay,' Strélnaya, or Strelétskaya, 'arrow bay,' Pestchánnaya, 'sandy bay,' Karantýnnaya, 'quarantine bay,' where stood once a formidable battery, and Artyllereyskaya, 'artillery bay'; some of these bays offer fair anchorage to small vessels, but they are all open to the north.

On the point exactly opposite to Fort Constantine stood Fort Alexander (84 guns), and Fort Nicholas (192 guns) was on the next point to the right, near the entrance to Yoúgenaya, 'south bay'; in front of Fort Nicholas was Fort St. Paul (80 guns), that commanded the entrance to the creek; all formidable defences which, being on the south side, were destroyed by the Allies after the fall of the city. To the east of 'south bay' is a small creek named Karabélnaya, 'ship port,' at the head of which were the splendid docks also blown up by the Allies.

The bay of Sevastópol, about four miles in length and nearly a mile at the widest part, with ten fathoms water, is one of the finest harbours in the world, and was possibly not known to the renowned Admiral Andrew Doria, who was fond of repeating that May, June, July, and Port Mahon were the four best ports in the universe. On the north shore of the bay, and abreast of Fort St. Paul, was the 'fowl's ravine battery' (34 guns), and on the heights above are the earthworks that were hastily thrown up by the Russians after they evacuated the city. The small fishing village beyond the defences on the north side of the bay is the Tatar village Ak-yar, 'white cliff,' opposite to 'careening bay' on the south side, above which had stood the Salynghýnsk redoubt, and at the head of this great harbour is the estuary of the Tchórnaya-retchka, 'black river,' called also Byouk-ouzýn.

Returning to the Yoúgenaya, on the east side are the conspicuous ruins of barracks that received the full fire of the Allies during the fearful bombardment, September 7 and 8, 1855, and on the west are the tottering walls of the Admiralty buildings, the whole exhibiting a melancholy picture of desolation!

The town of Sevastópol, built on the slope of a hill and extending to the water's edge, was completely destroyed during the late war, and is rising but slowly out of its dust. The Hall of Nobles, the Clubs, the Museum on the model of the Temple of Theseus, the Admiralty, and Naval Library, or what remains of these and other edifices, attest to the former proud condition of the city; the house in which Catherine II. resided in 1787 when she visited the Crimea attended by Potyómkyn,[1] who desired *to point out to her the road to Byzantium*,[2] is still shown. These wrecks, however, are being carted away, and new houses appear as the ground is cleared. Plans for laying out a new town have been approved by the Imperial Government, and among the earliest undertakings will be the construction of spacious quays along the shore of the 'south bay.'

When the Crimea was annexed to Russia in 1783, Ak-yar was the chief village. Potyómkyn was the first to recognise the immense advantages possessed by the bay and harbours, and upon the representation of her favourite, the Empress issued an *oukaz*, February 10, 1784, a few weeks after the treaty was signed that

---

[1] Usually spelt Potemkine: the minister and favourite of Catherine II.

[2] *By this the way leads to Byzantium*, was written in Greek characters over a gate at Kherson through which the Empress passed.

gave to Russia the sovereignty over the Crimea, directing the creation of a military port and fortress to be named Sevastópol.

There are no formalities to go through on landing from a Russian port, whether in the matter of passport or luggage; we took up our quarters at Wetzel's Hôtel, where we received every attention from the landlord, who arranged for the hire of boats, carriages and horses.

At 10.30 A.M., three hours after disembarking from the steamer, we hired a wherry at the *Gráfskaya prístan*, 'Count's landing-place,' so named after the late Count (afterwards Prince) Woronzoff, a handsome flight of steps at the foot of a screen of columns; and pulling up the great bay, we landed amid the rushes on the banks of the Tchórnaya-retchka, near the piles of the bridge that was thrown across the stream by the Russians in their advance to attack the Allies. To our right was the gaping ravine up which the Russian force advanced the morning of the memorable November 5, 1854,[1] and to the left the cliff of Inkerman surmounted by a ruined fortress, and pierced with the crypts of pre-historic times. Some of these crypts were converted into Christian places of worship, it is said in the first century, when Pope Clement I., who was exiled to this part of the Taurida by the Emperor Trajan, spent his time in prayer and the conversion of the barbarians; he suffered martyrdom by being thrown into the sea, A.D. 100. On each anniversary of his death the sea receded during the space of seven days, leaving his body exposed on the shore; this was repeated until the ninth century, when Cyril and Methodius had it interred at Cherson: the sainted remains were afterwards carried away to Kieff by the Grand Prince Vladimir

[1] Battle of Inkerman.

upon his conversion to Christianity. Clement was subsequently canonised.[1]

The crypt church of the Monastery of St. Clement is complete in every particular, for it has a portico, nave, transept, dome, and vestry, with a liberal allowance of the dusty bones of saints kept in stone sarcophagi; much of the church furniture and a balcony that overlooks the valley, will be found riddled with shot-holes, mementos of the battle of Inkerman.

From these crypts, a flight of steps cut through the rock conduct to the ruined fortress at the summit, believed by some to be the site upon which was constructed the defence by the General Diophantes, which he named Eupatorium in honour of his sovereign Mithridates Eupator;[2] but it is difficult to conceive what object the royalist commander could have had in view, in building a fortress as a defence against the Tauro-Scythians at so great a distance from the city of Chersonesus, the base of his operations; and as in the time of Bronovius, 1578, there were Greek inscriptions and armorial bearings over the gates and on the public edifices, there is some probability that these remains are of the prosperous city of Calamita[3] mentioned by the Venetian traveller Josephat Barbaro, in the fifteenth century, marked Chalamita in the old Italian charts, and known to the Tatars as In-kermen.[4] A Russian priest, Jacob Lyzloff, has left the following account of Inkerman in the seventeenth century:—

'During the blessed reign of the Emperor and Grand Prince

---

[1] The Church of Rome asserts that the relics of this pontiff are preserved in St. Clement's on the Esquiline; and its legends of his martyrdom are differently narrated.

[2] Strabo, *Rerum Geog.* VII. iv. 7.

[3] *Notices Hist. et Topog. concernant les colonies Italiennes en Gazarie.* Ph. Bruun, St. Petersburg, 1866.

[4] *In*, cave or crypt; *kermen*, castle.

Mihail Feódorovitch, Autocrat of all Russia, and under the protection of the great lord, the Reverend Joseph, Patriarch of Moscow and of all Russia, I happened, great sinner that I am, to visit, in the year 1634 from the birth of Christ, the land of Crimea, in company with the Ambassador Boris Dvoryanyn. In the Crimean land on the south side, on the shore of the Black Sea, opposite to the town of Ak-yar, and across the arm of the sea between Kozloff and Balaclava, there is a great mountain; a hard rock like a wall, the height of which mountain is 100 *ságens* (700 feet), and is distant 3 *versts* from the sea. On the top of that mountain is a small stone-built, scantily-peopled town, called, by the Tatars, Inkerman.' The priest goes on to describe the crypts as dwellings in the mountain like birds' nests, chamber over chamber for a great distance, some of which were inhabited by Greeks.[1] Another priest named Jacob (1647) relates that merchant ships were in the habit of anchoring in the port of Inkerman.[2] Of the village of Calamita or Inkerman nothing is left.

Looking to the north-east from the ruined tower are seen the remains of the Russian batteries, and away to the east, to the right of some small wood, is the hollow where the Russian *corps d'armée* was encamped previously to the battle of November 5. A good and extensive view of the pleasant meadows in the valley of the Tchórnaya is also obtained, but the site of Lord Raglan's bivouac at the *traktyr* bridge on the night of September 25, and the battle-field of August 16, 1855, are hidden by the formation of the heights.

From the left bank of the Tchórnaya-retchka we ascended

---

[1] *Zapysky Odess. obshtch. istor. y drev.* ii. p. 683.
[2] Ibid. p. 688.

by the Quarry ravine to the field of the battle of Inkerman on Sapounn-garà, 'Mount Sapounn,' and soon found ourselves at the 'Barrier,'[1] the standpoint of the British force throughout the action, and where 3,000 of our valiant troops held their own in deadly struggles against five times their number. Close by is the obelisk that marks the disputed ground, and at a very short distance is the Guards' battery, which remains perfect in its outline, though the parapet is falling away. Among young pollards are the graves of our warriors who fell on November 5, and over the brow lie their brave enemies, where they were interred by the Allies upon Prince Mentchikoff's declining to send a party for the purpose.

Keeping within the line of earthworks we got to the camp of the 2nd Division, and halted to lunch, when we observed that the ground was covered with rusty fragments of iron, portions of provision tins, and pieces of glass bottles. But there was little enough time for loitering, so we pushed on in front of the old telegraph station to the Sapounn ridge where Lord Raglan stood in amazement while the 'six hundred' charged. The plains of Balaclava, the Turkish redoubts on the Causeway ridge that is traversed by the Woronzoff road, the Kamara heights overgrown with the pollard and juniper, the village of Kadykyuy, and a part of Balaclava, are all taken in at a glance from this position. To the right in the distance, on Mount Hiblah, is the obelisk to the memory of General Rudolpho Gabrielli di Montevecchio, Lieut.-General Alessandro Ferrero della Marmora (the originator of the corps of Bersaglieri), General Georgio Ansaldi, and other officers of the Piedmontese army; and still away to the right, and still higher up Mount

---

[1] Kinglake's *Invasion*, &c., V. p. 164 *et seq.* The events of the war in the Crimea are of too recent occurrence to be reproduced here.

Hiblah, stands out in bold relief the Nightingale cross of white marble. At our feet were several cemeteries, with broken tombstones and rotting head-boards that lay about in disorder.

The farmhouse which had been the British head-quarters is the property of Colonel Bracker, who takes justifiable pride in keeping it in good repair, and especially the room in which the Waterloo veteran breathed his last. An inscription on the wall is in these words :—

'In this room died Field-Marshal Lord Raglan, G.C.B., Commander-in-Chief of the British Army in the Crimea, June 28, 1855.'

About twenty yards down the garden walk, under the shade of a large tree, is a slab to the memory of the Field-Marshal, which marks the spot where that noble soldier loved to sit and take his rest. His body having been embalmed, some of his remains were deposited under this stone. Colonel d'Estcourt, the chief's aide-de-camp and fellow victim to cholera, is buried close to the farm.

We returned to Sevastópol by the French head-quarters, stopping to look at the cemetery of the Light Division, and the cemetery on Cathcart's hill, at both of which we found the walls pulled down to admit cattle. Two handsome memorials, the one to the officers of the Royal Artillery, the other to the officers of the Coldstream Guards who fell at Inkerman, were completely overturned; broken slabs, in marble and stone, lay scattered, and every monument that had borne a cross was mutilated—wanton destruction committed through the fanaticism of the Tatar herdsmen, veneration for a cross and superstition being ample guarantees that the offenders were not to be looked for amongst the Russian population.

Such a state of things is now in all probability partly remedied, by the carrying out of the recommendations of a military commission that was sent to Sevastópol in the autumn of 1872, by an officer who has been employed on this special service during the year 1875. The walls of the several cemeteries were to be levelled; such of the monuments as happened to be in good condition were to be removed to Cathcart's hill, and the ground covered with sufficient earth to raise a mound over the once consecrated sites.

CASTLE OF CALAMITA, AND CRYPT MONASTERY OF ST. CLEMENT.

CHAPTER III.

FOURTH DAY.

Monastery of St. George—Miss Nightingale—The Criumetopon—The Tauri—The Chersonese—A Black Sea fog—Allied camps—Balaclava—Ancient history—The Greek battalion—Ulysses—British occupation—Genoese Castle—The Sutherland hillock—Scarlett's brigade—Lord Cardigan's cavalry charge.

TAKING the road between the British lines on the left attack, and the French parallels in front of the flag-staff battery, 'bastion du mât,' we passed the 'white house,' French camp, and French head-quarters, over a rocky and bleak tract lorded over by the bustard; the road is good, and a drive of seven miles brought us to the wall that encloses the Monastery of St. George. After passing the deep gateway, the traveller is spellbound at the transformation scene, when he is welcomed by the monks, and invited to ramble at will about the narrow walks ingeniously practised on the steep slope facing the sea, amid lilliputian cascades, and a luxuriancy of varied vegetation, garden flowers, vineyards, &c., which extend almost to the seashore.

The church, situated at 500 feet or 600 feet above the water's edge, is of modern construction, and contains the remains of such men as Prince Galitzin and General de Witt, who were among the first to appreciate the beauties of the south coast of the Crimea, and who died where they loved to live. The apartments within the monastery which were occupied by Miss Florence Nightingale during the war, are shown by the inmates with unaffected satisfaction, for the remembrance of that lady is respectfully preserved; they are available to pilgrims and strangers desiring to pass the night. The great festival at this place is the name's-day of the patron saint, when Greeks and Russians flock to the monastery with offerings, picnic about the verdant ridges, and drink at the holy fountain of the water which they believe to be invigorating and sanctifying. Little is known of the history of this monastery, owing to the absence of documents, and as it was subject to the patriarchate of Constantinople up to the year 1794, the archives are believed to be preserved in that capital. It is said that the monastery was founded in the tenth century, and that the first church was built in 891 by some Greek seamen miraculously saved during a fearful storm by St. George, who himself appeared, and left his portrait among them; the picture was kept in the church until 1779, when it was removed to Marioúpol.

Upon either side of the monastery extend lofty precipices 1,000 feet above the sea, the huge overhanging rock to the west at Cape St. George, or Fiolente, being at one extreme of the bay of Balaclava, which is enclosed to the south-east by Cape Aïa, partly seen from the church. Dubois de Montpéreux believes the Criumetopon of Strabo to have been at Ayou-dagh, a promontory to the east of Yalta; but I am inclined to the opinion of Mouravieff and Bruun who place it at Cape Aïa, the 'ram's head' according to the great geographer being opposite to Carambis (Kerémp boúroun) in Paphlagonia, the two points forming a strait.[1] It has been stated that Criumetopon, the abode of Iphigenia,

[1] Strabo, VII. iv. 3.

was at a distance of 120 stadia[1] from Lampadum[2] (Lambat), that is to say, at or about Aïtodor; the greater probability therefore remains that the name of the 'ram's head' was given to the formidable range of cliffs that line the south coast from Aïtodor to Cape Aïa.

We read in Herodotus that the Tauri who inhabited these parts, seized the Grecians they found on their coast and all those who suffered shipwreck, and sacrificed them to the virgin goddess by striking the victim on the head with a club; they then precipitated the body from a hill on which their temple was built; by their own account the goddess to whom they sacrificed was Iphigenia, the daughter of Agamemnon.'[3] It would be difficult to select a more fitting situation in the Crimean peninsula than that offered by Cape Aïa, at which the Tauri could have exercised their cruelties. Their goddess would appear to have been worshipped afterwards under a changed designation, for Strabo relates that 'towards the south of Carcinites (Eupatoria), in the territory possessed by the Tauri, there was a large promontory which was part of the great Chersonese; upon this promontory stood a city of the Heracleotæ, colonists from Heraclea (Bender Eregly) in the Euxine, which bore the same name as the territory, that is to say, Chersonesus. In this city was a temple to a virgin, a divinity,' whose name unfortunately has not been preserved, 'and on another promontory, which was called Parthenium, in front of the city, and distant from it one hundred stadia, there was a shrine of the goddess.' The text goes on to say that, 'between the city and promontory were three harbours, next to the promontory the ruined city of old Chersonesus, and beyond, the Symvolon-limen a

---

[1] One stadium = ·1144 mile.
[2] Scymnii Chii. *frag.* 118. Letronne edit. Paris, 1840.   [3] Herod. iv.

harbour with a narrow entrance.'[1] Now if the fact be admitted that the distances noted by Strabo agree in general with the conformation of the line of coast, then the promontory Parthenium, 100 stadia (10·44 miles) from the city of Chersonesus, should be looked for at Cape Chersonese or Fanary; we have the three harbours between the city and promontory, in the bays of Strelétskaya, Kroúglaya, and Dvoynáya, sometimes called the bay of Fanary, and on the supposition that the site of the old Chersonesus, to judge by the remains of ancient foundations with which the ground is covered, was to the south-east of the isthmus at the head of the bay nearest to the lighthouse, we find a city to have been on the seacoast beyond the promontory, and the harbour of Balaclava is at once recognised as being the port with a narrow entrance.

Whilst enjoying the view from the top of the monastery grounds, we were afforded the opportunity of witnessing the formation and approach of one of the thick fogs for which the Euxine is noted. It got into a sort of consistency suddenly, gathering in density from every quarter as it neared the land, and rolled over and onwards, uniting and forming a compact mass until it reached the shore; here the fog seemed to avoid contact with the cliffs, for as it continued rapidly to roll and touch, it would divide and dissipate, still touch, to divide and dissipate again. Its troubled surface by no means reached to the tops of the cliffs, and from our own lofty position we were enabled to view the clear sky and a horizon beyond.

Quitting the monastery we drove past the hamlet of Karany, once the head-quarters of Omar Pascha, and on through the Turkish camp, and the camps of the British Cavalry and Royal Horse Artillery, to within a short distance of the village of

[1] Strabo, VII. iv. 2.

Kadykyuy, when we turned to the right, and soon alighted at the silent and almost deserted village of Balaclava, eight miles from the Monastery of St. George.

The Symvolon-limen, 'port of signals,' is mentioned by Strabo as being a harbour with a narrow entrance, 1,000 stadia from Theodosia; it is subsequently referred to as being the 'calm port of the symbols';[1] that port is now Balaclava. The Genoese, who occupied it a short time previous to the year 1345, called the port Cembalo, a corruption of the Greek, Symvolon. An inscription discovered amid the ruins of the fortress in 1861, given further on, attests that its construction was commenced in 1357, during the consulate of Simone dell' Orto. Cembalo, the westernmost possession of the Genoese on the Crimean coast, was at one time constituted a bishopric. In 1433 a revolt among the Greek population was successful in subverting the authority of the Italians, and they tendered their submission to Prince Alexis (father-in-law to David, the last sovereign of Trebizond), then residing at Mangoup; the Republic, however, despatched a fleet the following year, having 6,000 troops on board, and Carlo Lomellino reduced Cembalo to submission.[2] After the conquest of Caffa and Soldaya by the Turks, Cembalo with the rest of the peninsula fell to the sovereignty of the Khan, upon his return from bondage in Turkey to rule as a vassal of the Sultan.

ARMS OF THE EMPERORS OF TREBIZOND.

The Genoese fortress consisted of the citadel on the summit of the cliff that commands the harbour; it was at the apex of a tri-

---

[1] *Anon perip.*, 55.
[2] *Le colonie commerciali degli Italiani in Oriente*, &c., G. Heyd. Trans. G. Müller, Venezia. 1868. ii. p. 145.

angular wall, the base of which was parallel to the port, with a tower at each end.

The origin of the name of Balaclava has been ascribed to Παλάκιον—Palakion, one of the three fortresses constructed by the Tauro-Scythian king Scylurus and his sons. Blaramberg,[1] who quotes Pallas, places Palakium on the same cliff as the Genoese defences, and supposes it to have been founded by Palakos, one of the sons of the king; he further suggests that Λαβα-Λαμβάνω—to take, to seize (?)—may have been added by the Greeks of the Chersonese upon their acquisition of the port; thus, Palakon-lava, Palaklava, Balaklava. The word is also said to be a composition of *bella* and *clava*, 'fine port.' In 1472 a Russian merchant, named Nikitin, landed at Balykleï, on his return from India,[2] and in the MS. of an Italian traveller of the seventeenth century,[3] Baluchlacca was inhabited by Turks, Greeks, and Armenians, when the fortifications were entire. In view of these two records, for the Genoese do not appear at any time to have called their settlement otherwise than Cembalo, one is led to the conjecture that the Balykleï of Nikitin and the Baluchlacca of the Italian may have been after a name given by the Turks from *bályk* (fish), and *óra* (a place), that is, Balyk-óra, a place where are fish; indeed the sole trade of Balaclava is in fish, fresh and salted, such as turbot, haddock, mackerel, bream, mullet, whiting, and the *kephály*, 'pilchard,' the smoked roe of which is prized as a delicacy at the Russian *zakoúska*.[4]

[1] *Trois forteresses Tauro-Scythes*, &c. Blaramberg, Odessa. 1831. p. 19.
[2] Bruun, *Gazarie*, p. 67.
[3] *MS. travels of Nicholas Barti of Lucca into Tartary, Circassia, and Mingrelia, from 1632 to 1639*, quoted in *Russia on the Black Sea, and Sea of Asoff*, &c. H. D. Seymour, M.P. 1855.
[4] Every Russian whets his appetite before dining with a *zakoúska*; caviare, anchovies, salted herrings, pickled mushrooms, radishes, cheese, &c., are always on a sideboard for the purpose.

During the Russo-Turkish war in 1769, Count Orlóff, who commanded the naval forces in the Mediterranean, issued a manifesto inviting foreigners to enter the service of Russia on liberal terms. The manifesto was followed up by a flattering letter from Count Pánin to the Greeks of the Archipelago. Under a leader named Mavromihail, the Hellenes formed themselves into eight battalions, and having embarked on board Russian vessels of war, did good service as marines from 1769 to the peace in 1773. Alarmed at the prospect of retribution with which Turkey would probably visit them, they sought the protection of Russia after the peace of Kaïnardjee (1774), and availed themselves of the offer of new homes at Kertch and Yeny-Kaleh, finally ceded to Russia by that same treaty; at those two places they were formed into a battalion which was styled the Army of Albania. Upon the annexation to Russia of the Crimea (1784) these troops were removed to Balaclava, which thereafter became their head-quarters, and they were employed on coastguard service between Sevastópol and Theodosia. The officers and men were treated with every indulgence, land was liberally bestowed on them, and they were exempt from taxes. At this time they were engaged afloat against the Turks at Kinbourn, and at the destruction of the enemy's flotilla near Hadgy bey. In 1797 they were entitled the Taurida, and later the Greek battalions, when they were placed on the same footing, and allotted a uniform similar to that of the Cossacks of the Don; at this period they numbered 400 rank and file. They were good agriculturalists, and the villages of Kady-kyuy, Kamara, Karane, Kermentchyck, and Lakou have been cited as evidence of their industry and good management. They were useful in suppressing a revolt among the Tatars in 1812, and in 1818 they received decorations and were granted more land upon the occasion of the Emperor's visit to the Crimea. Their last service in war appears to have been in 1842, when they occupied the fortress of Soudjouk-Kaleh, now Novorossisk, on the coast of Circassia.[1] To the remnants of this battalion, under the command of Col. Monto, was entrusted the defence of Balaclava, when, on the morning of September 26, 1854, Lord Raglan, having quitted his night bivouac at the *traktyr* bridge, marched in his 'unconditional resolve to seize the port,' and Lord Lyons, on board the Agamemnon, was 'keeping his tryst' off its entrance.

Dubois[2] has taken some pains in various portions of his work to confirm the views expounded by different authors, that the scenes of the wanderings of Ulysses were on the shores of the Black Sea, and we cannot fail to recognise in the features of Balaclava the port of the Læstrigons, with the description of which, in the Odyssey, it so precisely accords.

> Within a long recess a bay there lies,
> Edged round with cliffs high pointing to the skies;
> The jutting shores that swell on either side
> Contract its mouth, and break the rushing tide.
> Our eager sailors seize the fair retreat,
> And bound within the port their crowded fleet;
> For here retired the sinking billows sleep,
> And smiling calmness silver'd o'er the deep.
> I only in the bay refused to moor,
> And fix'd, without, my hawsers to the shore.
> From thence we climb'd a point, whose airy brow
> Commands the prospect of the plains below:
> No tracks of beasts, or signs of man, we found,
> But smoky volumes rolling from the ground.

In the relation of Ulysses, where

> proud Lamos's stately towers appear,
> And Læstrigonia's gates arise distinct in air.

[1] *Zapysky Odess. obshtch.* i. p. 205.
[2] *Voyage autour du Caucase*, etc. Ouvrage qui a remporté le prix de la Société de Géographie de Paris, en 1838. Par Frédéric Dubois de Montpéreux. 1843. vi. p. 110-115.

Dubois has pictured the palace of Antiphates built by Lamos an ancient king of Læstrigon, as being on the heights upon which are now the remains of the fortress of Cembalo.

With the barbarity of the Læstrigons, Dubois has associated the cruel practices of the Tauri, who put to death all navigators and strangers that chanced to fall into their power:—

> They went; but, as they entering saw the queen
> Of size enormous, and terrific mien,
> (Not yielding to some bulky mountain's height,)
> A sudden horror struck their aching sight.
> Swift at her call her husband scour'd away
> To wreak his hunger on the destined prey:
> One for his food the raging glutton slew,
> But two rush'd out, and to the navy flew.
> Balk'd of his prey, the yelling monster flies,
> And fills the city with his hideous cries.
> A ghastly band of giants hear the roar,
> And, pouring down the mountains, crowd the shore.
> Fragments they rend from off the craggy brow,
> And dash the ruins on the ships below.
> The crackling vessels burst, hoarse groans arise,
> And mingled horrors echo to the skies:
> The men, like fish, they stuck upon the flood,
> And cramm'd their filthy throats with human food.
>   *Odys.* x. 101–144.

while the only spring of water near the head of the harbour of Balaclava is presumably 'the stream of Artacia,' the sole supply of the Læstrigons.

Stepping into a Greek fishing-boat, we pulled out of the dark blue waters of the land-locked haven, the rocks on both sides having painted on them names in giant letters as they were left by our seamen—such as Cossack Point, Castle Point, Castle Bay, &c.; and to the left on entering the harbour, high up the steep cliff, where only the intrepid British sailor would venture to climb, are the initials of our beloved Queen surmounted by a crown. The fog had completely cleared, and we enjoyed a row beneath the majestic cliffs of pudding-stone, first to the west, where we saw stretched at a considerable depth, for the water was of surprising clearness, a chain cable of size and length, which the boatmen insisted had belonged to the ill-fated steamship 'Prince,' foundered during the terrific gale of November 14, 1854 ; but this could not be the case, for the transport was lost to the east of the entrance. The Greeks were chatty ; they were kind enough to wish for another war, which they said must be profitable to everybody—for it had been to themselves ; they toiled much now and gained little ; they had toiled less during that war, and gained more ! Under the shade of a projecting cliff where the Genoese parapet overlooks the sea, we lunched on the refreshing waters.

On the wooded height opposite to the Genoese Castle, is a cemetery, where, among the many by whom he was beloved, lies Rear-Admiral Boxer, C.B. Other cemeteries, including that of the Royal Marines, are among the vineyards and shrubberies on Mount Hiblah, within the British line of defence in front of Kamara.

The ascent to the old fortress is over rough ground strewn with blocks and fragments of masonry, and is more easily made from the rear of the village. The remains of two crenelated walls which united the large tower or citadel of St. Nicholas to two turrets, and a tower and lower wall which appear to have formed the base of the triangular fortification, are all that is left of the ancient defences. In 1855 the Sardinians carried away two slabs, now at Genoa, which bore the following inscriptions :—

I.   MCCCL . . . .
HIC OPUS FIERI FECIT SPECTABILIS ET
HONORABILIS BARNABAS GRILLUS

II. MCCCLXVII
HIC OPUS FACTUM FUIT TEMPORE CONSOLATUS IOANNIS BAPTISTE DE OLIVA HONORABILIS CONSULIS CEMBALI HANC TURRIM CUM MURO

and on a slab found by M. Jurgievitz of Odessa, in 1861, now preserved in the village church, is inscribed—

✠ 1357 DIE
(OP)US INCEPTUM FUIT
TENPORE REGIM(INIS)
DISCRETI VIRI SI
MONIS DE ORTO CON
SULIS ET CASTELANI

Leaving Balaclava and the village of Kadykyuy behind us, we drove straight for the plains in a northerly direction, passing to the left of a small eminence named by our troops the Dunrobin or Sutherland hillock, from which the 93rd Highlanders, 550 strong, with 100 invalids and a few hastily-collected men under Sir Colin Campbell (afterwards Lord Clyde), checked the advance of four squadrons of Russian cavalry numbering 400, on the morning of the memorable October 25, 1854. Not unnaturally, the Russian horsemen imagined that they were falling into some ambush, as was afterwards communicated by the Russian officers to our own; and, on the other hand, the men of the 93rd with a wild impetuosity which was characteristic of the battalion as then constituted, showed a mind to rush forward as though undertaking to charge and exterminate cavalry in the open plain; but in a moment Sir Colin was heard crying fiercely: 'Ninety-third! Ninety-third! damn all that eagerness!' And the angry voice of the old soldier quickly steadied the line.[1]

---

[1] The whole of the particulars on the movements of the British troops in the Crimea are taken from Kinglake's *Invasion*, &c.

We quitted the carriage directing that it was to wait for us where the Woronzoff road rises over the ridge above the plain, and walked towards General Scarlett's field of victory [1] at the vineyard enclosure, round which that gallant officer advanced at the head of his force of 300 horse, to the immediate discomfiture of Ryjoff's 3,000! 'It was truly magnificent,' so spoke a French general officer who had witnessed the fight, to Colonel (afterwards General) Beatson—'it was truly magnificent; and to me, who could see the enormous numbers opposed to you, the whole valley being filled with Russian cavalry, the victory of the Heavy Brigade was the most glorious thing I ever saw!' Lord Cardigan, who chafed with envy while this action was going on, impatiently ejaculated: 'Damn those Heavies; they have the laugh of us this day!'

Crossing the Woronzoff road in the midst of the old Turkish redoubts on the Causeway heights, we dipped and fancied we had guessed the spot where the twelve 12-pounders had stood, which the Earl of Cardigan so bravely attacked and carried with his brigade of 673 horse. Walking along the North valley with the Fedioukine heights on our right, and the Causeway heights to our left, our hearts thrilled with just pride as we thought of the deeds of our heroes, so many of whom had moistened the sod with their life's blood! [2]

> When can their glory fade?
> O the wild charge they made!
> All the world wonder'd.
> Honour the charge they made,
> Honour the Light Brigade,
> Noble six hundred!

[1] Scarlett's brigade was composed of two squadrons of the Inniskillings, and two squadrons of the Scots Greys.
[2] Of the 673 horsemen that went into action, 198 only returned.

'Despite all Lord Raglan's anger and grief, despite the kind of protestation he judged it wholesome to utter for the discouragement of rash actions on the part of his officers, still he wrote in private of the Light Cavalry Charge, that it was perhaps the finest thing ever attempted.

The well known criticism delivered by General Bosquet was sound and generous. He said of the charge: *C'est magnifique; mais ce n'est pas la guerre.* " It is splendid ; but it is not war." This was said by General Bosquet to Mr. Layard in the field, and at the time of the charge. He spoke with a most exact justice ; but already the progress of time has been changing the relative significance of that glory and that fault which his terse comment threw into contrast. What were once the impassioned desires of the great nations of the West for the humbling of the Czar are now as cold as the ashes which remind men of flames extinguished ; and our people can cease from deploring the errors which marred a battle, yet refuse to forget an achievement which those very errors provoked. Therefore the perversity which sent our squadrons to their doom, is only, after all, the mortal part of the story. Half-forgotten already, the origin of the Light Cavalry Charge is fading away out of sight. Its splendour remains. And splendour like this is something more than the mere outward adornment which graces the life of a nation. It is strength—strength other than that of mere riches, and other than that of gross numbers—strength carried by proud descent from one generation to another—strength awaiting the trials that are to come.'

The Greeks of Balaclava who had witnessed the actions of the 25th October, and other engagements, volunteered their opinion of the respective merits of the contending forces, in words to this effect: 'Certainly the English got the best of it, for they never fired unless they were certain of hitting; our Russian soldiers always fired too soon, and then rushed at the English, who shot them down. They were brave fellows, but of course they did as they were ordered.'

GENOESE CASTLE, BALACLAVA.

CHAPTER IV.

FIFTH DAY.

The Malakoff Redan—French cemetery—The ancient Chersonese—The defences of Diophantes—Ctenous—Free Institutions of the Chersonians—Their wars—Treachery of the Bosporians—Ingratitude of the Chersonians - Vladimir the Grand Prince—His conversion—Decadence of Chersonesus—Its destruction—Ruins of the city—Christian churches—The Alma.

ON reaching the Malakoff tower this morning, we were accosted by a little man who introduced himself as an old French soldier, then employed on the new railway works; his delight is to recount over again the capture of the Malakoff, in which dashing affair he took a part. 'Turn the soil up where you will,' he said, 'and you will find the bones of my comrades and countrymen. How impatiently we awaited the signal for the assault, and when it was given we all felt as if *saisis de convulsions*, and our brave Chasseurs and Zouaves rushed to the attack; they had only 25 mètres (27 yards) to run, from that parallel to this ditch, and yet they fell by fifties under the hellish fire of the Russians as they tried to reach it, and those that did get to it only helped to fill it up with their bodies. Then came the Reserves; I was in the Reserve, and away we went over the dead bodies of our own soldiers, and in a moment the parapet was ours!'[1] It will never be known how many Frenchmen

---

[1] 'At noon the French were observed to start *en masse* from their trenches and possess themselves in gallant style of the Malakoff battery, on which the tricolour flag was

have fallen here; but never mind, we won the day, and our flag floated here. The Russians returned to the attack after this fort was ours, but we were too quick for them, and when they again tried to recover this position, they found us too well prepared, and brave though they were they had at last to retire, and that night the city was in our possession! But we found nothing in it, there was no *butin* for us; the *gaillards* left nothing behind them but burning houses.' In his excitement, our new cicerone began to dig, and we found that the old soldier was right; bones were plentiful just beneath the surface, and so were bullets and grape-shot.

The view from the round tower of the Malakoff is superb, for the eye sweeps the positions of the allied land forces from the French batteries and works on the right attack, to the flag-staff battery on the left attack; and the Mamelon, French trenches, and Victoria redoubt to the right of the middle ravine, and the British rifle-pits and parallels and Naval Brigade battery on Gordon's or the right attack to the left of the middle ravine, are easily distinguishable; while to seaward every movement of the allied ships to the south of Wasp battery could be observed.

On descending the Malakoff we drove to the Redan, which we approached on foot. An obelisk marks the spot where our gallant Second and Light Divisions, with the ladder parties of the 3rd and 97th Regiments, advanced to storm the salient angle in their front; the ditch is almost filled up, and it is now easy enough to mount the parapet inside which the deadly struggle for victory took place between the Russians and their determined

hoisted and the Imperial eagles planted within ten minutes of their quitting their trenches.' *Letter from Captain the Hon. Henry Keppel, R.N.*, commanding Royal Naval Brigade, to Sir Edmund Lyons, Naval Commander-in-Chief.

foes. Here the remains of the brave are mingled, and bleach above ground as the earth falls away; as at the Malakoff, a search for bullets and fragments of shells is quickly rewarded.

From the Redan we proceeded to the French cemetery, a neat and well-kept enclosure, prepared and maintained by a grateful country to do honour, to the valiant sons who perished during the war. A mausoleum in the centre is the last resting-place of the superior officers of the French army, and beneath other monuments around, lie interred officers and men according to their corps and divisions. The Russians also have erected at great cost a memorial to their brave defenders, and England—wealthy England alone—has left the graves of her fallen neglected and uncared for; the walls of the British cemeteries have been pulled down by the Tatar herdsmen, monuments have lain mutilated and overturned, and in many instances the remains have been desecrated. The indignation of English travellers frequently met with the sympathy and powerful support of the Press, in exposing the disgraceful condition of the British cemeteries about Sevastópol, until at length, in September 1872, a military commission was sent to the Crimea to examine and report their state; but it was not until March 1875 that an officer was ordered to Sevastópol, empowered to carry out the recommendations of the commission with the sum of 5,000*l.* that was granted by the Government two years previously, a sum, however, totally inadequate to any creditable and integral reparation.

We now hurried over that part of the steppe on which the French were encamped, until we alighted at the gate of the monastery on the site of the ancient city of Chersonesus.

The first locality to which the Heracleotes and Delians came, when they founded the colony of Chersonesus[1] in the third year of the thirtieth Olympiad, 658 B.C., was near the promontory at Cape Fanary, and probably between the head of the creek nearest to the lighthouse point at Cape Chersonese (Fanary) and the head of what is now Cossack bay, about which I have clearly traced many ancient foundations. As the Grecians increased in prosperity and power, they selected a more suitable spot for a settlement, and established themselves on that peninsula between Quarantine and Pestchánnaya bay, or Bay of Soses, where was previously a place called Megarice,[2] in all probability the *emporium* of Scylax. The Chersonians occupied the entire plateau, triangular in form, that extends from Ctenous to the Parthenium promontory, thence to the port of Symvolon, and back in a direct line across the isthmus to Ctenous.

In the time of Strabo, Chersonesus was a flourishing city under the domination of the Kings of the Bosphorus, who were elected from Rome. Chersonesus had been independent, but the citizens were unable to withstand the continued attacks of the Tauro-Scythians, and they applied for succour to Mithridates (Eupator), who sent to their assistance a general named Diophantes, by whom was built for their protection the Castle of Eupatorium. Of another fortified place, Strabo[3] relates that at

---

[1] Scym. Ch. 118. Anon. perip. 55.
[2] Pliny iv. 26. 7.
[3] Ἔστι δ' ἄκρα διέχουσα τοῦ τῶν Χερρονησιτῶν τείχους, ὅσον πεντεκαίδεκα σταδίους, κόλπον ποιοῦσα εὐμεγέθη νεύοντα πρὸς τὴν πόλιν· τούτου δ'ὑπέρκειται λιμνοθάλαττα, ἁλοπήγιον ἔχουσα· ἐνταῦθα δὲ καὶ ὁ Κτενοῦς. "Ἵν' οὖν ταῦτ' ἔχοιεν οἱ βασιλικοὶ πολιορκούμενοι, τῇ τε ἄκρᾳ τῇ λεχθείσῃ φρουρὰν ἐγκατέστησαν, τειχίσαντες τὸν τόπον, καὶ τὸ στόμα τοῦ κόλπου τὸ μέχρι τῆς πόλεως διέχωσαν, ὥστε πεζεύεσθαι ῥᾳδίως, καὶ τρόπον τινὰ μίαν εἶναι πόλιν ἐξ ἀμφοῖν· ἐκ δὲ τούτου ῥᾷον ἀπεκρούοντο τοὺς Σκύθας. Ἐπεὶ δὲ καὶ τῷ διατειχίσματι τοῦ ἰσθμοῦ τοῦ πρὸς τῷ Κτενοῦντι προσέβαλον, καὶ τὴν τάφρον ἐνέχουν καλάμῳ, τὸ μεθ' ἡμέραν γεφυρωθὲν μέρος, νύκτωρ ἐνεπίμπρασαν οἱ βασιλικοὶ καὶ ἀντεῖχον τέως, ἕως ἐπεκράτησαν. Strabo VII iv. 7.

'a distance of fifteen stadia (1·7 miles) from the wall of Chersonesus, there was a promontory that formed a large bay and that inclined towards the city, above which were salt-lakes full of salt. Ctenous is here. Thus the besieged Royalists enclosed the place with a wall, and stationed a garrison at the promontory alluded to, having filled up the entrance of the bay which conducted to the city, with the view of facilitating communication on foot, and to constitute of the two places one city. Consequently they easily repulsed the Scythians. But as they (the Scythians) attacked the wall that divides the isthmus, near Ctenous, they filled the trench with reeds. This kind of bridge, laid across during the day, was burnt by the Royalists at night; in this manner they continued their resistance until they finally defeated the enemy.'

It is the practice to attribute the original construction of the castle on the rock above the Tchórnaya-retchka to Diophantes, calling it the Castle of Eupatorium,[1] identifying it with the fortified place on the promontory 15 stadia from the city, and assigning to Inkerman the port of Ctenous. But Strabó has given no clue whatever as to the situation of the fortress of Eupatorium, any more than he has to the fortresses of Palacium, Chabum, and Neapolis that were constructed by the Tauro-Scythian king Scylurus and his sons; and although the wording of the text leaves us somewhat in a difficulty, it must be borne in mind that Ctenous was at the head of a bay at a distance of 40 stadia only from the Port of Symbols [2] (Balaclava); it should therefore scarcely be looked for where the Tchórnaya flows into a bay at a considerably greater distance than 40 stadia (4½ miles) from Balaclava, and 15 stadia (1·7 mile) from the peninsula between Quarantine bay and Pestchánnaya bay, but rather in the Yoúgenaya, 'south bay,' which is

---

[1] See page 23.   [2] Strabo VII. iv. 2.

within a radius of two miles of the site of ancient Chersonesus, and the extreme inlet on a coast of many harbours, a coast κτενοειδής, 'like a comb,' whence probably the name of Ctenous; and the head of which inlet, previously to being filled in, may have extended two thousand years ago a mile or more further inland, and in the direction of Balaclava.

In persisting in their attacks on that part of the wall that was nearest to Ctenous, the barbarians may in the first place have sought the destruction of the ships of the Chersonians, for the better protection of which the Royalists kept up a line of defence and communication to the promontory now called St. Paul's point, 15 stadia (1·7 mile) from the city, but not at Inkerman which is double that distance, by means of an agger and vallum that crossed the bay, where it had been filled in to shorten the way. With regard to the great wall of the Heracleotic Chersonese, the nature of the country renders it equally possible for that wall to have been constructed from Balaclava to the head of the 'south bay' as to the cliffs at Inkerman; but whichever the direction of the wall of defence built by the Chersonians, it is very certain that there are now no vestiges of it left.

Constantine Porphyrogenitus, who has furnished us with an account of the wars that were fomented between the citizens of Chersonesus and their rivals the Bosporians, includes one of the most romantic episodes in history, which gives us an insight into the manners of a community of Hellenes who preserved their independence, and owed their prosperity and high state of civilisation during the space of one thousand years, to the free institutions they enjoyed, and to their own competence for self-government.

In the reign of Diocletian and the chief magistracy at Chersonesus of Themistos, Sauromates [1] of the Bosperians, the son of Crisconorus, after having overcome the Lazi, reached the banks of the Halys,[2] where he was encountered by Constantine *Chlorus*, who checked his further progress. The Emperor having in the meantime called upon his federates at Chersonesus to attack the Bosporians, Christos, then chief magistrate, held council, and war having been determined upon, the Chersonians proceeded to the Bosphorus, and seized the city (A.D. 304). For this timely service the Chersonians were liberally recompensed, for the Emperor bestowed on them many privileges, including, on their own supplication, immunity from all tribute.

When the Goths rebelled in the reign of Constantine the Great, the Chersonians were summoned to attack the common enemy; Diogenes their president despatched his forces to the Danube, and the Goths were defeated. Thereupon, as a mark of his favour, the Emperor sent to the Chersonians a statue in gold of himself wearing the *chlamys*,[3] and also granted them a yearly subsidy for the supply of warlike engines and men.

Some years after these events, Sauromates, the grandson of the Sauromates who had ravaged Lazia, declared war against the Chersonians, that he might revenge himself for the humiliation to which they had subjected his grandfather; but he was defeated at Caffa by Viskos, and Caffa thereafter became the frontier town of the victors.

After a time, another Sauromates (VII.), desiring to recover Caffa, provoked a war with the Chersonians by insulting them, for he relied greatly upon his own gigantic stature and on the strength

---

[1] This Sauromates could not have been king of the Bosphorus, for Thothorses was the sovereign from 279 to 308.

[2] Now the river Kyzyl Ermaak.

[3] A mantle.

of his forces. When the contending armies met, Pharnaces, the president of Chersonesus, who was a little man, at once engaged with his adversary in single combat, and having slain him, dismounted from his horse and severed the head of the king from his body. With the death of Sauromates his dynasty came to an end, and the Bosporians having declared themselves free, erected a statue in their city to Pharnaces as their deliverer. The boundary of the Chersonian territory now extended to Kimmericum.[1] (A.D. 322.)

Whilst Lamachus was president at Chersonesus, and Asander by election king of the Bosporians, the latter, who was desirous of maintaining friendly relations with his powerful neighbours, sent ambassadors to their city to propose for his son the hand of the daughter of Lamachus; the proposal was accepted on the conditions that the son of Asander should never seek to return to his father's capital, and should even suffer death were he surprised in the attempt. Now, Lamachus had the reputation of being very rich in gold and silver, in slaves, in cattle and estates, and he lived in a magnificent palace near the Bay of Soses.

In due course the nuptials of the son of Asander and Gycia, the daughter of Lamachus, were celebrated. Two years after this marriage Lamachus died, and Gycia bound herself by an oath to celebrate the anniversary of her father's death annually for the rest of her life, by inviting all the citizens and their wives to a banquet. Her husband, who was secretly watching his opportunity, lauded her filial piety, and expressed his own desire to pour out libations in honour of her parents.

After the first banquet had been given, he privately communicated to the Bosporians his plans for rendering himself

[1] At Opouk.

master of Chersonesus, and demanded that ten or twelve youths, well armed, should be sent from time to time by sea to Symvolon, whence they were to proceed on foot to the city. This being done, the armed men were concealed in the house of Gycia as fast as they arrived there to remain until the next commemoration, when they would fall upon the defenceless people in the midst of their diversions, and put them to the sword.

It so happened that while preparations were being made for the second celebration, the handmaid of Gycia who had incurred her mistress's displeasure, was confined in a chamber over that in which the Bosporians were concealed. As she sat spinning, her spindle fell and rolled into a hole near the wall, and not being able to recover it, she removed a piece of the pavement, and happening to look through the opening she had made, saw a number of men assembled; replacing the stone, she immediately sent for her mistress, saying that she wished to speak with her in private. Gycia repaired to the girl's chamber, and discovered the plot; she forgave her maid's transgression, and summoned two of her own relatives in whom she could best confide, to entrust them with a message to the authorities. Having obtained from them the promise, that as a reward for her patriotism she should at her death be buried within the city walls, though contrary to custom, she disclosed to them her husband's treachery.

When the night of the feast came, Gycia commanded that wine should be liberally served; and she herself encouraged others to drink, by pretending to empty a crimson goblet in which diluted wine was repeatedly poured out to her. After the entertainment, the citizens returned to their homes at the usual hour, but some there were that remained, for they were overcome with wine; among these was Gycia's husband. At that moment, Gycia who was attended by her maids bearing her jewels, left the house stealthily, and locking all the doors behind her, caused it to be fired, and the enemies of the Chersonians were consumed. The citizens desired to reconstruct the palace, but Gycia refused the gift, and ordered the site to be made a dungheap which thereafter was called the Den of Lamachus.

In testimony of their gratitude, the citizens caused two statues in bronze of Gycia to be erected in the market-place; one represented her youthful figure as the deliverer of her country, the other as the avenger of her countrymen.

A few years later, when Stratophilus was chief magistrate, Gycia, desiring to put to the test the gratitude of the Chersonians, feigned to be dead, and her friends asked instructions as to the place for her interment. The Chersonians deliberated, and having resolved that Gycia should be buried outside the walls, she was conveyed thither, and so soon as the couch on which she was borne was laid in the vault, she rose, and looking around on them that had followed, said: 'It is thus you observe the promise that was made! Woe be to all who shall hereafter confide in the citizens of Chersonesus.' The Chersonians were put to shame, but they renewed the promise, and forthwith caused a tomb to be prepared with a statue over it, which was completed in the lifetime of Gycia, and in which she was eventually laid.[1]

Although the Emperor Theophilus (833) replaced the *protevontos*, or chief citizen of Chersonesus, by appointing a prefect, whereby the city became a dependency of the empire, it continued to preserve its freedom under its own municipal administration, and the Chersonians were still in the height of their prosperity when

[1] Abridged from *De Administrando Imperio*. Constantine Porphyr. Bonn edition. pp. 144-155.

Vladimir the Russian prince sailed into their bay, and laid siege to the city. The Chersonians opposed a determined resistance and rejected all terms, for they hoped to receive succour from Constantinople; but there was a traitor among them, one named Athanasius, who shot an arrow into the enemy's camp that bore this missive: 'Thou canst stay or divert the course of the springs that are behind thee to the east; it is thence that the city is supplied with water.' 'If this be true,' cried Vladimir, 'I vow to receive baptism.' The inhabitants being driven to extremities for want of water, were forced to yield.

The conquest of this celebrated and opulent city only served to augment the pride of the Russian prince, who now sought to gratify his ambition by allying himself to the powerful Emperors of the East; he accordingly sent to Basil and Constantine to demand their sister Anne in marriage, threatening, in the event of refusal, to seize on Constantinople. The moment was propitious for the Grand Prince, as the Emperor was engaged in suppressing the revolt excited by his general, Phocas, and the hand of the princess was promised to Vladimir on condition of his receiving baptism.

After the celebration of the nuptials at Chersonesus, Vladimir despatched his troops to the support of his imperial relative, and the overthrow of the rebels was accomplished. Vladimir also ceded Chersonesus to his new allies, and being fully initiated in the rites of the religion he had so lately embraced,[1] took his departure for Kieff, where he flung the god *Peroün* into the Dnieper, overturned the pagan altars, and constrained his subjects to receive baptism.[2]

---

[1] Catherine II. instituted the order of St. Vladimir in 1782.

[2] *Histoire de l'Empire de Russie.* M. Karamsin. Paris. 1820. I. p. 265.

The decadence of Chersonesus and the diversion of its extensive commercial relations into other channels, dates from the time when the Genoese obtained the monopoly of trade in the Black Sea, through their influence at the Byzantine Court;[1] but the Christian population in all probability went on increasing, for in 1333 Pope John XXII. constituted Cherson a bishopric, appointing to the see an Englishman who was styled *Ricardus Anglicus*, and in 1384 there was a Metropolitan at Cherson, who disputed with the Metropolitan of Gothia the jurisdiction over the parishes of Sikita (Nikita), Partenite, Lambad, Alousta, Phouna (?) and Alania (?).[2] It was in 1363, however, that Cherson met with its destruction at the hands of Olgerd, Grand Prince of Lithuania, the invader of Russia, who, after leading his armies through Podolia to the Dnieper and defeating the Tatars, pushed his successes into the Taurida, where he slaughtered the Chersonians and denuded their churches. Turkish misrule followed from the reign of Mahomet II., who subjected the whole of the Crimea; and such of the venerable remains of the once proud city as escaped the desolating hand of the Ottoman, were removed by the Russians and utilised in the construction of the city of Sevastópol.

When Dubois de Montpéreux visited the site of Cherson in 1835, spending two months in diligent research, he was able to trace the streets and public places, and where the public buildings of the ancient city had stood; all is much changed since, for the ground has been ploughed up by Russian shells, and the construction of the Bruat battery and French line of attack during the late war have displaced nigh every vestige of anti-

---

[1] Cherson at this epoch was called Sary Kerman, 'Yellow Castle,' by Eastern writers; and Carssona by the Genoese.

[2] Bruun, *Cæsaric*, &c., p. 53.

quity. The walls of the city,[1] in some parts 8 feet thick, that extend from Quarantine to Pestchánnaya bay, and the remains of one tower and a portion of the gate of egress to the Bay of Soses, have alone escaped the general destruction. Within them still stands the imperishable monument of infamy, raised by Gycia to her husband, and near it is a small outlet that led to the landing place at the pier, submerged but still visible beneath the ripple of the waves.

To the west and east, beyond the precincts of the city, are the tombs and sepulchral vaults of the Chersonians, hewn into the rocks that are seen pierced with crypts by fifties, for the most part shapeless and defrauded of their interest from having been wantonly destroyed and converted to various purposes. Many are occupied by fishermen or are the haunts of shepherds, who are ever ready to exchange for a piece or two of imperial silver currency, old coins in bronze of Chersonesus, usually in poor preservation, and of Byzantium in silver and bronze, sometimes in fair condition.

The ruins of three Christian temples have been disinterred at Cherson. Over the remains of one was constructed, in 1853, the Church of St. Olga;[2] it suffered during the war, was restored and reconsecrated in 1857; but the sanctuary of paramount interest is the Church of the Mother of God, in which it is believed that the Grand Prince Vladimir received baptism. The Cathedral Church, still far from completion, which is to enclose and preserve to future ages this interesting monument of the

---

[1] An inscription removed from one of the towers many years ago, recorded that the walls were erected by the Emperor Cæsar Zeno, in the year 512 of the era of Chersonesus, indiction 14 = 476 or 491 A.D. Dubois vi. p. 139.

[2] Olga, a canonised Russian princess, was baptized at Constantinople in the reign of Constantine Porphyrogenitus. She was the widow of Igor.

tenth century, was commenced in 1861 under the auspices of the Emperor, who presented to the adjoining monastery the relics of Russia's sainted prince. The enclosure near the Cathedral inside which are ranged broken shafts, capitals, and other fragments in marble, is pointed out as having been the palace of Vladimir.

We found the monks very civil, but quite unable to give any information on the subject of the churches, except that the 15th of July is their great festival, when the baptism of Vladimir is commemorated by processions, and services celebrate the proclamation of peace after the Crimean war. On sending our cards to the Archimandrite we were admitted to his apartments, and shown a small collection of Chersonian antiquities.

It takes a day to visit the heights of the Alma; the road is dreary and uninteresting; we therefore abandoned the idea of going, and decided upon leaving Sevastópol in the morning.

RUSSIAN MONK.

CHAPTER V.

SIXTH DAY.

Departure from Sevastópol—Valley of Baidar—The betrothed Tatars—A Tatar cottage—The Pass of Phoros—The Chaos—Aloupka—The late Prince Woronzoff—'Trois femmes célèbres'—Dolmens—Pelasgic remains—Imperial residences—The Bay of Yalta—Gourzouff—Ayou-dagh—Lambad—Aloushta—The ancient Chabum—Athenaon.

THE journey from Sevastópol to Yalta, to include a visit to Aloupka, the seat of Prince Woronzoff, may be accomplished within the hours of daylight by taking post-horses, a comfortable carriage being obtainable for 25 to 30 roubles. At seven o'clock on a fine bright morning we left the Hôtel, keeping on the Woronzoff road across the plain of Balaclava with which we had become well acquainted, and passing the Turkish redoubts, beyond which to the right at about the 14-*verst* post, may be traced the old British road to Balaclava, now disused and covered with turf; farther on were the British and Sardinian camps, while on the heights behind the village of Kamara appears here and there the parapet of the British line of defence.

Horses are changed at Tchatall-Kayà, where the country assumes a different aspect, groves and wood succeeding to the bare and stony downs about Sevastópol. A dip in the road brought us to the famed valley of Baïdar, perhaps a corruption

VALLEY OF BAÏDAR.

of the Tatar *bagh*, 'vineyard,' and *deré*, 'valley'; the villages, embosomed in the midst of truly lovely scenery, with luscious pastures, brooks, copses, and cornfields with green hedges, reminding one much of an English landscape. It is to the plentiful irrigation occasioned by numerous small streams, among which is one of the sources of the Tchórnaya-retchka, that is due the verdure of the meadows and the richness of bright foliage. The valley is 12 miles long and 6 miles wide, closed in on the north and south by rocky cliffs above the wooded slopes; to the east by the *jayla*[1] of Ouzountchou, and on the west by the forests of Varnoutka. The oak, which abounds, is small; the next tree in abundance is the juniper, and there are large orchards of fruit-trees of excellent quality, for the apples of Baïdar are pronounced by many to be equal to those of the valley of the Salghyr.

We had some difficulty in persuading the *yamstchyck* to pull up for a few moments that we might look into the village of Baïdar, until a *bakshysh* settled the point. Meeting a Tatar with a handkerchief over his head, its folds hanging down in front and concealing his face, we asked the meaning of a friend by whom he was accompanied, and were informed that this man 'with shame' was to be married in a day or two! We offered to shake hands with him, when he bowed to the outstretched hand and meekly kissed it; we then asked to see the bride, and were invited in a very pressing manner to go to her house; the man 'with shame,' however, did not accompany us. We were shown into a room expressly darkened, in one corner of which crouched the bride, screened by curtains formed of various articles of linen, a proud display of her own trousseau; for three

---

[1] The grassy plateaux on the mountain tops of the south coast, where herds and flocks are kept to graze during the summer months, are called *jayla* by the Tatars.

days preceding the wedding-day, no person may see the bridegroom's or bride's face, 'for it is a shame that they should show themselves.' K—— was permitted to approach the screen, and kindly took the bride's hand, but she turned away her face, which was thickly veiled, and sobbed quite audibly, it being the custom for brides to sob when they become the objects of attention. Nuts, biscuits, coffee and *vodka*[1] were served, and K—— was presented with a towel of the bride's own embroidery in gold and

A TATAR INTERIOR.

coloured threads; we gave *bakshysh* to the children gathered in the room, and were then shown over the rest of the house.

There is little enough mortar employed in the construction of Tatar cottages, which are kept whitewashed without and within, *kil*, 'fuller's earth,' being largely employed for cleaning

[1] The Tatars *on the south coast* eschew wine, but many drink spirits.

purposes and especially for the floors. The apartments for females —the *hárèm*—are on an upper storey, quite separate from those of the men; in the room set apart for receiving visitors are laid mattresses covered with carpeting, which form a *sóffa*, for there are no chairs, and refreshments are placed on a *koursou*, a small stool, in the absence of a table. The females were all unveiled and entered the room and conversed freely; they and the men were most assiduous in their attentions, and we observed that none would seat themselves in our presence, evidently from a feeling of deference.

Loud shouts of *Gaspada, pajálouytye, pajálouytye!*—'Gentlemen, deign to come, deign to come!' repeated in a painfully supplicating voice, reminded us that we were exceeding the limits of even a *yemstchyck's* patience and indifference; we thanked the Tatars for their hospitality, and were soon on the hill that leads to the post station of Baïdar, whence we walked to the Baïdar gate at the summit of the pass of Phoros while the horses were being changed. Upon gazing through the gate—it is a frame to the picture—one of the grandest sights that it is possible to imagine, offered by a combination in close proximity, of mountain, cliff, and beautiful region, to the open sea, presents itself to the view; of its kind there is probably nothing like it elsewhere. In front rise perpendicularly to many hundreds of feet bold precipitous cliffs, the sturdy pine and hardy juniper looking like tufts of verdure as they overhang the perilous brinks from the *yaylas* above, while here and there from fissures in the rock strike forth again the pine and juniper or the beech. Lower down, declivities extend to the right, their irregular surfaces, overspread with a compact growth of garden, orchard, and wood, projecting into the sea, and shaping the most fantastic of sea-boards. Far below, and only just above where the waves beat, appear the residences of the opulent, and occasionally a Tatar hamlet. It would be scarcely possible not to experience some kind of delight at the novelty of the scene.

The carriage joined us, and we commenced a winding descent skirting the foot of the cliffs, which increase to quite 1,000 feet in height; again their grandeur lessens, and small rills oozing through the clefts, course away almost in a whisper down the slopes and into the waters of the Black Sea. Several landslips will be noticed on this road, a remarkable sight being at Kastropolo.

Horses are again changed at Kykeneïs, a good-sized Tatar village, where cultivation is sumptuous; the Genoese called it Chinicheo, and appointed a priest. Beyond Kykeneïs is Lymena, above which are the ruins of a fort called by the Tatars, Khazar, and on approaching the village of Symeïs, more gigantic rocks of granite are seen scattered in an almost direct line from the foot of the cliff to the sea; on one of these formidable masses, now a seaside rock, are the ruins of an old fort. Dubois writes of these convulsions of nature: 'Les grands agents de ce formidable acte de puissance sont deux jets porphyriques, qui ont percé à travers le schiste entre Limène et Kikineïs, et qui, s'élevant à une hauteur considérable, sont allés heurter jusque sous la voûte de la muraille calcaire. Brisée par cet effort, la muraille s'est séparée et forme dans la Yaïla une espèce de golfe et même des îles de schiste, élevé ici à la plus grande hauteur qu'atteigne le calcaire. Dans ce schiste refoulé en haut par la force du jet igné, nulle trace de couche régulière. L'on voit des fragments de schistes empâtés en entier dans les porphyres, ce qui prouve qu'ils étaient dans un état liquéfié quand ils ont formé leurs jets.'[1] The best view of the remarkable chaos of Symeïs, is obtained by looking back from between the ninth and tenth *verst* stone, on the high road between Mysh'orr and Kykeneïs, when for the first time the mansion of Aloupka appears; a little way beyond is the descent to the valley of Aloupka, where we had decided on spending a few hours. The post station of Mysh'orr, the Mouzacori of the Genoese, is just above Aloupka, but beyond the turn off the post road that leads to the valley; here a difficulty arose—how were we to reach Aloupka, unless our carriage conveyed us, and so long as the *yemstchyck* refused to proceed elsewhere than to the station? Recourse was had to purse-strings, and a rouble satisfied his scruples; the horses' heads were turned, and in twenty minutes we were set down at the inn, seven hours after quitting Sevastópol.

The grounds at Aloupka are open to the public; but the house can be seen only on making special application. After some consideration, and the assurance of the innkeeper, a tenant on the estate, that Prince Woronzoff was ready at all times to gratify strangers, Mr. S——[2] addressed a note requesting the favour of being permitted to view the mansion. One of our party was a lady, and, like a gallant knight, the prince shortly appeared in person, and expressing the pleasure it would afford him that we should visit the estate, placed at our service his head gardener, by whom he had come attended.

At the appointed hour we walked to the castle, which has been the subject of criticism of every traveller. Constructed of ophitic granite, it is a combination of the Moorish and decorative Gothic, surmounted by castellated turrets. A gem in itself, it is ill supported by two irregular wings of an uncertain style of

---

[1] Dubois vi. p. 82.   [2] The late Mr. J. Coysgarne Sim of Coombe Wood.

architecture, wanting in harmony and solidity, and although various architects were employed in the completion of this mansion, the coach-houses, stables, and offices remain attached to the house. Of the decorations and fittings of the interior there is nothing to record, for they are of the simplest kind. Owing to the sloping nature of the ground, the principal entrance to the building, in front of which are two cypresses said to have been planted in 1787 by Potyómkine, is in a confined situation, but the façade to seaward, partly a sectional reproduction of the Alhambra, is fine. The steps from the front lead to where innumerable paths diverge and traverse the grounds, which are an interesting exhibition of the vegetation of all climes, thriving in perplexing confusion. One sees the pomegranate, fig, and mulberry, huge magnolias, sycamore and lotus trees, the graceful wild vine, and the Judas tree without end: here and there a cypress or cedar, the almond and wild chestnut, cork, medlar, pistachio, tamarind, turpentine, the arbutus, the *Arbutus andrachæ* a curious-looking tree without any bark, and thickets of laurel, myrtle, laurestinus, rhododendron, &c.; everywhere a tangle of the clematis, while the walks are bordered with the wild rose; nowhere has nature so bountifully lent its aid to art. East of the mansion, a labyrinth of footways lined with a liberal supply of unpretending fountains, conducts to a series of grottoes, some of natural formation, others artificial, and in the midst of them is a large basin in which trout revel unmolested; it is near this pond that two *Wellingtoniæ giganteæ* were planted by the Prince and Princess of Wales in 1869. At the rear of the pond is 'the Chaos,' where lie in marvellous disorder monstrous masses of granite: 'Il m'a paru probable,' wrote Dubois, 'que le granite ophitique formait une couche solide. Une rude commotion aura brisé cette roche et en aura jeté les débris dehors, en les entassant autour du point d'éruption.'[1] But the attraction, the spell at Aloupka, is the enchanting situation of the house. Fifty years ago a traveller wrote : ' Il seroit à désirer que quelque grand propriétaire fit l'acquisition d'Aloupka ; il ne faudroit pas beaucoup d'art pour en faire le séjour le plus enchanteur, tandis que l'indolent Tatar ne songe pas même à remplacer, par un nouvel arbre, l'arbre qui dépérit.' At 150 feet above the sea, a great excavation was made in the hill-side, and on it stands the mansion and its appurtenances facing the Euxine ; the ground to the rear is a continued slope to the foot of Aïpetry,[2] a stupendous cliff rising perpendicularly with scarcely a break to a height above the sea of 3,798 feet. The two points, Aïtodor and Kourtyry bouroun to the south, form the extremes of the little bay of Aloupka.

Near the mansion is the old country house of the late Prince Woronzoff, in which he planned, carried out, and perfected with singular success his great conception in the creation of Aloupka as it is. The Genoese called the place Lupico.

The late Prince Mihail Simiónovitch Woronzoff, born at St. Petersburg in 1782, was the son of a distinguished statesman, Count Simon Woronzoff, who died in London, whither he had been sent as ambassador. Mihail Woronzoff received his education in England, and commenced his military career in the Caucasian corps commanded by a Georgian, Prince Tzytzyanoff ;[3] he remained in the Caucasus until 1805, when the Prusso-French war called him to Germany. In 1807, war broke out with Turkey,

---

[1] Dubois, vi. p. 81.
[2] There is a bridle road over the Aïpetry to Baghtchasarai.
[3] Tzytzyanoff was a man of undaunted courage. It is related that Souvaroff was in the habit of encouraging his men when in action, by telling them to fight 'like the brave Tzytzyanoff.'

and Woronzoff went to that country as a colonel; in 1810 and 1811, he distinguished himself considerably, and was advanced to the rank of major-general. In 1812, Napoleon commenced the Russian campaign; Woronzoff took part in the war, and commanded a division of 12,000 men (the Grenadiers) at Borodino, where he was severely wounded and had the whole of his division cut to pieces; to a sergeant-major was left the command of the survivors, all the officers having been either killed or wounded. Woronzoff commanded the Russian Chasseurs in support of the Swedish battalions at Leipzic, and offered so obstinate a resistance to Napoleon himself at the battle of Craone in the campaign of 1814, as to elicit from the Emperor the flattering observation: 'Voilà le bois dont on fait des maréchaux.' He drove before him the divisions of the Generals Mensnier, Curial, and Boyer de Rebeval, and subsequently conducted a masterly retreat when the Cavalry of the Guard were directed by Bonaparte to turn the Russian right, and was again personally opposed to Bonaparte, who held the village of Clacy.[1] He subsequently commanded the Russian army of occupation in France after the peace of 1815, and when, on leaving, many of his officers, seduced by the temptations of that delightful country had contracted debts, and left that country without paying, he, in order to save the honour of the Russian name, ordered all the bills to be brought to him, paid them out of his own pocket, and burnt the whole of them. After the conclusion of the war he went to England, where he was always fond of residing, until he was recalled in 1823 to undertake the government of Bessarabia. In 1844 he was made *namestnyk*[2] or Lieutenant of the Emperor in

---

[1] *Memoir of the Operations of the Allied Armies*, &c. by Major-General Lord Burghersh. 1822, p. 194.

[2] An exalted rank rarely conferred.

the Caucasian provinces, Commander-in-Chief of the Army of the Caucasus, and Admiral of the Caspian Sea, so that he held the supreme command over all the country from Poland to Persia.

After Prince Woronzoff's assumption of government in the Caucasus, the whole aspect of the country became changed; towns were built, roads made, peculation checked, honourable feelings stimulated in the officers, and the condition of the private soldiers was greatly improved. The natives were raised to a level with the Russians, and all were alike treated with respect and urbanity. He displayed administrative abilities of the highest order, and possessed the rare quality of securing the affection and raising the tone of all around him. Those who hated the Russian name made an exception in his favour, and the chivalrous Georgians would have died to serve him. Mr. Seymour adds: 'I never yet have met an individual in whom the fundamental virtues of courage, prudence, generosity, and magnanimity were enhanced by such acute sagacity, such delicate refinement of sentiment, such simplicity of manners, and a modesty which, when it survives the trial of power, is the surest sign of a superior mind.'[1] Woronzoff died in 1856.

There was no hesitation on the part of the post-master at Mysh'orr to send horses to us at Aloupka; and after an early dinner at the inn, where are some of the best wines of the Woronzoff estates, we got away in ample time to enable us to complete before dark our journey along the delightful coast.

At a short distance beyond Mysh'orr is Gaspra, where, during the reign of Alexander I., three ladies—the Princess Galitzin, the Baroness de Krüdener (who coolly told the Emperor

---

[1] *Schamyl and Circassia*, Dr. F. Wagner, p. 113. Seymour, *Russia on the Black Sea*, &c., p. 207.

he was a sinner), and the soi-disant Countess Guacher—took up their residence after their banishment to the Crimea, and entered upon the task of trying to convert the Tatars to Christianity. A few years after the Countess died, it was discovered that she was the Countess de la Mothe who was publicly whipped and branded on the Place de la Grève, as an accomplice in the scandalous affair of the diamond necklace of Marie Antoinette. The history of the three ladies is admirably told by the graceful and vigorous pen of Madame de Hell, in the chapter entitled 'Trois femmes célèbres.'[1]

The headland with the lighthouse is Aïtodor, the east extreme of the Criumetopon, and here the mountains begin to recede. Twenty yards off the road to the right, in a direct line with the third *verst* stone, are three dolmens similar to the dolmen at Trie described by Ferguson,[2] except that these are not holed; they are set north and south; the largest is almost perfect, the others have suffered most perhaps at the hand of man; the following are the dimensions of the large dolmen :—

	Sides.		Top.	
	Ft.	In.	Ft.	In.
Length	7	0	8	0
Depth	3	6	5	6
Thickness	0	10	0	14

These dolmens are on the property of the Grand Duke Michael, brother to the Emperor, who will no doubt take good care that such relics of antiquity shall suffer no further injury.

Happening to visit the lighthouse upon one occasion, I

---

[1] *Les steppes de la Mer Caspienne, &c.*, X. Hommaire de Hell, 1845. Seymour, l.c. p. 209.

[2] *Rude Stone Monuments in all Countries*, &c., Jas. Ferguson, D.C.L., 1872.

came to some Cyclopean remains—enormous masses of stone are laid above each other, appearing to have formed part of a bulwark of defence on the land side; but there are now no means of tracing its extent. Numerous graves of comparatively modern construction have been disturbed about these ruins; they are of hewn stone covered with slabs, and were found filled with earth. I obtained a few bronze coins of Bithynia, Chios, and the Chersonesus, that had been turned up in the little garden attached to the lighthouse.

We passed *Verkʼnaya* Orianda, 'Upper Orianda,' once the property of General de Witt—Orianda, which belongs to the Grand Duke Constantine; and Livadia, the summer residence of the Empress—and at 6.30 P.M. we reached the little town of Yalta.

The anchorage at Yalta, in 13 fathoms, is exposed to east and south-west winds, and a south or south-westerly breeze is usually accompanied by a disturbed sea, which renders the process of embarkation or landing very disagreeable, and at times prevents all communication between a ship and the shore. We repaired to the office fully an hour before the time appointed for the departure of the steamer, 8.30 P.M., to secure cabins for our voyage; various delays, however, caused by the want of efficient means for the transport of passengers and goods, for there was an unpleasant swell at the time, detained the vessel until 9.45 P.M., when we steered out of the little bay, every part of the steamer being crowded with passengers. It is singular that the Steam Navigation Company, which is in such prosperous and wealthy circumstances, should be so niggardly in its administration, regardless of the comfort of passengers and the safety of merchandise, notwithstanding the high charges made for passage and freight; small steam launches might easily be provided at Yalta at an insignificant cost, to replace the clumsy and insufficiently manned boats so totally unsuited to an open roadstead.

On leaving Yalta, the course lays near enough to the coast to be able to distinguish[1] the properties and hamlets that dot the declivities abutting from the cliffs as far as Aloushta. The more remarkable are Lower and Upper Massandra, the properties of Prince Woronzoff, Magaratch and the Botanic Gardens of Nikita, both belonging to the Crown, and Aïdanyll, again an estate of Prince Woronzoff. On rounding Nikita point, the picturesque bay of Gourzouff opens out, with its Tatar village rising terrace-like amid rich vegetation; it has a small mole below the cliff that is capped by the ruins of a fortification attributed to Justinian, called by Procopius the fortress of the Gorzubitæ,[2] and off the shore are two high insulated rocks; the fortress was restored by the Genoese, who called the place Garzuni, Grasni, and Gorzanium, and appointed to it a consul or chief magistrate. The adjoining promontory Ayou-dagh 'bear mountain,' which rises to 1,800 feet above the sea, and has precipitous sides covered with wood, projects with much originality of form, and receives the name from its resemblance to a bear stooping to drink.

Beyond Ayou-dagh is the small cove and Tatar hamlet of Partenite; this place appears to have been of sufficient importance in the fifteenth century to have necessitated the appointment to it of a consul by the Italian Republic, and a

---

[1] When the voyage east from Yalta is performed during the day, the steamers leave that port at 7 A.M.
[2] Procopius, *de Ædif*. iii. 7.

century later the Metropolitans of Cherson and of Gothia disputed the cure of the parish. Another small cove is that of Lambad—Lambadie of Gothia, having behind it Mount Babougan, which ends the range on the south coast. In ancient times Lambad was distinguished as Lampadum.[1]

In the mediæval Italian charts, notably in that of the Brothers Pizzigani, 1367 (preserved at the Biblioteca Nazionale, Parma), a harbour named Pangropoli appears between Laspa and Austa (Aloushta), and was in all probability identical with this ancient port of Lampadum, which affords a more secure anchorage than does Partenite.

By a little bay on a lovely shore, is Aloushta the ancient Alustum, another fortress of Justinian, and a consular station of the Italians as Lusta and Lusce; behind it is the great Tchadyrdagh. The land thence becomes almost a desert in appearance, and trends away to the north-east, while the vessel's course lies for Cape Tchóbàn-bash, 'shepherd's head,' inside which is the vine-growing district of Soudàk.

After passing Cape Tchóbàn-bash the coast becomes abrupt and inhospitable, except at the little anchorage of Otouz, near which are said to be the ruins of Chabum,[2] one of the fortresses mentioned by Strabo as having been erected by the Scythian king Scilurus. The high point of land that erects itself so gloomily is appropriately called Kàra-dagh, 'black mountain,' and farther on is the Bay of Koktebel, where was probably the port of Athenaon which Arrian found deserted. Athenaon was 200 stadia from Theodosia,[3] and 1,125 stadia from Symvolon,

---

[1] Seym. Ch. 824.
[2] Blaramberg, *Trois forteresses Tauro-Scythes, etc.*, p. 27.
[3] Seym. Ch. 834.

distances that somewhat exceed the actual length of coast, but careful measurements made on the presumption that modern Theodosia [1] is near to where stood the ancient city, will, I think, point to Koktebel as having been the site of Athenaon.

[1] Pronounced Feodosia by the Russians.

DOLMENS AT AÏTODOR.

CHAPTER VI.

SEVENTH DAY.

Arrival at Theodosia—Earliest history—The Genoese—The Turks—Our passengers—The Karavy rocks—Ancient Kimmericum—Grecian colonies—Pavlovsky fortress—Port of Kertch—Panticapæum—Kingdom of the Pontus; of the Bosphorus—The Alans—Huns—Goths—Kyertcheff—The Museum—Mount Mithridates—Catacombs—The Bashlỹk—Excavations—Scythian burial.

Soon after daylight we rounded Theodosia point and steamed alongside the pier; there is good anchorage in 8 to 10 fathoms, with deep water close in shore. The moment is opportune, during a short hour's stay, whilst passengers and goods are being landed and embarked, for reviewing the history of this ancient and more than once opulent city.

The earliest appellation of Theodosia appears to have been Ardavda, 'City of the Seven Gods';[1] it fell into the possession of the Milesians who colonised it in the seventh century B.C., and so great was the fertility of the neighbouring country, that Leucon, king of the Bosphorus, 393–353 B.C., who seized on it, is stated to have sent 2,100,000 *medimni*[2] of corn to the Athenians, and Theodosia[3] won for itself the distinction of being called the 'granary of Greece.' That such a prodigious quantity of corn should have been shipped from one place in a year, has been

---

[1] Ἐπτάθεος, *Anon. Perip.* 51. [2] Medimnus = 12 gallons.
Θεοῦ δόσις, 'Gift of God.'

a subject for doubt, but as one-third of that amount is exported yearly from Odessa, it is very possible that even the great supply quoted by Strabo could have been collected at one time for the purpose of relieving a famine, as conjectured by Demosthenes in his celebrated oration. After the assumption of power by Mithridates in the Bosphorus Theodosia paid tribute to that monarch, but when Arrian visited the coast, two centuries later, he found the place deserted.

Of its modern history we learn that, about the years 1263-67, the Genoese fixed upon this desirable port for their headquarters in the Black Sea; the new colony soon afterwards found support under the auspices of the Emperor Michael VIII. (Palæologus), who conceded to the Italians the monopoly of trade above the Thracian Bosphorus; and so rapidly did the importance of Caffa increase, that in 1289 the colony was enabled to fit out a squadron of three ships which was despatched under the command of the Consul Paolino Doria to the relief of Tripoli, a sister colony in Syria. Such prosperity excited the malevolence of the Venetians, whose influence at the Byzantine capital had waned, and in 1296 they sent a fleet of 25 sail, commanded by Admiral Soranzo, who destroyed the town of Caffa and reduced the Genoese naval force. The colony soon recovered from this disaster, but only to receive another check at the hands of the Khan of Kiptchak, who in 1308 sought to punish it for kidnapping Tatar children and sending them as slaves into Egypt. The indomitable energy of the Italians was not to be repressed, for Caffa again recovered, and in 1318 the city was raised to a bishopric.[1] Peace was

---

[1] The eparchiate extended *e villa Varia in Bulgaria usque ad Seray inclusive in longitudinem; et a mari Pontico usque ad terram Ruthenorum in latitudinem.* Bull of Pope John XXII. Dubois. v. p. 283.

enjoyed until 1344, when the Khan, desiring to avenge the death of one of his subjects who had been killed in an altercation with an Italian, lay siege to Caffa, but was repulsed with loss; and then were erected by Goffredo di Zoagli, 1352-53, for better security against the enemies of the Republic, the proud fortifications of which some traces still remain. Caffa continued to be a powerful and prosperous city, and the chief centre of the Genoese commercial relations in the Black Sea, extending from Moncastro[1] on the Dniester, along the shores of the Crimea and of the Caucasus, to Trebizond, Simisso,[2] Sinope, and Samastro,[3] on the southern shores; but after the capture of Constantinople by the Turks, followed by the destruction of the Empire of Trebizond, and the submission of all the ports in Anatolia, the Genoese at Caffa became apprehensive of attack, and they accordingly strengthened their fortifications by erecting new walls of defence, and they also sent embassies to seek the alliance of the Holy Father and of the sovereigns of the West. But discreditable intrigues and internal dissensions led to strife with the Crim-Tatars, who appealed to the Sultan of Turkey for support, and thenceforth the Genoese power became doomed to extermination,[4] for Mahomet II., *Alèm ghyr*, 'conqueror of the world,' followed up his conquests by despatching his Vizir, Ahmet Pasha, with a fleet of galleys to subdue the Crimea. In June 1475 Caffa was bombarded, and the inhabitants surrendered at discretion after a feeble resistance: the foreigners found in the city were heavily fined, some being sent into slavery, and the Genoese had to yield large contributions, after which they were transported *en masse* to Constantinople. The Turks gave

---

[1] Ancient Tyra, now Akerman.   [2] Samsoun.
[3] Ancient Amastris, now Amastra.   [4] Heyd, *Le colonie, etc.*, ii. p. 157.

Caffa the name of *Yárym Stámbol*, 'half Stamboul,' and *Koútchouk Stámbol*, 'little Stamboul,' in regard to its considerable size, for at that time it included a population of 100,000 Christians, and could boast of having 50 Christian churches, numerous mosques, synagogues, and other public buildings. Under Ottoman misrule the glory of Caffa soon passed away, and in more recent times the soldiers of the Tzar completed the destruction of its monuments.

The origin of the name of Caffa is not known; it is presumed by some to be a corruption of Χάβον (Chabum), the Tauro-Scythian fortress, believed to have been on the adjacent coast; or it may be from *kjafyr*, the Turkish for infidel, were there any evidence of the place having been occupied by a Christian people before the reign of Constantine Porphyrogenitus, in whose works the name appears for the first time with reference to events that had taken place in the fourth century. Nothing more is heard of 'Capha' until the tenth century, when it is mentioned in a Hebrew MS. as being inhabited by Karaïm Jews.[1]

We left many visitors at Theodosia, the most favoured if not the most fashionable watering-place in the Crimea, for the busy season on this coast is from May to September, when the steamers are overcrowded with passengers: those on deck supply themselves with their own provisions, and a *samovar*[2] on the funnel casing, kept filled with boiling water, is at their service for the favourite occupation of tea-drinking, so that they make themselves comfortable and happy with very little trouble. Few there are who do not carry their own bedding, which they spread where they please; and they are permitted to smoke everywhere, undoubtedly the safest method for ensuring security from fire, as in this way none

---

[1] Bruun, *Căzarie*, &c., p. 65.   Russian tea urn.

are under the necessity of resorting to shifts for enjoying a coveted whiff.

Beyond Cape Tash-Kyryk, the east extreme of the Bay of Theodosia, are seen the *Karazy*, 'ship' rocks, called by the Tatars *Sytchan kalch*, 'rat fortress,' a mile or two off that part of the coast where was the ancient Kimmericum, 'a port sheltered from westerly gales,'[1] called Ciprico in the Middle Ages, and now the Tatar village of Opouk. Dubois[2] has given a long description of his researches among the considerable ruins of Kimmericum. At Cape Yaynysh Takyl are numerous tumuli, which perhaps denote the site of Cytis, and after doubling the lighthouse on that cape, we passed the Salt-lakes of Tobetchyck, near the ground where stood Accra, mentioned by Strabo as being within the territory of the Panticapæans, and separated from Corocondame by a channel 70 stadia wide. We had now entered the strait of Kertch, steaming off a rocky shore to Kára-boúroun, 'black cape,' between which and Kámysh-boúroun, 'reed cape,' was once 'the good port' of Nymphæum, a Milesian colony, now the Salt-lakes of Tchourou-bash, separated from the waters of the strait by an isthmus formed of the accumulated sand borne from the Sea of Azoff during many centuries.

Outside Ak-boúroun, 'white cape,' is the shelving shore where the Allies landed in May 1855.[3] The batteries that were attacked by a British gunboat have been superseded by the Pavlovsky fortress, a combination of masked batteries and covered ways over an extent of two miles, the casemates being masked by massive earthworks supported in their rear with buttresses of masonry; there are also embrasure batteries, at present showing

---

[1] Seym. Ch. 835. [2] Dubois, v. p. 258.
[3] The British, French, and Turkish force amounted to 15,000 men.

from 100 to 120 guns, the whole being surmounted by the citadel, Fort Todleben, whence the fire is directed by means of telegraphic communication, the entire view to seaward being comprehended in a camera. At night a lime-light will be burnt at the lighthouse, when required during hostilities.

Fortifications one-fifth the size of the Pavlovsky, and a few torpedoes, would have sufficed to defend the entrance, half a mile in width, between the Touzla bank and the works. When it is considered that this fortress might be invested by an enemy without a mighty effort, and the supply of water at the rear cut off, it is difficult to conceive the object with which these enormous defences have been erected, defences which in time of war will necessitate a garrison of many thousand men. A second Sevastópol has been raised, without the advantages of a good port.

Two miles beyond Ak-boúroun, which the Italians called Aspromiti, is the town and harbour of Kertch, where we came to an anchor at 1 P.M. The strait was filled with shipping, large vessels lying in mid-channel, the shallows at 15 feet only, extending fully two miles from the quays. The town presents a striking appearance, rising as it does from the water's edge, and is built over the ruins of the most ancient of the Grecian colonies that lined the shores of this strait 2,000 years ago.

In the sixth century B.C., the Ionic Grecians founded a colony here, which was named Panticapæum; the probability of its having been dedicated to the god Pan is indicated by the autonome coins, which bear on them the effigy of that divinity. Some writers have derived the name from πάντα κῆπος, 'ever a garden,' perhaps because Pliny has stated that fruit-trees were abundant in the Bosphorus.[1]

[1] Pliny, xvi. 3.

In the year 480 B.C., Archæanax became the chief ruler, and his dynasty, known as that of the Archæanætidæ, was succeeded by that of Spartacus, 438 B.C., which preserved its independence until 115 B.C., when Parisades, the last sovereign, surrendered his kingdom, which included the two cities of Panticapæum and Phanagoria, to Mithridates (Eupator), king of the Pontus, that he might escape the oppression of the Royal Scythians who occupied the country about the Mæotis (Sea of Azoff), and the Taurida; it would appear by this that the Grecian colonists, and there were many about the Cimmerian Bosphorus,[1] did not in any way promote the civilisation of those barbarians. Thereafter, Panticapæum with other Greek towns became a dependency of the Pontus, and was given in appanage to Machares, a son of Mithridates, who chose to die rather than fall into the hands of his father, after having been obliged to subject himself to the dominion of the Romans.

After the victories of Lucullus and the pursuit by Pompey, Mithridates fled to the Bosphorus, 64 B.C., but the treachery of both his sons disconcerted the scheme the aged king had formed of invading Italy, at a time when the Romans in large force under Pompey were far away; and fearing to fall into the hands of the enemies ever so bitter to him, he destroyed himself by taking poison. Peace followed for a time, until Pharnaces, the late monarch's eldest son, who had been suffered by Rome to assume the sovereignty of the Bosphorus, impatient of his subjection, and aspiring to the recovery of his father's lost kingdom, clutched at the Pontus, defeated its governor, and carrying his victories into Bithynia and Cappadocia, was on the point of

---

[1] Herodotus, Strabo, and other ancient authors have written this name, Bosporus, with π.

attacking Armenia, when Cæsar marching against him overthrew him in a great battle at Zelah (Zileh), the very field on which Mithridates had defeated a portion of the army of Lucullus. Such was the celerity with which Cæsar overcame his enemy, that he laconically reported his victory in the well-known words, *Veni, vidi, vici.*

Strabo describes Panticapæum at about this period as being inhabited for a circuit of over two miles; the harbour, which had docks capable of receiving thirty vessels, is now filled in.

After the defeat of Pharnaces, and the violent death he met with upon his return to his states, 39 B.C., the kingdom of the Bosphorus continued subject to Rome, and Mithridates of Pergamus was sent by Cæsar to rule over it. He was, however, resisted by Asander, one of the generals of Pharnaces, who had revolted and rendered himself independent, assuming the title of Archon; he afterwards became king by authority of Augustus, and reigned from 39 to 11 B.C. At his death the crown passed to Polemo I., king of Cilicia and a portion of Pontus, who married Dynamis, the widow of Asander, and afterwards Pythodoris, the daughter of a wealthy citizen of Tralles, by whom he had three sons, who all occupied the throne. One of his sons and successors, Polemo II., was invested by Caligula with the kingdom of the Bosphorus and Pontus, A.D. 38; he married Berenice, the daughter of Agrippa, and embraced the Jewish religion, which he renounced when his wife deserted him.[1] This line of sovereigns ended with Rescouporis VII. A.D. 335.

About A.D. 62, the Alans, a ferocious people in war, whose earliest migrations to the West had taken place during the first hundred years before the Christian era, carried their rapine

---

[1] *Souvenirs de Kertch et chronologie du Royaume de Bosphore.* J. Sabatier, 1849, p. 49.

beyond the Palus Mæotis and attacked the Tauric-Scythians;[1] they were dislodged by the Goths who remained in peaceable possession, until the Huns in 376 swept over the peninsula, carrying destruction before them. Panticapæum was then known as Bosporus.[2] The Huns, however, passed on to the Ister (Danube), and the Goths resumed their agricultural occupations on the shores of the Taurida, those who occupied the Cimmerian Bosphorus being distinguished as the Tetraxite Goths. The Goths became Christians, and the seaboard was called Gothia until the sixteenth century, though ceded to the Genoese by treaty *circa* 1380. In the Italian charts of the fourteenth and fifteenth centuries, Panticapæum or Bosporus appears as Cospo, Cospro, Bospro and Pondico, also Bosphorio Cimmerio; it was likewise called Cerchio, possibly from the Russian name of Kyertcheff, in the eleventh century. In 1332, Vospro was the seat of a Metropolitan, twenty-ninth in order of precedence, and became a settlement of the Venetians, with the permission of the Crimean Khan, after their loss in 1343 of Tana,[3] which was situated where now is Azoff; but it is not clear when the Venetians quitted Vospro to be occupied by the Genoese settlers, for whose protection a consul was appointed in 1449. In 1771, Kertch (called Ghersety by the Turks) was ceded together with Yeny-Kaleh to the Empress Catherine II., by the Khan Sahym Ghyrey, in grateful acknowledgment of her support at a time when he had incurred the displeasure of the Sultan, but the aid and protection afforded to the usurping Khan was only the customary prelude to conquest, repeated over again in the history of Russia; the cession of the two fortresses

---

[1] Josephus, *Wars of the Jews*, VII. v.i. 4. Ammian Marcell. lib. xxxi.

[2] Procopius, *De bello Gothico*, iv. 5.

[3] Descendants of the Italians were at Azoff as late as the year 1665; among them were the Spinolas of Genoa. Heyd, *Le Colonie*, &c., ii. p. 164.

was confirmed by the treaty of Kaïnardjee, which opened the Euxine to the Russian flag, and Ghersety was immediately named Kertch.

Upon landing from the steam-tender in the midst of strange confusion and disorder among the servants of the Steam Navigation Company, we proceeded to the Hôtel de St. Petersburg, a sorry house, though the best in the town. In due course, a *droshky* was hired at sixty copecks the hour (for country or town), and we drove to the Museum, removed from a worthier building since the war. A few duplicates of the relics of people long passed away are allowed to remain at Kertch; but it is in the magnificent room prepared for their reception at the Hermitage, St. Petersburg, that are to be seen the exquisite golden ornaments and trinkets, most perfect specimens of the high condition of art in Greece, as far and as immeasurably superior in their workmanship to anything of their sort that has been found elsewhere, as Greece itself was ever superior to Rome in the production of art. Among the interesting relics at the Kertch Museum are some laurel crowns of beaten gold that encircled the brows of the dead; there are also many amphoræ, vases, figures in terra-cotta, and osseous remains, all from the tumuli and catacombs that are explored in the neighbourhood year after year; a few inscriptions on marble, and some coins, complete the collection. The need of a catalogue is greatly felt.

From the Museum we drove through the market-place to the foot of a flight of steps of modern construction, fast going to decay from neglect. Ordering the carriage to meet us on the Theodosia road near the catacombs, we mounted the steps to the Russian Church, an edifice erected in 1823 on the model of the Temple of Theseus to receive the antiquities of Kertch, and which continued to be the Museum until the town was evacuated by the Russians in 1855. From the Church we completed the ascent over *debris* of pottery, fragments of marble and brick, to the summit of the hill, an irregular cone, crowned by a mass of rock that has been hewn into shape, there being on the west side some steps leading to a niche known as the armchair of Mithridates, the sovereign of twenty-two nations, who dispensed justice to each in its own language, without the aid of an interpreter.[1] Here had stood the Acropolis of his predecessors, and on the hill-sides are still to be seen the remains of masonry. Local tradition asserts that Mithridates was buried here, hence the name of the hill, 'the Mountain of Mithridates,' Mytrydátskaya garà—notwithstanding the certainty that the monarch was interred at Sinope by direction of Pompey, with all regal honours. Souvaroff is stated to have knelt and wept on this spot, believing it to have been the sepulchre of the great king. Dubois, with much reason, conceived the rocky summit to have been part of an edifice that probably had a religious destination, from the circumstance of a fine torso of the statue of Cybele, of colossal dimensions, having been found at the foot of the rock.

The tasteless erection overlooking the town, is a tribute to the memory of a governor of Kertch, named Stempkoffsky, an antiquarian of some merit. A grand view is obtained from this site, 400 feet above the strait, which includes the horizon of the Black Sea and of the Sea of Azoff, and the intervening coast on the opposite shore between Cape Kyshla to the south and Cape Kamny on the north; it is in contemplation to construct a

[1] Pliny, VII. xxiv.

fortification here, as an outpost to the Pavlovsky fortress. To the rear of the mount lie a succession of conical elevations connected by a ridge of coral rag, there being in the range the regal sepulchres known as the Zolotoï Kourgan, or Altynóda, 'Golden Chamber,' and the Kyoul-óda, 'Chamber of Ashes.'

We descended the hill in the direction of the village of Glynytchye, and got to the catacombs, distant 1½ mile due west of the town, where a large number of graves are laid open, also other excavations that are entered by a doorway and contain from four to eight niches of a size to hold a body at full length. Among them were made some interesting discoveries in 1872.

In one catacomb, found emptied of its contents, the ceiling and champs are plastered over and painted with a variety of subjects. We see a combat between two horsemen; one holds his lance pointed at an adversary, who lies wounded beneath his horse; near these warriors is another horse bending over his fallen rider, who lies decapitated;[1] some of the men are represented in shirts of mail, trousers with belts, and high conical head coverings. In another picture is a wood with stags and tigers, and on three sides of the chamber are niches having above them beasts, winged genii, a peacock, and some scolopendra. In another catacomb are more battle scenes, between beardless men, and their vanquished enemies who have beards and thick hair; the former are in a kind of armour, and provided with two

---

[1] It has been noticed elsewhere how the last of the Sauromatian dynasty met with his death in single combat with Pharnaces, ruler of the Chersonians, and was decapitated by his foe. The Bosporians, who erected a statue to the victor whose prowess had rendered them a free people, may have sought to represent in this regal catacomb the discomfiture of their king.

javelins and a shield; the latter are armed with bows, a lance and shield; again is seen the conical but sharper-pointed cap. There is also a variety of birds, wild beasts, and flowers; two statuettes in terra-cotta were the only articles found. These two catacombs are walled up to save them from destruction, but the drawings have been reproduced on canvas, and are to be seen at the Museum on application.

The pointed head covering is greatly worn in Russia, where it is called a *bashlyk*, and is in all probability the most ancient portion of dress that has descended to our own times. We read in Herodotus, that in the mighty army of Xerxes the Sacæ or Scythians 'wore a cap rising to a point in the form of a pyramid';[1] and on the golden ornaments found in Scythian tombs, near Kertch, and in the South of Russia on the banks of the Dnieper and Don, Scythian warriors are represented wearing the pointed cap.

We watched some excavations that were being conducted at the graves of a child and of two adults; the bodies had been laid in wooden coffins without regard to position, and covered with earth. The director of the Museum, who has held his appointment twenty years, and has superintended all researches during that period, informed us that the remains are usually found lying north and south; the graves were at a depth of eight feet, of which four feet was artificial soil.

The process of removing the earth in search of relics is heedful and diligent. Portions of a coffin were recovered with some shavings it had contained; also the occiput with matted hair, some of the larger vertebræ, and one finger-bone much oxidised having on it a bronze ring; at the feet were fragments of lachry-

[1] Herod. VII.

matories. The graves hitherto laid open are evidently those of the poorer classes among the Bosporians, and the works are continued in the search for objects that will tend to throw further light on the history of that people. The tumulus was the earliest form of sepulture among the Milesians, who adopted it from the Scythians, and these graves may be considered as being of a subsequent period, probably of the first or second century before the Christian era.[1]

Within a short distance of these tombs, is the principal gate of Panticapæum on the road to Theodosia, now reduced to two pilasters, each surmounted by a sphinx, the symbol of the ancient city; near it are many small tumuli. At the gate we found the carriage, and drove to the 'Golden Chamber,' two miles from Kertch, which we found in a completely ruined condition. The original form of this tumulus was that of a cone; the dimensions, according to Dubois, were 100 feet in height and 150 feet in diameter, the crest of the hill upon which it is raised being 323 feet above the sea. It has been walled from top to bottom with large blocks of masonry, but a small portion only of the casing is left; indeed we found labourers at work detaching stones and preparing them for removal. In 1832, thirty-five men were employed for fifteen days attacking it from the south, and when the tomb was reached it was found empty! The gallery that conducted to it has fallen in, and the chamber remains roofless; the tomb being on one side and not beneath the apex of the cone, it is very possible that the mountain encompasses one or more other sepulchres. We next ascended the Kyoul-óda, the tomb of one of the dynasty

---

[1] A skull in fair preservation from one of these graves, is now at the Royal College of Surgeons. I am indebted to Professor Geo. Busk, F.R.S., for the description of this skull, which will be found in Appendix III.

of Leucon, and found it in an equally ruined condition and scarcely worth the trouble of a visit.

Herodotus, whose birth took place about 413 B.C., has described in full the forms observed at the burial of their kings by the Scythians, customs that were followed by the first Milesians who settled on these shores. The entertaining historian relates, that when a king died, his body was embalmed, and carried about the country until it was finally laid in a tomb with one of his wives and several attendants, who were all strangled for the day of burial; the monarch's horses, his weapons, gold cups, and many other objects of daily use, were placed in the same sepulchre; the earth was then piled high above the tomb, until it formed a kind of mountain. The contents of the tomb of Kyoul-óda, believed by Dubois to have been that of Leucon or of Parisades I., fifth century B.C., both kings of the Bosphorus, were found to agree with the account just quoted, for near the remains of the King were the bones of the Queen, of an attendant, and of a horse with helmet and greaves; also various arms, cups in gold, silver and electrum, some amphoræ, and bronze vessels in which were found mutton bones.[1]

A somewhat similar usage was in vogue in Russia in much later times. Nestor the chronicler, 1056–1116, confirms the statement of an Eastern traveller in the tenth century, who witnessed the disposal of a corpse on the banks of the Volga. The Arabian relates that on the occasion of the death of a wealthy merchant, one of his male and female slaves were required to die; volunteers immediately offered themselves for

---

[1] For a detailed account of the Altyn-óda and Kyoul-óda, see Dubois v. p. 186. or Seymour, *Russia on the Black Sea*, &c., chap. xvi.

the sacrifice, and after certain feasting and much drinking, the merchant, his two slaves, and all his wives, who were obliged to suffer death, were burnt together. Warriors had their arms burnt with them, artificers their tools, and sailors were burnt afloat.

TERRA-COTTA MASK FROM A TOMB OF PANTICAPÆUM.
(SCALE ¼ TO I INCH.)

CHAPTER VII.

EIGHTH AND NINTH DAYS.

Yeny-Kalch — Tzarsky-kourgan — Mud volcanoes — Byzantine Church — Antiquities — Embarkation for Taman — Cimmeria — The Bosphorus — The Cymri — Tmoutorakan — Mstislaff — Matracha — Taman — Ancient remains — Sennaya.

Six miles east of Kertch is the old Turkish fortress of Yeny-Kalch, 'new fort,' which commanded the entrance to the Sea of Azoff; we found it in a hopeless state of ruin, the only occupants being some naval officers employed in topographic and marine surveying, who had pitched their tents at an angle of the fortification. The village, though a poverty-stricken looking place, is inhabited by Greek well-to-do fishermen and thriving pilots for vessels entering the straits. We visited the burial-ground of the Church of St. Nicholas, where several officers of the Turkish contingent are interred, and then started upon our return, stopping on the way to see the Tzarsky-kourgan, 'royal mountain,' an artificial mound 56 feet in height, and 840 feet in circumference, inside which is a royal tomb in perfect condition, thanks to the care taken for its preservation by the Archæological Society of Odessa. Three years, 1833–36, were consumed in the exploration of this great tumulus, it having been unsuccessfully attacked in several quarters before the gallery that leads to the vault could be found; the entrance was at last discovered on the south side, and measures 112 feet in length and 8½ feet in width, the chamber, nearly in the centre, being 9 feet square; it is believed to be one of the most ancient tombs yet brought to light. The roofs of the gallery and chamber are constructed of tiers of large blocks of hewn stone that project, the one over the other, until they meet. The tumulus is formed of a deep layer of earth immediately over the sepulchre, then a layer of sea-weed, again earth, stones, and lastly a covering of earth over all. The objects found in this tomb are at the Hermitage.

The road from Tzarsky-kourgan to Kertch lies between rows of crowded barrows, the necropolis of the ancient town of Myrmecium that lay on the northern shore of the Panticapæan Gulf, and of the town of Porthmion, according to Dubois;[1] these barrows have all been explored. The largest is the Salantchyck-kourgan, in the Melektchesmaky, a suburb of Kertch; it is a reproduction on a smaller scale of the Tzarsky-kourgan.

In the afternoon we drove to see the mud volcanoes to the south-west of the town of Kertch. We approached a large space about 20 feet in diameter, having an irregular leaden-coloured surface and rising to a centre not exceeding 3 feet in height above the level of the ground, whence the mud which bubbles actively, but irregularly and silently, from several openings, runs over to swell the mound. Occasionally, as if the result of a violent internal effort, the cold black mud is thrown up a foot or two into the air; the odour is faint and we could not perceive any exhalation. When dry, the mud turns to a greyish colour and is brilliant. An analysis exhibits the following composition:

---

[1] According to others, Porthmion was at Yeny-Kalch, marked Pondico on the Italian charts.

Carbonate of lime	52·10
Carbonate of magnesia	23
Carbonate of iron	18
Clay	6·90
	100 [1]

Taking advantage of our proximity we proceeded towards the fortress, in the vain hope of seeing the works in progress ; but as we neared the glacis, some soldiers from an encampment outside hurried with the evident intention of cutting us off before reaching the gates, we therefore turned the horses' heads and returned to the town. Permission to see the fortress was refused, on application being made to the *gradonatchalnyk*, 'governor' of Kertch, no foreigners being allowed to pass the lines under any pretence ; there has been one exception, however, in the person of an Englishman who was *invited* to enter the fortress, where he was asked professional advice by an officer employed in the direction of the works.

After the Russians had taken possession of Ghersety, they demolished an old fortification of Genoese origin that had been restored by the Turks ; it enclosed the most ancient and perfect specimen of Byzantine ecclesiastical architecture in the Crimea. This church is in the form of a cross, with short transepts and narrow aisles ; at a disproportionate height for the size of the edifice is the cupola, supported by four heavy pilasters, which rest on four marble columns of the Corinthian order ; on one of these columns is the date of foundation, the year 6265 from the creation ; 757 A.D.[2]

Jewellers and watchmakers deal in old coins and antiquities, for which they ask high prices, though they are open to offers.

---

[1] Sabatier, *Souvenir*, &c., p. 11. [2] Dubois, i. 405 ; v. 113.

The authorities require all finds to be delivered up, that the Crown may have the option of retaining them; but the general complaint is, that they who minister in the name of the Crown are unfair in their valuation. The Jews, Armenians, and Greeks who trade in such objects, seek opportunities to tempt foreigners with the cloked goods in the hope of effecting more advantageous bargains. The money-changers in the market-place and the watermen at the quays are many of them amateur dealers, being the first to purchase of the country people coming into town, whether from the neighbourhood of Kertch or from the opposite shores. Ask any of these people the simple question, *Yest-ly ou vas stary'ye veshtchy*, or *Yest-iy ou vas stary'ye monyety*—'Have you any old things?'—'Have you any old coins?' you are immediately invited to a stall or shed, and coins, pottery, fragments of glass, beads, and occasionally ornaments in gold, will be offered to you piecemeal, one article at a time, with an air of the profoundest mystery.

At nine the following morning we embarked for Taman in a small steamer of the Russian Company at Odessa; the discomfort experienced on board this dirty vessel was extreme, for the quarter-deck was crowded with labourers and people of the working-class with their tools, luggage, and insects, while the fore-part of the boat was entirely taken up with carts, horses, and bullocks, the only advantage offered to holders of first-class tickets being the privilege of sitting in a small, close, and offensive cabin.

The dull state of the weather befitted the memories attached to the localities by which we were surrounded, for a heavy leaden sky, and a sullen stillness in the air, well accorded with the description of them given by the greatest of the poets of Greece:—

> There in a lonely land and gloomy cells
> The dusky nation of Cimmeria dwells ;
> The sun ne'er views th' uncomfortable seats,
> When radiant he advances or retreats.
> Unhappy race ! whom endless night invades,
> Clouds the dull air, and wraps them round in shades.
> ODYSS. xi. 15.

What are those numerous dismal-looking hillocks, small and great, that meet the eye on all sides, but silent and imperishable monuments of an ancient, great, and wealthy people? Each an indication—a memory ; they laid their dead, the needy and the opulent, and thus piled the earth over them. Sabatier justly observes that it would be difficult for the coldest heart to remain indifferent at the aspect of these classical sites.

The strait of Kertch or Azoff was for many centuries called the Cimmerian Bosphorus, after the Cimmerians, a people whose earliest history is lost in obscurity. They were known, as we have seen, to Homer, and Herodotus has related in what manner they abandoned their country, which extended from the Ister to the Tanaïs (Don), upon the invasion of the Scythians, an Asiatic people. The Cimmerians fled into Asia Minor, 680-631 B.C., along the shores (?) of the Euxine, and settled in a place where the Grecians afterwards founded a colony, which was named Sinope. 'While the Cimmerians whom they drove before them with such ease on their first passage of the Tanaïs, continue to exist as Cymry in the mountains of Wales, and the Getæ their neighbours upon the west, have their descendants among the great Gothic or Teutonic family by which nearly one half of Europe is still occupied, the Scyths have disappeared from the earth. Like the Mexican Aztecs, whom they resemble in some degree, they have been swept away by the current of immigration, and, except in the mounds which cover their land and in the pages of the historian or ethnologist, not a trace remains to tell of their past existence.'[1]

Besides the Bosphorus, some fortresses preserved the name of the Cimmerians. Bosphorus, from Βοὸς-πόρος, 'passage of an ox,' is an ancient designation, and denoted in all probability a tract of water of a width to permit of an ox crossing it by swimming, as in the instance of Titan, who traversed this outlet of the Mæotis seated on a robust bull.[2]

The Scythians, scarcely a barbarous people, whose customs are described by Herodotus, held the whole country of the Cimmerians, with the exception of the mountainous region inhabited by the Tauri[3] on the southern shore of the Tauric peninsula. The Tauri were savages who performed cruel rites, as has already been noticed when visiting the coast of the Chersonese; in their territory was included Trapezus (Tchadyr-dagh) and the hill of Kimmericum (Otouz). They were possibly a remnant of the Cimmerians, and had taken refuge in the mountains; they could scarcely have been Scythians, for we read that in the sixth century B.C. they had their own king, who was invited by the Scythians to assist in repelling the invasion of Darius.[4] Soon after that event, the Grecians founded their colonies in the strait and on the adjacent shores, where the Scythians never ceased to disturb their peace.

At mid-channel, as we steamed across the strait, the numerous tumuli at Cape Touzla, where was the ancient Corocondame,[5] be-

[1] *History of Herodotus*, Geo. Rawlinson, M.A., 1862, iii. p. 167.

[2] *Orph. Argonaut*, Trajecti ad Rhenum edit. 1689, p. 72, 1054.

[3] *Teira*, in Assyrian, is a mountain, or a chain of mountains; in the Chaldean it is *tyren*, and in Syrian *touro*. In Asia Minor the alps are *taer*; with the Turk races, *tau* signifies a mountain; the Celts called a tower or rampar, *ter*, *tour*. In Greek ὄρος oros means a mountain. Dubois, vi. p. 12.

[4] Herod. i. iv.

[5] Corocondame was separated from Accra in the territory of the Panticapæans by a channel 70 stadia (7 miles) wide.

came more distinguishable, as did also the barrows about Roubanova point, close to which was Patraeus, and where has yet to be determined the site of the monument of Satyrus.[1] The nearer we approached the eastern shore, the more did the tumuli seem to multiply on the higher land which extends north-east on the peninsula of Taman, towards the sites of Phanagoria and Cepi.

Strabo has asserted that Neoptolemus a general of Mithridates defeated the Scythians in the Cimmerian Bosphorus, first in a naval action during the summer season, and afterwards in a cavalry engagement on the ice, and the geographer further observes that waggons frequently performed the passage from Panticapaeum to Phanagoria as the freezing of the sea in the strait was an event of ordinary occurrence; thus corroborating the statement of Herodotus, that the Scythians were in the habit of driving their chariots and leading their armies over the ice in this Bosphorus.[2]

In 1793, an inscription was discovered at Taman which records that a measurement was made on the ice, of the distance across the strait, by Prince Gleb, son of Sviatoslaff; the slab was sent to St. Petersburg, but the Empress Catherine commanded that it should be returned to Taman, as being the proper place at which it should remain. It is now in the Numismatic department at the Hermitage. The inscription, in Slavonic, is a precious relic to Russia, and of great value in throwing a light upon the history of her early possession of the peninsula of Taman:—

✠ IN THE YEAR 6576, 6TH INDICTION,[3] GLEB THE PRINCE MEASURED THE SEA ON THE ICE FROM TMOUTORAKAN TO KVERTCHEFF. 8054 SAGENES.[4]

[1] Strabo, XI. ii. 8. Satyrus, King of the Bosphorus 407-393 B.C., the ally of the Athenians, was killed at the siege of Theodosia.
[2] The strait was traversed on foot over the ice, from the Kouzla bank, in April 1875.
[3] 1068 A.D.
[4] Vtorytcheskoye yzdolavanye o myestopologényye drévnavo Roséisskavo Tmoutorakánskavo Knyagéstva. St. Petersburg, 1794.

If the actual distance from Kertch to Taman somewhat exceeds the measurement of the eleventh century, it should be borne in mind that the landslips on the shore of the little bay of Taman, although of small proportions, are of frequent occurrence, and it is while the newly fallen soil is being gradually washed away by the sea, that numberless coins are picked up.

Tmoutorakan was conquered by Sviatoslaff in 965, and when Vladimir determined in 989 upon the partition of his states into principalities, he gave Tmoutorakan in appanage to his son Mstislaff; it is mentioned in Russian chronicles as a principality, for the last time in 1127. In the twelfth century, Tmoutorakan was named Matracha, as appears in a treaty concluded, 1170, between the Emperor Manuel Comnenus and the Republic of Genoa, wherein it was stipulated that the Genoese should trade unmolested in all parts of the Byzantine empire, 'except in Russia and Matracha';[1] this article of the treaty was subsequently rescinded, probably when the Genoese had conferred upon them the monopoly of trade in the Black Sea, for in the fifteenth century they had commercial establishments at Matrica, watched over by a president. Matrica was for a long time a flourishing seaport, at which the monk Rubruquis saw at anchor some large vessels that were unable to enter the Sea of Azoff because they drew too much water.[2] Taman is now a small village unproductive in itself, but a place of transit for the large supply of cattle on their way from the Tcherkess lowlands to

---

[1] Heyd. *Le colonie*, &c., i. p. 55. The date of the treaty in which the above-named places were styled *Rusia* and *Matica*, see *Della colonie dei Genovesi in Galata*, Lud. Sauli. II., was more correctly 1169, the third indiction of the year 6678 of the council of Constantinople.

[2] William de Rubruquis, or de Rubruk, a Grey Friar, sent in 1253 by St. Louis, King of France, on an embassage to Mangou, the Great Khan of the Mongols. *Recueil de voyages et de mémoires*, &c. publié par la société de Géographie. Paris, 1839, iv. p. 215.

the Crimea, and thence into Russia; the animals are shipped in barges and towed to Kertch by the steam ferry-boat.

On landing at Taman we failed to obtain saddle horses, but secured a *droghy*, a long four-wheeled springless cart used for travelling on cross roads. We went in the first place to the Church of Bogya-mater, 'Mother of God,' founded by the Russian Prince Mstislaff in thanksgiving for the victory he obtained over his neighbours the Kassogues, or Cossacks, in 1022. The first church was of bricks, but the present edifice is built of fragments of stone and marble of antiquity, that have been recovered from the sand drifts around; some Greek inscriptions difficult to decipher are let into the walls, and in the churchyard are the Ionic capitals and shafts of two marble columns, the latter having on them a large cross in relief; there are no other visible remains of antiquity on this part of the island of Eion, by which name it was known to Pliny. The surface soil at Taman is artificial to the depth of several feet, as was evident where labourers were at work preparing for the foundations of new houses; within a short distance of the village are the remains of the fortress erected by the Russians in 1794, and named Phanagoria, ground now occupied by the works of a naphtha company.

At 3 P.M. we left Taman in a *pereclodnáya* and *troïka* [1] of post-horses; the *yemstchyck* was a woman of thirty, who complained of the hard work she had to go through to obtain a livelihood; her husband, a mason, had been in prison two years on a charge of breaking into a public-house, and there was no knowing when he would be tried, for the required witnesses could not be found!

We passed large herds of cattle and horses grazing on the vast pasture lands, where there is not the sign of a habitation, nor was

---

[1] Three horses harnessed abreast.

a living being to be seen; an hour's drive brought us to a narrow strip of what appeared to have been the bed of a river or canal, the earth seeming impregnated with the water from the sea, and on which grass refuses to grow.

When we reached Sennaya at five o'clock, my travelling companion, Professor Bruun of Odessa, was welcomed by a member of the Archæological Commission of St. Petersburg, who was conducting a series of excavations in the neighbourhood. We passed the night in a cottage, the head-quarters of the society in this peninsula.

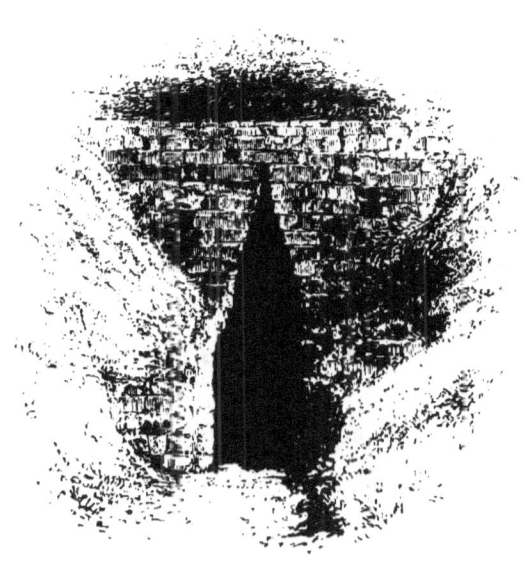

ENTRANCE TO THE TOMB. TZARSKY-KOURGAN.

CHAPTER VIII.

TENTH DAY.

Jewish tombstones—The Khozars—Their conversion—Their disappearance—Phanagoria—Its Necropolis—The Corocondamitis—Exploration of Tumuli—The 'Great Twins' Tumuli—Their antiquity.

THIS day was spent in interesting rambles about Sennaya, and in surveying the country from the tops of the hills. We first moved from the village in a south-westerly direction, until we got to a flat piece of ground about 600 yards wide and exceeding one mile in length, that inclines slightly from a range of hillocks towards the Gulf of Taman, where it meets the sea in an abrupt bank 12 or 14 feet in depth. Numerous excavations have been made about this ground and on the hillocks, which show the earth to be an artificial deposit,[1] composed largely of pieces of pottery, charcoal, the bones of animals, shells, &c. In the lower cuttings were found some inscriptions and fragments of sculptured marble, and among the hillocks were brought to light many curious slabs without inscriptions, but on which the seven-branched candlestick of the tabernacle like the golden candlestick represented on the Arch of Titus at Rome, and the sacrificial knife, are clearly defined. They may possibly be the tombstones of the Khozars

---

[1] In March 1875 a boring was made at the seaside, about two thirds of a mile to the north of Sennaya, when from a depth of 14 ft. of yellow clay was brought up a small fragment of red pottery.

who wrested the Taurida from the Goths, and renouncing Islamism, embraced Judaism in the ninth century.

The Khozars were a Turk-Scythian people from the north-west shores of the Caspian Sea, who had become so formidable as to necessitate the construction of the great wall at Derbent by Chosroes *Anoushirvan*,[1] the great King of Persia, as a protection against their attacks. Their ruler at that time was called the Khagkhan.[2] In the seventh century, the Khozars allied themselves to the Emperor of the East, and aided in the overthrow of Chosroes II., the monarch of their old enemies. Their chief city was Balangiar (the present Astrahan) near the mouth of the river Itil, 'large stream,' and in 834 the Byzantines constructed for them the frontier fortress of Sarkel, 'white town,' as a defence against the Petchenegues. The place is now called Byelovaya.

In the ninth century many Khozars were converted to Christianity by Constantine,[3] the Apostle of the Slaves, who prepared himself for his task by learning their language at Chersonesus, but all creeds were tolerated by the Khagkhan, and his subjects of all nationalities enjoyed equal rights of citizenship The Khozars were then at the zenith of their power, their sovereignty extending from the Yaïk to the Drieper and Boug, and from Kieff and the Oka to the mountains of the Caucasus. The victorious Oleg, regent during the minority of the son of

[1] 'The new sovereign of sovereigns.'

[2] *Historia Armeniaca*; Moses Chorenensis, Whiston edition, 1736; p. 356. Moses Chorenses, the Armenian chronicler of the fifth century, was surnamed *Khertogh*, the grammarian, from the elegance of his style.

[3] Constantine assumed the name of Cyril on being consecrated a bishop. Aided by his brother Methodius, he originated the Slave alphabet, consisting of forty-five letters, thirty-six of which, slightly changed, are used in the Russian language. Cyril and Methodius were the first to translate the Holy Scriptures with the new alphabet.

TOMBSTONES DISINTERRED AT SENNAYA

Rurik, was the first to deprive them of some of their territory, and in 965 the Grand Prince Sviatoslaff seized upon Sarkel after a great battle, and on Tmoutorakan and their dominions to the east of the Cimmerian Bosphorus. Notwithstanding these losses, the Khozars continued to hold the Taurida until 1016, when the Emperor despatched a force from the Byzantine capital to invade the peninsula, while Mstislaff,[1] the son of Vladimir, attacked them from his appanage. The Khozars withdrew to the shores of the Caspian, which still retained the name of Khazar-dharyn, and Bahr-Khazar, 'Sea of Khazar,' and then disappeared an extensive monarchy, leaving only its name, for the Crimean peninsula was known as Khazary up to the thirteenth century, whilst among the Karaïm Jews of South Russia we see some of the descendants of those Khozars who remained behind.

But the slabs found at Sennaya may be of greater antiquity than the time of the Khozars, for it appears that the descendants of Abraham found a refuge on the shores of the Cimmerian Bosphorus long before the spread of their religion upon the conversion of that people, the existence of a synagogue at Panticapæum in the 377th year of Pontus, 81 A.D., being established by an inscription that is preserved at the Imperial Hermitage, St. Petersburg.[2]

Beyond the hillocks are larger mounds, likewise artificial, into many of which, vertical cuttings 40 feet in height have been made, but they have yielded nothing of interest. On the land side of these mounds is the vast necropolis, a succession of tumuli that stretch away towards Pyrnava in one direction, and

---

[1] In his chronicle, the monk Cedrenus records that Spheng, brother of Vladimir, and not Mstislaff, was the Emperor's ally. *Compend. Hist. Georgii Cedreni.* Parisiis, 1647. ii. p. 710.

[2] Bruun, *Gazaria*, &c., p. 33.

Ak-tanys[1] in the other, on the shore of which lake Dubois naturally places Cepi, the birthplace of the mother of Demosthenes; it was near these tumuli at Sennaya, on the border of the Gulf of Taman, that had stood Phanagoria, the metropolis on the eastern shore of the Bosphorus. From the heights on which are some mud volcanoes[2] similar to those at Kertch, we were able to trace the continuation of the arid strip of land we traversed the previous day, and which we became convinced had been a water communication between Ak-tanys and the Gulf of Taman.[3]

Strabo's description of these localities is clear enough where he tells us that 'there is a large lake beyond Corocondame, which is called Corocondamitis; that upon sailing into that lake, Phanagoria and Cepi are on the left hand at the entrance.' The sites of those two cities may be pretty well determined, if it is assumed that Ak-tanys is the lake of Strabo, and that the lake was entered by the now dried-up channel; but the remainder of his

[1] The Lower Temrouk lake in the Admiralty chart. Ak-tanys is a corruption of the Turkish Ak-denghyz, 'white sea'; it is a fresh-water lake 16 miles long, 5 miles broad, and averages 8 feet in depth. Large quantities of crucian carp and pike are taken in it, and salted.

[2] There are numerous mud volcanoes on both sides of the strait, and some naphtha wells on the Taman side. Strabo quotes Homer, who represented the Cimmerians as being dwellers in northern and distant lands near the Bosphorus, and *in the vicinity of the Hades*. Strabo, III. ii. 12.

[3] It is in contemplation to unite Ak tanys with the Gulf of Taman, a distance of 7 *versts*, by making a cutting in the presumed ancient channel, with the object of facilitating the transport of goods between Russia and the Caucasus, *via* the Kouban, from the Crimea. At a series of borings made in March 1875, between the gulf at a point 7 miles to the south of the village, and the Vanoffsky liman, the small lake to the west of Ak-tanys, dry yellow clay was found to a depth of 7 feet below the surface. Over a distance of 2 miles where the ground gradually rises from the lake, the borings brought up moist yellow clay with traces of very fine sand, like the sand on the west shore of the Ak-tanys. The highest part of this isthmus is 27 feet above the gulf, but the land to the south being much lower, the channel between the sea and lake may have formed a bend.

relation becomes somewhat entangled upon examination of the country, from the difficulty experienced in determining where the branch of the Anticeitis emptied itself into the lake, and how the island was formed that was surrounded by the waters of the lake, of the river, and of the Mæotis. Professor Bruun is persuaded that the Anticeitis fell into the Mæotis at Peresypnoyè-ghyrlò,[1] between the Ak-tanys and the Sea of Azoff—that the village of Tytorovko is over the ruins of Hermonassa—and that the Temple of Venus (Apatura) was on the point of land that projects into the Ak-tanys, now called Doubóvy-rýnok, 'oak mart,' on the Russian map. But with all due deference to the learned Professor, there appears to be some ground for objection to these convictions, for the great geographer represents Hermonassa and the temple as being on the right hand of the entrance to the lake of Corocondamitis, in Sindica beyond the Hypanis, and it is not shown what was the course of the Hypanis in his time, nor is the extent of Sindica in a northerly direction clearly defined.[2]

It has been already stated that Phanagoria was the principal city on the eastern side of the strait, and a capital of the kingdom of the Bosphorus; but when that kingdom was confirmed to Pharnaces by the Senate of Rome as a recompense for his treachery to his father, Phanagoria was excluded and raised to a free city, in consideration of having been the first to revolt against

---

[1] From *peresypatt*, to strew over ; *ghyrló*, an estuary.

[2] The difficulty experienced in the attempt to reconstruct a map of these parts on the geography of Strabo, is best illustrated by Scymnus, who wrote before Strabo, that the island upon which were the cities of Kimmerion, Cepi, Hermonassa, Phanagoria, and the Sindic port, was rendered impracticable by reason of its many marshes and rivers. Ταύτης παρείχει τὰς πόλεις διακειμένας ἡ νῆσος κατὰ Μαιῶτιν ὄχρι Βοσπόρου, χώραν ἀπολαμβάνουσα πολλὴν πεδιάδα· ἥτις τὰ μὲν τοῖς ἕλεσι, τοῦτί τε ποτομοῖς ἀδιάβατος, τενάγιοί τε τοῖς ἐν τῷ πέραν, τὰ δὲ τῇ θαλάττῃ, τῇ τε λίμνῃ γίνεται. Seym. Ch. 902.

the late great monarch. Phanagoria and Cepi were totally destroyed in 541, in all probability by the Outougours, who were settled near Heptali Portus, now Ghelendjyk.

At each of six large tumuli that were being explored near Sennaya by direction of the Archæological Commission, we found from 15 to 20 men employed either in making vertical cuttings or in hollowing out galleries. In the more important of these sepulchral mounds the tomb of solid masonry is found above the level of the ground near the centre; but it is sometimes below the surface. There are instances in which a tumulus covers two or three tombs irregularly placed, and there being no accepted rule or indication by which they may readily be reached, much labour is in such cases expended before the exploration is completed; fourteen days is the time required to search a large tumulus thoroughly, the cost amounting to 200*l*., labourers being paid 2 roubles for each square fathom excavated. Many tombs are found pillaged and even destroyed, although there are seldom any outward traces of an entrance having been effected. In 1431 the Venetians directed their attention to the opening of tumuli in search of treasure, but there is much reason to believe that the dead were disturbed at a remoter period.

The most interesting discovery of late years was made at a large double tumulus near the hamlet of Stable'evsky, south of the Yanoffsky-liman,[1] opened in 1864, and named the Balshy'ye-blyznytzý, 'Great Twins.' In the middle of the larger mound, near traces of burnt lime, was a funeral pile, a heap of ashes which included the carbonised bones of various animals, and some fragments of pottery; the altar of sacrifice consisted of two large stone slabs laid horizontally the one above the other, both having

---

[1] The natives call these limans *váryky*.

a funnel-shaped hole found covered with a stone ; beneath the altar, an indentation in the ground was filled with a bluish soil, and behind it were the fragments of a vase showing in relief a female figure seated on an ox. Near the altar under 4 feet of earth was a vault, and inside it resting on three slabs, a wooden sarcophagus with bronze corner-pieces and handles, which was unhappily crushed by the falling of a stone ; it is believed to have contained the remains of a priestess of Demeter, because of the sphinx and griffin on some circular gold ornaments that lay with them ; there were also many gold buttons with other adornments for dress representing dancing figures, and portions of two leathern sandals. On the right side of the sarcophagus were several rings, one being a scarabæus in gold, ornaments in gold-leaf representing winged figures, the head of Pallas, or of Medusa with the tongue protruded, and a quantity of bronze arrow-heads ; on the left side was a golden wreath of olive branches of surpassing beauty, a bronze helmet shaped like a Phrygian cap, some portions of armour parcel-gilt, and the fragments of a black vase with a gilt garland round the neck. The other objects were a mirror in a bronze case with Venus and Cupid in repoussé work, several bronze φαλαρά, 'cheek pieces,' the remains of four horses and their gorgeous trappings. The head-dress of the dancing figures on the trinkets is the κάλαθος, 'basket,' which was at one time made of plaited reeds and afterwards of more costly material ; the *calathus* of the priestess[1] was of gold, having represented on it, in relief, a combat with griffins ; and there were other large ornaments in gold that were attached to the head-dress in such a way as to cover the ears. All these relics in the precious metal

---

[1] The Greek divinity Demeter was the Ceres of the Latins, represented in ancient sculpture with a basket on her head.

are exquisitely wrought, and among the richest specimens of
Grecian art at the Hermitage. The date of these tumuli is
presumed to be of the fourth century B.C., from the circumstance
of a gold coin of Alexander the Great, a brilliant specimen,
having been found near the remains of a female, in one of the
other tombs of minor interest that were covered by the twin
hillocks.

THE PERECLODNAYA.

CHAPTER IX.

ELEVENTH AND TWELFTH DAYS.

Ak-tanys-liman—Tytorovko—Black Sea Cossacks—The sect of the Shalapoutts—River Kouban—Its navigation - Commerce—Michelthal—The farmer's curse—Anapa — Ancient inhabitants — Prince Mentchikoff — Raïeffsky — Saints and Sinners.

NOTHING can be more uninteresting and forlorn than the appearance of the country after the necropolis of Phanagoria is left behind: our good-natured *yemstchyck* spared us the longer drive on the post-road, by striking across the isthmus straight for the Liman Ak-tanys, where herds of cattle and horses were watering. We saw the last of the tumuli on the peninsula, in a cluster of barrows at the western extreme of the lake, where the land southwest of Rah'manovsky point is fully 600 feet above its waters; according to Dubois, the temple consecrated to the divinities Anerges and Astara (the Astarte of the Phœnicians) by the queen of Parisades I., 349–311 B.C., was erected on the Rah'manovsky peninsula.

At noon, four hours after leaving Sennaya, we reached the smiling little village of Tytorovko nestled in a grove, a pleasing change from the arid uplands we had passed over with the thermometer at 97°. We asked to see the *starshyná*, 'elder,' of Tytorovko, who appeared in the person of a fine-looking Russian, a pompous man in Cossack uniform; he quickly informed us that he was a descendant of the Zaparojsky'ye Kazakў, and in command of a detachment of the Tchernomorsky'ye Kazakў, ' Black Sea Cossacks';[1] he found quarters for us in the cottage of an elderly female, a *starozyórka*, 'old believer,' where we enjoyed a rest after some severe jolting in the *perecladnáya*, and were soon supplied with fresh eggs, milk, and good black bread; but our hostess was in great trouble, for one of her kindred had deserted the faith of his fathers and joined a new sect called the Shalapoutt, in the Government of Yekaterynadar.

Little is known as yet of the Shalapoutts, who meet for worship of an evening in each other's cottages, with closed doors and windows, when the preliminary ceremony is the washing of hands; hymns are sung and prayers repeated, at the same time that supper is being served and wine freely indulged in, for the Shalapoutts eschew *vodka*; they also renounce tobacco. They have no regard for the established Orthodox Church, though they make the sign of the cross and burn incense at their meetings. The Shalapoutts carefully avoid the police, who report that when married men and women join the sect, they abandon their wives and husbands to lead with their co-sectarians the most dissolute lives.

From Tytorovko we descended to the lowlands of the river Kouban, and entered a large tract of country, all marsh, river, and lake, each feature being indiscriminately called *járyk* by the

[1] The Black Sea Cossacks separated in 1792 from the Zaparogues, who proudly dated their origin from the ninth century. Catherine mistrusted their power and influence, tempted them to the Kouban with grants of land, and gave them a chief town at Yekaterynadar, 'Catherine's gift.' The Zaparogues were subdued for the first time in 1021, by Russia, and in the sixteenth century they formed an alliance with the Poles, which, however, was of short duration. In 1708, Mazeppa their Hetman joined the cause of Charles XII. of Sweden, and after the battle of Pultowa the Zaparogues were decimated by order of Peter I. In 1750 the Cossacks elected Count Rasumoffsky to be their Hetman (an office that was abolished in 1722, which election was approved by the sovereign.

people; an excellent road traverses this pestiferous-looking district, in which the Kouban is twice crossed, over bridges of boats. The river here, considerably smaller than the Protchock, as the Russians call the northernmost arm of the Kouban which falls into the Sea of Azoff, is possibly that branch of the Anticeitis which Strabo informs us was the Hypanis, and flowed into the lake Corocondamitis. The sturgeon, ἀντακαῖος, *Antacæus*, which gave its name to the river, is taken in abundance, also the sterlet, and it is said the salmon, with other small fish. The word Kouban is of Tatar origin, but the signification I am unable to learn; the Italians called the river Chopa.

In 1777-78, Souvaroff fortified the right bank of the river against the attacks of the Circassians; he then took command in the Crimea, but returned to the Kouban in 1782, and in 1790 the imperial troops of Russia traversed the territory of the Kouban for the first time, under General Bibikoff. The river is now navigated from Temrouk to Tifliskaya, a distance of about 170 miles on what is called the Yekaterynadar line, by vessels belonging to the Russian Company at Odessa; the voyage is performed in twenty-four hours, the return journey occupying twelve hours, more or less, according to the strength of the current. Passengers are conveyed each way, twice weekly, and *berlins*, 'barges' with goods, are taken in tow.[1] The exports from Circassia, which include maize, rye, barley, oats, and a little wheat, are landed from the river boats at Temrouk, where they are shipped on rafts for the navigation of Lake Kourtchansky, and re-shipped on the Azoff in

---

[1] During the year 1874 the steamers conveyed 1,200,000 *pouds** of goods, &c., on the river. Population of the government of the Kouban, 719,969. (Census 1873.)

* A *poud* (40 Russian pounds) = 36 lbs. 1 oz. 12 dr. 5 gr. avoirdupois.

sea barges that are towed to Kertch, where the cargoes are transhipped to British steamers. The imports are limited to agricultural implements and hardware, chiefly foreign, and cottons from Russia. This service is hazardous, for Temrouk alone is free from fever.

We passed the night at Michelthal, a small German colony, where a happy-looking and tidy *frau* prepared an excellent supper and clean beds in her cozy little cottage. Seven years ago, these colonists, some forty in number, left their homes in Bessarabia, where they were tenants only, to become the owners of the land and habitations at Michelthal, by periodical payments that were to extend over ten years. The *thal* is treeless and cheerless, the downs close around shutting out the distant view, but the soil is productive and remunerative, particularly in corn, and the Germans live on contentedly at the prospect of soon becoming the possessors in freehold of the land they cultivate.

On leaving Michelthal at an early hour on the following morning, we drove for miles through golden fields, to the incessant warbling of larks :

> Als der Herr die Lerch' erschaffen
> Sprach Er : Flieg empor und singe !

until we reached the shore of the Kyzyl-tash liman, where the land was overrun with the *Trifolia gigantesca*, known in England as the farmer's curse ; it is grown for cattle food, and for an oil that is extracted from it, of which the natives are very fond. At 10.30 A.M. we entered the town of Anapa, its dilapidated condition recalling to our minds the events of the late war.

Anapa was taken, for the first time, by the Russians under General Goudovitch in 1791, when Mansour the fanatic prophet and enthusiast was made a prisoner; and again in 1807 by

Admiral Potoshkyn and General Govoroff, who destroyed the town; the place was given up to the Turks, in whose possession it remained until 1829, when Admiral Greig and Prince Mentchikoff besieged and took it, and Anapa was finally ceded to Russia, together with Gouria and the pashalik of Ahal-tzykhè, by the treaty of Adrianople.

When the Turks founded Anapa in 1784, they constructed a fortress to mount 84 guns, for the defence of what they considered to be their most important possession on the eastern shore of the Black Sea, a port that enabled them to keep up their communications with the Mahommedan populations on the frontiers of Russia, and was the great mart from which the harems of Constantinople were supplied with the vaunted beauties of Circassia. The Russians destroyed the lines of defence at the approach of the Allies, and the fortifications, no longer formidable, were temporarily strengthened, during their final struggles with the mountain tribes, in 1859. The port remained unnoticed and uncared for until 1867, when it was opened to foreign trade, a wise measure, for already in 1873 the value of imports and exports amounted to 2,000,000 roubles.

Anapa occupies the site of the ancient Sindica, where Professor Stephani of St. Petersburg thinks it probable that a community of Hebrews dwelt in the first century, from an inscription that has been found there, corresponding in date to A.D. 42. This country, at one time inhabited by the Toreatæ, and others of the Mæotæ, was also called Evdousia or Evlisia, having become peopled by the Eudosians or Tetraxite Goths, who spoke the Gothic or Tauric tongue.[1] In later times the Genoese had a settlement at Mapa,

---

[1] *Tchernomòrskyje Goty.* Prof. Ph. Bruun. St Petersburg, 1874.

where a president was appointed in 1449 to watch over their interests.

We called upon the chief of police, governor of the town, a most polite officer who placed his *droghy* at our disposal. He showed us fragments of Greek inscriptions found of late years, and took us to some rising ground east-south-east of the church, where two headless statues of white marble were discovered in 1871, at a depth of 3 feet below the surface. They were forwarded to the governor at Novorossisk, on their way to the Museum at Tiflis, but Russians seldom do things in a hurry, so the statues remain at Novorossisk for the present.

Four miles from the town are three large tumuli, called 'The Sisters,' and other tumuli of smaller dimensions that stand invitingly on the plain. It is to be regretted that the Archæological Commission at St. Petersburg does not extend its labours beyond the radius of Kertch and Sennaya, and explore some of the many barrows on the Caucasian shores.[1] The excavations that have been conducted under its direction in other parts, seem in general to have been wanting in system and perseverance.

We left Anapa at 5.30 P.M. in a pelting shower, passing through the waste lands of H'maraka, a country that has remained desolate since Prince Mentchikoff destroyed by fire every Circassian habitation within a radius of 10 miles, when besieging the town in 1829. We sheltered ourselves in our *pereclodnaya* as best we could against the tempest, and when in the midst of a severe thunderstorm, we reached Raïeffsky at 7.30, we at once determined upon staying for the night. The post station was full of travellers,

---

[1] During the summer of 1875, the 'seven brothers' tumuli, distant 7 *versts* from Michelthal, were explored with brilliant results. Among other objects were many golden ornaments evidently of great antiquity, and apparently of Iranian origin.

SAINTS AND SINNERS. 111

but we had no difficulty in securing a room in this Russian settlement, where a *samovar* was soon hissing at our elbows. Our hostess had the walls of her apartment covered with the images of saints and martyrs suspended side by side with the portraits of imperial personages, who rank in Russia next to, and immediately after, the many divinities mentioned in the calendar.

ARMORIAL BEARING OVER A STABLE-YARD DOOR, ANAPA.

CHAPTER X.

THIRTEENTH AND FOURTEENTH DAYS.

The sect of the Douhobortsy—Their doctrines—Sacraments—Sanctity of churches—Persecution and exile—Morality—Arrival at Novorossisk—A market day—The inhabitants—Ancient localities—The ship 'Vixen.'

AMONG the villagers at Raïeffsky are many of the sect known as that of the Douhobortsy,[1] who resemble the Malakany in some respects; the Douhobortsy, Malakany, and other sectarians are now permitted to move from place to place without molestation, but when banished in the reign of Alexander I., they were deported to certain districts in Transcaucasia and to other distant parts of the empire, their most pernicious doctrine in the sight of the Government of Russia being the rejection of monarchy; for, they say, that as all men are fallen, so are all men equal and without distinction, and as Christ Himself said that He and his were not of this world, therefore there can be no earthly power.

The Douhobortsy fully believe the Scriptures to be the revelation of God, and as such to be alone accepted, to the exclusion of all traditions and acts of councils, which are of no avail, for nothing holy can proceed from men; on these grounds they are opposed to the Orthodox Church, believing the real church to be constituted only

---

[1] From *douh*, spirit, Holy Ghost; and *borotya*, to wrestle—i.e. 'Wrestlers with the Spirit.'

of such people as are chosen by God to dwell in *light* and *life*, admitting the right of Mahommedans and Jews to enter into that community, if they work to do good by inward spiritual light. The priest of the visible church having no inward conviction, performs its ordinances mechanically, and speaks the words of his imagination only; he cannot *lift up the inner curtain*, is therefore not competent to preach the Word, and leaves his hearers to trust to visible forms; thus is it that priests of the visible church, being themselves sinners, cannot lead others to salvation. Christ alone is the Word; He is the bishop and priest to whom we look for the salvation of our souls; His priests can only be they who feel the power of His *word* in their hearts, which word does not remain unfruitful.

Christ is God and man, and the regenerator of the human race. He is spiritually incarnate in our souls, having been born into the world like the rest of mankind. It is by inward faith in Him alone that we can be saved, and by receiving *light* from Him we shall rise again, though not in the same body. In the Trinity, Christ is *life*, the Holy Ghost is *peace*, in one with the Father who is *light*; for God is the spirit of strength, of wisdom, and of will.

There can be no outward forms in the true church where all is measured by the *inner workings of Christ*; the sacraments must therefore be understood spiritually.

The Douhobortsy maintain that baptism, such as we are in the habit of seeing performed, is fruitless, for of what avail can it be with infants that do not feel, and cannot comprehend, or indeed with adults even, if they be not baptized by the *spirit* and with *fire*! The church has no power to loose and bind sins, true confession being that of a contrite heart before God; the ceremonial of marriage they consider superfluous, if the union be contracted at a reasonable age in

VOL. I.   I

mutual love and esteem, and with a firm purpose; but the sanction of parents is imperative.

The Douhobortsy do not recognise the sanctity of a church, for it is a *building made with hands*, whereas the Saviour taught, saying: *Thou, when thou prayest, go into thy chamber*, &c.; they condemn the practice of raising images or idols,[1] for God commanded Moses, saying: *Thou shalt not make to thyself any graven image*, &c.; and they refuse to make the sign of the cross, because prayer must be offered in the *spirit* and by the *word*; nor do they fast there being no command to do so in the Scriptures.

These are the people who, 'because they would not turn away from their errors,' were persecuted, and exiled by command of the Emperor Paul to the mines at Yekaterynbourg. The origin of this sect is not known, and when a commission sat in 1802 at the Alexander-Nevsky Monastery, St. Petersburg, for the purpose of inquiring into its history, and qualifying its tenets, the more prominent members, summoned to give their evidence, were only able to state that their teaching had come to them from the Ukraine.

The Douhobortsy are good agriculturalists, steady in their habits, and trustworthy in business; the majority are able to read, and many can write; the humane treatment of their horses and cattle is in striking contrast to the barbarous cruelties practised by other people in the Caucasus and Crimea.

Beyond Raïeffsky we passed through more waste land entirely uninhabited, with an abundance of vegetation, but where, from some unexplained cause, so said some woodcutters on the road, the trees never attain their full growth; hence the name Varyann, 'bad trees,' given to the plain. The drive over the Seragar

---

[1] The Douhobortsy are also called Ykonobortsy; *ykone* is any image used in prayer.

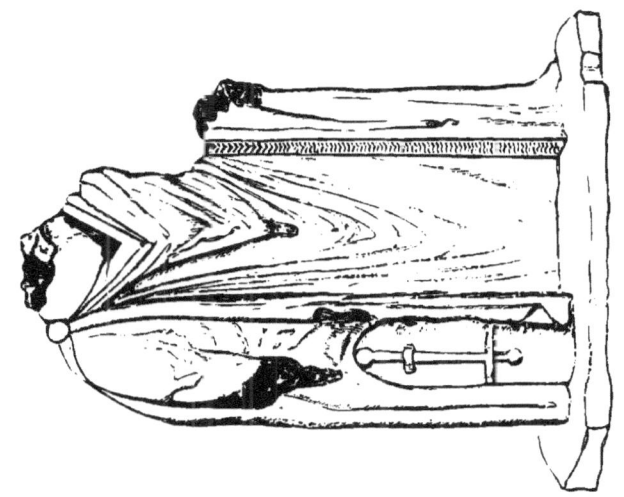

Fig. 1.
Length of hand to wrist—9 in.
 ,,   middle finger—5 ,,
 ,,   thumb—2 ,,

Fig. 2.

pass is very beautiful, and when we descended on the south side into the valley of Novorossisk, we were surprised to find it well peopled and in a high state of cultivation, being laid out more especially in orchards and kitchen gardens, for corn does not grow. In this valley, watered by the Tzemess a rivulet that flows into the head of the bay, is the model farm of Heydouk, so named after the proprietor who receives 3,000 roubles yearly from the Crown, for the cultivation of fruit-trees on the imperial estates of Dourso and Abrao, and for keeping a nursery from which young trees are supplied at cost price, with the view of encouraging the culture of fruit.

At Novorossisk we put up at a dirty little inn kept by an Armenian, and were detained at this miserable seaside village over twenty-four hours, awaiting the arrival of the steamer from Kertch. It was a market-day, and the Circassians mustered in force at the bazaar to dispose of eggs, vegetables, poultry, and a few hides, their only produce brought in clumsy carts from long distances; the following morning at an early hour they were again on the road homewards, with cotton goods, crockery, oil, salt, and tobacco, purchased or bartered for among the Armenians and Jews, who keep every stall in the village; the seafaring population, however, is Greek.

Our search for the site of an ancient city said by Dubois to be on the seashore opposite to the large Turkish fortress of Soudjouk-Kaleh, 'dry sausage fort,' now crumbling away to dust, was unsuccessful. This fortress was taken by the Duke de Richelieu in 1811, restored to Turkey the following year, and finally ceded to Russia by the treaty of Bucharest in 1829. The spacious barracks in the town, of modern construction, were occupied by 100 men of the line.

In the garden of the governor's residence we saw the two statues found at Anapa. Although the arrangement of the drapery about the male figure is peculiar and unusual, both statues would appear to be Roman, and are probably of the period of the decadence of the empire.

In the port of Tzemess, the name given to it by the natives, we see the port of Hieros near which was the town of Bata, called also τὸ Νίκαξιν; on the Italian charts Hieros is noted as Calolimene, and Trinixe or Trinica. It was here, in the Bay of Tzemess, that the 'Vixen,' a British trading vessel, was seized in 1836 by a Russian ship of war, an act which for a time rendered war imminent between England and Russia.

CIRCASSIAN CART.

CHAPTER XI.

FIFTEENTH AND SIXTEENTH DAYS.

Departure from Novorossisk—Ghelendjyk—River Pshad—Dolmens and barrows—Touapse—Camara and Katchermà—The coast of Abhase--Pytzounda—Soukhoum-Kaleh—Its prospects—The Eucalyptus globulus—Climate—Dioscurias and Sevastopolis—Superb vegetation—Elbrouz—Grotto of Gounasky.

OUR feelings were certainly those of delight on seeing the steamer come to an anchor off the little town early in the morning, for we had had enough of Novorossisk ; at seven o'clock we left the bay.

A short length of coast formed of fantastically-shaped white cliffs, separates Novorossisk from the snug little harbour of Ghelendjyk, the ancient Toricos and Pagra, the Maurolaco of the Italians. The reddish cape beyond is Ydokopaz, between which and Cape Tsougou is the small river of Pshad, the site of Achæa, so named after the Thessalians of Phthiotis who formed part of the Argonautic expedition. On the right bank of the Pshad, in a pass leading to a village of the same name, are many dolmens, one beyond the village being 10 feet square ; other dolmens are on the seashore between Netchepsouko and Aderbyskoyou, and they are numerous in the passes about the North-west Caucasus, where sandstone is abundant.[1] On the hills near Pshad were opened, in 1818, some

---

[1] *Journal of a residence in Circassia*, J. S. Bell, 1840 ; i. p. 154.

barrows that were piled over with large stones ; in them were found urns of baked clay that contained ashes, also ornaments in copper, iron utensils, fragments of lacrymatories, and tusks of the wild boar.[1]

At Netchepsouko was the port of Lazica in the country of the Lazi, and in a bight a little to the east are the ruins of Nicopsis ; next is seen Fort Velyamÿnoff, now better known as Touapse, after the river it adjoins ; it was the Porto de Susacho in the Middle Ages. On the Netchepsouko was Mihaïloffsky fort, blown up by its Russian garrison rather than that it should fall into the hands of the enemy. At Touapse we anchored for one hour to land and embark passengers and goods.[2]

Beyond Touapse, on the promontory of Heracleum, is another Russian fort, named after General Lázareff ; farther on is the river Achæunta, now the Soubetchy, and the imperial property of Vardannè is near the ancient Masætica. This is the coast described by Strabo as being mountainous and without havens, and where the natives subsisted by piracy. The sea robbers had long slender boats called *camaræ*, capable of holding twenty-five to thirty men, and as they were light they were easily carried into the forests for the want of safe shelter afloat. It is only since the complete subjugation of the country by Russia that piracy has been entirely suppressed, but fishing-boats and little coasters are still hauled up where there is a beach, as was the custom 2,000 years ago. The small coasting vessels that trade on the eastern shore of the Black Sea, many under the Turkish flag, are called *katcherma* and *katchmar*, into which it seems possible to 'glide'

---

[1] *Voyages en Circassie*, de Marigny, 1836, p. 119.

[2] The steamers now call at many other intermediate stations on the coast. See Appendix II.

the word *camara* of the Greeks. It was here also that the Genoese carried on an extensive trade, bartering the produce of their salt lakes in the Crimea, and the wines and salted fish of Trebizond, for fair slaves to be sent to the Egyptian market.

The broad and well-wooded valley that reaches to the shore at Sotchabytke point, marks Nisis; here the steamer stopped to communicate with the shore. A little way beyond was Borgys or Bruchonte, where the forest land sinks to the river M'zymta at Cape Adler. It was hence that the Grand Duke Michael, Commander-in-Chief of the forces in the Caucausus, sent to His Imperial Majesty the comforting despatch, dated July 21, 1863, announcing the termination of the war. From Cape Adler the mountains again grow at the rear of Gagra, Cacari on the Italian charts, the ancient Nitica or Stennitica, the abode of the Phthirophagi, 'lice eaters.' We then passed Pytzounda, ' the great Pityus,' the 'most opulent city' of Pliny, to which place, when it was the limit of the Empire of the East in this part of Asia, St. John Chrysostom was condemned to banishment at the instance of the Empress Eudoxia in the fifth century; but the archbishop expired at Comana in Cappadocia, before reaching his destination.

Pytzounda has a well-sheltered anchorage, open only to the south, at which vessels are continually loading with timber from the neighbouring inexhaustible forests. A striking object in passing, is the large church which stands enclosed by 'sacred woods,' for Pytzounda derives its name from the πίτυς, 'fir tree,' which abounds, and reaches an enormous size; this church of Pytzounda, on which Dubois expresses himself enthusiastically,[1] was founded

---

[1] For a description of this interesting edifice, see Dubois, i. p. 221; and *Rapports sur un voyage Archéologique*, &c., M. Brosset, St. Petersburg, 1849, Rapp. viii. p. 127.

by Justinian, became the mother church in the Caucasus, and the seat of the patriarchate down to the twelfth century, the chief dignitary being styled the Catholicos of Abhase; it is now undergoing thorough restoration.

The arrival at daylight of the steamer at Soukhoum-Kaleh, and the delay occasioned by waiting for the steam tender from Poti with passengers for the Crimea and Russia, enables the traveller to land and spend several hours on shore. Soukhoum-Kaleh in Abhase is situated at the foot of some hills, and has an alluring aspect from the anchorage, owing to the luxuriant vegetation that overspreads the coast. Its commerce, which is principally carried on by Armenians and Greeks, who form the great portion of the population, is limited to a small export of local produce, such as corn, vegetables, and tobacco, and a minimum of import trade for transit; but there is the prospect of a change in the fortunes of Soukhoum-Kaleh, in the project of uniting it by rail with Novo-Senaky, the second station on the Poti-Tiflis railway, and of constructing a post-road to Starogevaya on the river Zelentchouck, in the Government of the Kouban; if these plans are found feasible, then it is in contemplation to make Soukhoum a naval station and military port.

The *Eucalyptus globulus*, or blue-gum tree,[1] has been extensively planted since its first introduction at Soukkoum in 1861; it grows rapidly, increasing in size 6 feet annually, and its property of largely absorbing moisture, will, it is believed, greatly improve the climate, which, at certain seasons, is one of the most pernicious on the coast; but some idea may be formed of its mildness from observa-

---

[1] The *Eucalyptus globulus*, discovered in Australia by the French naturalist La Billardière in 1792, was brought to Europe in 1834; the blue-gum tree is of the myrtle family, and it is said attains at Tasmania the great height of 350 feet; it is largely used in ship and house building.

tions made during the winter of 1873-4, when the mercury never fell below 3° Reaumur, and vegetation kept in leaf. Military patients suffering from affections of the chest are sent to serve at Soukhoum when possible; and were accommodation and medical comforts available, it would be a highly desirable station for the consumptive, to whom it is strongly recommended by the faculty.

Soukhoum is now largely admitted to be on the site of the ancient city of Dioscurias, named after the Dioscurii, Castor and Pollux, by Amphitus and Telchius their charioteers who were believed to have founded it. Dioscurias was the common mart of the nations situated above it and in its neighbourhood. There assembled at Dioscurias 70 nations, who all spoke different languages from living dispersed without intercourse; they resorted hither chiefly for the purpose of supplying themselves with salt, one of the principal imports.[1] In the second century Arrian inspected a fortress at this possession of the Roman Empire, named Sevastopolis;[2] it was destroyed during the invasion of Chosroes *Anoushirvan*, and rebuilt by Justinian, who surrounded the new city with a wall;[3] in the fifteenth century its last vestiges disappeared. Coins of Rome and of the Byzantine Empire are found from time to time, especially near the river Beslata, where the ground is covered with ruins; but the autonome coins of Dioscurias are rarely met with.

The governor of the province of Koutaïs,[4] who was taking a passage accompanied by his family, kindly invited us to join his party about to land for the purpose of visiting a stalagmite grotto

---

[1] Strabo, XI. ii. 16.
[2] *Castellum Sebastopolis.* Pliny VI. iv. 6. *Dioscurias sive Sevastopolis*, Anon. perip. 13.
[3] Procop. *de Ædif.* iii. 7.
[4] General Count Levaschoff, A.D.C.

discovered in 1871. We accordingly went on shore at noon, and started in two carriages, better by a long way than anything we expected to find in these parts ; the General, who sits his horse admirab'y, preferred to ride, and took the lead, attended by his aide-de-camps and the local officials.

From the landing pier we drove through an avenue of grand willows [1] which line the main street, and passing some gardens of fig, pomegranate, almond, hazel, and olive trees, ascended the hills at the back of the town, to dip on the other side into the midst of wild and marvellously beautiful scenery. The road, however, was abominable, and how the *yemstchyck* contrived to get us over the ground without upsetting the carriage must ever remain a mystery, for the ruts, certainly 18 inches deep in some parts, were here and there crossed by furrows, the action of water-courses from the broken ground above, and their united effect it is not difficult to conceive. A couple of Cossacks in attendance upon the General had to dismount occasionally to lift the vehicles on to the level, the excitement lasting over a distance of seven miles, but through a magnificent country where the acacia, the bignonia, the woodbine and clematis, with the box, holly, blackthorn, laurel, myrtle, azalea, and rhododendron vied with each other in profusion and gorgeous array ; no tall forest shaded our path, but trees there were in abundance, from the sprouted acorn to the giant poplar :

> Some trees their birth to bounteous Nature owe;
> For some without the pains of planting grow.
> With oziers thus the banks of brooks abourd,
> Sprung from the wat'ry genius of the ground.
> From the same principals grey willows come,
> Herculean poplar, and the tender broom.

[1] These superb specimens have been lately cut down.

But some, from seeds enclos'd in earth, arise :
For thus the mastful chestnut mates the skies.
Hence rise the branching beech and vocal oak,
Where Jove of old oraculously spoke.
Some from the root a rising wood disclose,
Thus elms and thus the savage cherry grows ;
Thus the green bay, that binds the poet's brows,
Shoots, and is shelter'd by the mother's boughs.

At one part of the road we chanced to get some way ahead of the second carriage, which was left to be helped in its turn over the rough ground by the Cossacks. The General and suite had galloped across a green sward in another direction, and we were thus proceeding alone, when the *yemstchyck*, suddenly pulling up, declared he would go no farther ; he was afraid, he said, of *rosboynyky*, 'brigands,' and sullenly insisted that we were nearing a spot where robberies were frequently committed on lonely travellers. There certainly was everything in the appearance of the locality to favour persons bent upon such illegal and objectionable practices, but somehow we did not share his alarm, and he appeared much relieved when the mounted guard cantered up to our side. A few moments after this, the *yemstchyck* became enthusiastic at the sight of Mount Elbrouz,[1] according to some, the rock to which Prometheus was bound. *Vott, nasha bolshaya gara, Vott !* 'There, (see) our great mountain, there !' he exclaimed as he pointed to the loftiest of the snowy peaks.

A two hours' jolting brought us to a richly carpeted dale, guarded at its entrance by 'herculean poplars'; it was the Gounaskaya-dalyna. The ascent to the grotto through dense

---

[1] The two peaks of Elbrouz have been ascended by Englishmen — the eastern (18,431 feet), on July 31, 1868, the western (18,526 feet), on July 28, 1874 ; the former by Messrs. D. W. Freshfield, A. W. Moore, C. C. Tucker ; the latter by Messrs. F. Gardiner, F. C. Grove, H. Walker, all members of the Alpine Club.

undergrowth and over moist and clayey soil, was a matter of no small labour for the ladies, but a prize awaited us at the goal. Our noble host had ordered hampers to be sent in advance, and their contents were spread invitingly at the entrance to the cave. After luncheon we explored the cavern, which measures 140 feet in length, in a direct line, south and north, varying in width from 30 in. to 22 ft.; at the extreme end it extends at a right angle 30 ft. farther to the west, this last chamber being entered through an opening at the level of the floor, 20 in. in diameter, and named the Emma *Salon*, after the wife of a police officer who had the resolution to squeeze herself through the narrow entrance; a few years ago, the crinoline would have quite precluded the accomplishment of such a feat! Stalactites had been knocked off by wanton hands, but the spar on the floors remained, very fantastic and beautiful; there being no geologist among us, I was unable to borrow a learned description of this grotto.

It was already dark when we re-embarked, and at 11 P.M. the steamer left the anchorage.

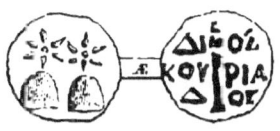

COIN OF DIOSCURIAS.

CHAPTER XII.

SEVENTEENTH AND EIGHTEENTH DAY.

Arrival at Poti—The great mountain range—The river Rion—Lake Paleostom—The Phasis—Ancient and modern fortresses—A breakfast party—Preparation for Gouria—Journey along the coast—Noblemen Cossacks—Evil practices—Swampy country—Nicolaya—Russo-Turkish frontier—Gouria labourers—The ancient Petra—Arrival at Ozourghety—Sovereignty of Gouria—Population—Costume—The (Prince) Gouriel—Monastery of Tchemokmedy—Travelling in the Caucasus—Coinage.

WE arrived off Poti at 7 A.M., and anchored two miles from the shore. It was a lovely morning, and though the vapours rising from the marshes through which the Rion wends its way, developed into mist, their expansion had a limit, for they left unobscured the summits of the majestic Caucasian range which stood out in bold relief against the eastern sky. It was so peradventure when the 'Argo,' 'sped by a favourable wind, reached the smiling banks of the Phasis at the hour when the dawn of day illuminating space, cast its rays towards the Hesperian shores of the inhospitable sea.' (Πόντος ἀξείνος).[1] The double-headed Elbrouz that claims its title to distinction as lord of the range, is seen, it is said, from this anchorage, but such, I believe, is not the case. To the right

---

[1] *Orph. Argonaut*, 755. The name 'Αξείνος, 'inhospitable,' was altered to 'Εὐξείνος, 'hospitable,' whence Euxine, in the fifth century B.C. Pliny VI. i. and Ovid IV. eleg. 4, have attributed the name 'Αξείνος to the inhospitable disposition of the people on the shores of the Black Sea. Sofocles called it 'Απόξεινος. In the Middle Ages it was known to the Italians as the Mare Maggiore.

is the Mossian, now the Adjaro range, the *Mooschici montes* of Ptolemy, with the mountains of Taghynaourou and Nepyss'-tzkaro, rising respectively 8,755 feet and 9,343 feet.

The small island upon which stands the lighthouse, forms the delta of the river Rion, and like the country around, is covered with exuberant vegetation. At the mouth of the northern arm an iron pier was constructed, where it was the intention to establish a port ; but the venture turned out a failure, owing to the exposed position selected. A new harbour is now in course of completion

DELTA OF THE RION.

under the direction of General Falkenhagen, to consist of a pier having a depth of 18 feet water at its sides, protected by two curving breakwaters. At the southern entrance to the Rion is a bar which prevents all but the smallest vessels from entering, and as the bank outside is shifting, great circumspection is needed in the navigation between the roads and the river, the maximum of water over the bar never exceeding 8 feet.

At eight o'clock the passengers were landed in a small steam tender, and we went to the Hôtel Colchide kept by Mons. Jaquot, one of the earliest settlers at Poti. We received an invitation from the Countess Levaschoff to breakfast at eleven, and made use of the intervening time by driving to Lake Paleostom, through a wild profusion of vegetation growing on the richest soil. In the park near the lake are noble forest trees of strength and beauty, and interspersed with them are huge ivies that emulate the wild vine in their loving embrace of the wide-spread branches; the oak alone seemed stunted in its growth.

As we neared the Paleostom, the swampy ground, overgrown with rushes, rendered impossible any approach to its border. The idea was at one time entertained by the Russian Government of converting this lake, which is $2\frac{1}{2}$ miles long, into a port, and connecting it with the Rion and the sea by navigable canals; the officer, who had himself conducted the survey, informed me that the scheme was abandoned solely on account of the cost. Had the plan been successfully carried out, the Paleostom in its importance and commercial prosperity would not have been second to any port in the Empire, upon the completion of the railway from Tiflis to Bakou. The line of rail from Poti to Tiflis and Bakou, and the road across the Kirghiz steppe after leaving Orenburg, will, for some time, be the two great arteries of communication between Russia and the Turcoman populations, thus renewing, after an ancient manner, the trade with the Khanates;[1] to these, however, should be added the efficient navigation on the Volga at certain seasons,

---

[1] In the Russo-Khivan treaty concluded at the Russian camp in the gardens of Gendemain, August 25, 1873, was agreed: 'Clause 5. Russian steamers and other ships, whether belonging to the Government or to private persons, will enjoy the right of free navigation on the Amu; the said right will belong exclusively to the said ships. Khivese and Bokharese ships will be permitted to navigate the Amu only with the special sanction of the supreme Russian authorities in Central Asia.' The Russians have now advanced to the waters of the Attreck.

and the Rostoff-Vladykavkaz-Petrovsk railroad, only partly completed.

The possession of the Phasis was coveted at a period when the conformation of the coast at its entrance rendered it probably better adapted to purposes of commerce than it is at present, altered as it has become by the retrogression of the waters of the Black Sea during many centuries. In his plan of conquest, the ambitious Chosroes[1] was fired by the hope of launching a Persian navy from the Phasis, of commanding the trade and navigation of the Euxine Sea, of desolating the coast of Pontus and Bithynia, of distressing, perhaps of attacking, Constantinople, &c.,[2] and similar designs were entertained by Abbas I. in the early part of the seventeenth century.

In the time of Strabo there was a city on the Phasis of the same name; it was a mart of the Colchians, bounded on one side by the river, on another by a lake, and on the third by the sea. After Arrian had visited the coast, A.D. 130, he reported that the fortress, garrisoned with 400 picked men, was formidable by its position, and a protection to all who sailed on the river.[3] The Turks built a fortress in the reign of Amurat III., 1574–95, which was destroyed by the Imeritians, who afterwards restored it; the ruins are seen in the public gardens at some distance from the sea; nearer to the river's mouth is a Russian fort of recent construction, which commands the entrance over the bar. The garrison at Poti consists of a thousand troops.

On returning to the residence of the chief of police, who does the duty of governor, we found a large party assembled, consisting chiefly of the officials of the province in full uniform and plentifully

---

[1] *Anoushirvan.* [2] *Decline and Fall of the Roman Empire*, chap. xlii.
[3] Arr. perip. 12.

decorated with stars and crosses, who had assembled at Poti to receive his Excellency; several were members of princely families in the Caucasus now sunk into insignificance, and one was a direct descendant of the last Crimean Khan. During the collation, a military band stationed under the windows enlivened the occasion by playing selections from 'Faust,' 'William Tell,' &c.; and when the entertainment was over, the Count and Countess added to their courtesy by inviting us to accompany them to Koutaïs in a special train which was placed at their disposal, and would leave in the afternoon.

For the journey to Ozourghety in Gouria, a saddle horse is to be had at Poti for four roubles, and the guide charges four roubles for his horse. Saddle-bags are readily procured at the bazaars, but they should be strengthened with a leathern lining; English groceries may also be obtained, for let it ever be borne in mind, that travelling must never be undertaken in the Caucasus without a sufficiency of provisions; another valuable hint is, that the traveller should avoid being overtaken on the road by darkness, if possible, unless attended by an escort.

His Excellency had kindly given directions that every facility should be afforded me for travelling in Gouria: in a few hours the requisite arrangements were completed, and at 5 P.M. I left Poti in a southerly direction with an officer of police and two Cossacks. As we kept along the seashore with dense woods to our left, we passed the wrecks of numerous *katchermas* that had been abandoned on taking the ground, and at 6.30 we crossed the Kappar-tchaï, a stream about 150 yards in width, on a floating raft; the Kappar-tchaï unites the lake Paleostom and the sea, but I doubt if there is much current; the lake, which was two miles distant, we were enabled to view from the top of a summer-house in the grounds of

Prince Vakhtang Gouriel. We proceeded through well-wooded land and fields of maize, crossing the Soupsa, the ancient Mogrus, at 7.30; these streams are very shallow, allowing of the rafts to be poled across. The shortest road to Ozourghety is from this river's right bank, and passes through two villages, called Tchotch'hat and Gouryam, thus striking across country, but I preferred keeping the seashore. We changed horses at Grygoretsky, a Cossack station, where the officer invited us to take tea; he was in command of a small detachment of the 200 men employed on this part of the coast for the suppression of smuggling and horse-stealing, both profitable occupations. The majority of these Cossacks are the impoverished princes and nobles of Gouria and Mingrelia, who give infinite trouble and are difficult to control; their feeling of independence ill accords with the position they hold, and the scanty pay they receive of five roubles monthly; but many there are, it is said, whose incomes amount to hundreds of roubles, because they share in the lawless spoil of the footpads and horse-stealers that infest the province, the very malefactors it is their duty to seize. Horse-stealers amuse themselves by carrying off across the Turkish frontier all animals they can lay hands on in Russian territory, while those stolen from Turkey are brought into Gouria; this traffic has succeeded to the kidnapping of females and boys, greatly in practice before the annexation of the province to Russia.

Beyond Grygoretsky is another stream, the Outchky-abano, 'foot-bath,' in Mingrelian, after which the road lies through thick jungle, at this time flooded by the late rains, the damp fusty feeling in the air making me apprehensive of fever at every respiration. As the evening advanced, I was glad to find that the path led along the shore, where we enjoyed the gentle breeze that helped the rippling waves to pet the sands under our horses' feet; but now and again we plunged into the darkness of a jungle illumined by the myriads of phosphorescent insects that played about us, many as they darted to and fro becoming for an instant a floating light, and then perishing. As we hastened over the sodden ground, our horses would splutter, stumble, and splash, until we neared Nicolaya, the frontier station, where the ground rises. At ten o'clock we entered the village, and were welcomed by the chief of customs, at whose house we passed the night; we should not have fared so well in one of the *doukanns*[1] for native travellers.

Whilst waiting in the morning for our horses, ordered for five o'clock, we strolled to the Natonyeba, anciently the river Isis, which, with the Tcholok'h,[2] is the line of frontier at the coast, between Russia and Turkey; the posts of observation of the two Powers are within pistol-shot, yet almost invisible to each other. The chief of customs, who had been many years at Nicolaya, told us that no communication had ever taken place between himself and the Turkish authorities, all necessity for any rencontre being carefully avoided. The trade at Nicolaya in maize and boxwood increases yearly, the maize being exported chiefly to Trebizond; its population varies according to the harvest;[3] the season of 1874 was good, and as many as one hundred hands had come from the country to load vessels. In the Natonyeba six *katchermas* were waiting for their cargoes.

From Nicolaya we struck inland into a beautiful country, the

---

[1] *Doukann*, a wine and provision store, where a night's lodging may be had.

[2] In the draft of the treaty at the termination of the war with Turkey, Russia, it is said, inadvertently inserted the name of the river Tcholok'h in place of the Tcholok-sou at Batoum, for the sea-board boundary, thus losing through an error of its own, the only desirable port on the east shore of the Black Sea.

[3] In the course of 1874, 2,600,000 *pouds* of maize were shipped for export at various parts of the coast, between Anaklia and Nicolaya, at 55 copecks per *poud*, delivered at the seaside.

hills and their acclivities being covered with forests of oak and box, and the valleys cultivated almost exclusively with maize, for there was little corn or barley growing; maize is sown in May and gathered in September, when it is temporarily stored and husked in *sassymyde*, 'lofts' constructed in the fields on spars, 12 to 14 feet above the ground, as a security against field mice. The Gourias would seem to be a noisy people, for as they toiled with their spades they kept up incessant and inharmonious cries, assimilating the public-house sounds that had disturbed us at Nicolaya the past night. We rode to a grassy plot where dinner was being got ready for those at work; a very comely young woman, the wife of the proprietor, was herself, according to custom, superintending its preparation by an elderly female; and the meal which consisted of broiled trout and broiled mutton, with boiled maize, and *gommy*, 'millet,' the universal substitute for bread, promised to be excellent. The extent of uncultivated land we passed is incredible, and landowners sigh for manual labour; it was a common occurrence to see children of both sexes, in their seventh or eighth year, employed turning up the soil.

We forded the Natonyeba, a rapid stream, repeatedly, also a multitude of rivulets, for this part of Gouria is well irrigated. Dubois, who believed that he had discovered the site of Petra the capital of the Lazi, destroyed in 550, places it to the east of the Skourdeby where it unites with the Natonyeba, and has gone into lengthened details to describe the ruins he saw.

At 10 A.M. we entered Ozourghety, the chief town of Gouria, and once the residence of its sovereigns; it has one long street, the bazaar, where the stalls are badly supplied, and a few *doukanns* scattered irregularly like the houses the people live in; it is a poor and unattractive town, but the vegetation and gardens that encompass the dwellings give it in reality a most picturesque appearance.

Gouria was a part of ancient Lazica, the theatre of the wars between Justinian and Chosroes. The first mention in the annals of Georgia of a Gouriel, the distinguishing title of the ruler of this province, is in the reign of Queen Roussoudan, 1223–47, from which period the country had its own governors. After the partition of the kingdom of Georgia in the fifteenth century, Vardanydze, *crystav* [1] of Swannety, became ruler of Gouria, and his successors held the sovereignty as vassals of the king of Imeritia. The last reigning Gouriel, Mamia V., recognised the suzerainty of Russia in 1810, and in 1829 Gouria was annexed to the Empire.[2] The present prince, Dmitri, claims to be the lineal descendant of Vardanydze.

The name Gouria is believed by some to be derived from Guebres, the fire-worshippers who were in the country during the Persian invasion in the sixth century; others conceive it to be from *Ourya*, the Georgian for Jews, many of whom were banished hither by Nebuchadnezzar.[3]

The small population of Gouria is eminently agricultural, less attention being paid to the rearing of cattle. The men wear trowsers fitting tight to the ankles, a jacket trimmed with lace, and the *bashlyk*; round the waist is a thick sash in many folds, inside which they stick their dagger and pistols.

The day turned out damp and disagreeable—Gouria is pro-

---

[1] 'Head of the people,' the title of the governor of a large province, during the Georgian monarchy, and now assumed by many nobles in Transcaucasia.

[2] *Histoire de la Géorgie*, M. Brosset, St. Petersburg, 1849, i. p. 521; ii. p. 252. Translated from the Georgian of the Tzarevitch Wakhoucht.

[3] *Description Géographique de la Géorgie*, M. Brosset, St. Petersburg, 1842, p. 414. Translated from the Georgian of the Tzarevitch Wakhoucht.

verbially a damp country. I called to pay my respects to the Gouriel, and present my letters of introduction; the Prince was too ill to receive me, and he subsequently sent his card, expressing his regret at being unable to show me any attention in consequence of the state of his health.

Saddle-horses were not to be had, so I took a post *troïka* and left Ozourghety at 1.30 P.M. for the Monastery of Tchemokmedy, the road lying through six miles of forest. From the hamlet we scrambled up a steep path to the Monastery, 800 feet above the woods, and had no sooner reached the gate, than a retainer arrived with a message from His Serene Highness, who placed a handsome horse at my disposal.

The ancient Monastery of Tchemokmedy, which enclosed the Episcopal Church of Gouria and was the residence of a Metropolitan in the eighteenth century, was a fortified position protected by massive walls, portions of which remain; the place was dismantled by the Russians on the suppression of an insurrection. The church, of irregular masonry, is vaulted and has two aisles, the walls of which bear traces of paintings in fresco; a smaller sanctuary, built of brick, adjoins it. Both edifices are in a precarious state, the restorations and repairs that have been made being rude and inefficient; the monks complain bitterly of their poverty and inability to keep the premises in good order.

The relics and precious objects are reduced to a mass of gold and silver fragments, destruction caused by a band of Mahommedan Gourias, who broke into the edifices in 1861, and carried off everything of intrinsic value. The sacrilege was quickly discovered and made known, when some 500 Gourias from the Christian villages turned out and tracked the robbers into Turkish territory, where they killed them, losing three of their own number in the conflict;

the stolen articles were all recovered, but battered and destroyed. The inscription on an image of the Virgin Mary is said to be of the eleventh century.

The disinclination on the part of the monks to show the relics was very marked, but being well supported by my companion from Poti and the messenger from the Prince, the archimandrite invited me with great solemnity to inspect them. Two objects only had escaped the complete destruction which was the fate of the rest, one

MONASTERY OF TCHEMOKMEDY.

being a golden chalice, the gift in 1713 of the Gouriel Mamia III., for some time king also of Imeritia; the other, a handsome Georgian work of art, is a small pedestal of solid gold, set in rubies and turquoises with an inscription in black enamel, which had supported a Christ in gold, now sadly mutilated. There were many pearls and precious stones, among the latter a rough ruby of size and colour, the price of which would alone restore the church and render the dormitories habitable.

The monks were painfully superstitious, and consequently ignorant. There was no end to the miracles that had been wrought through the intervention of their own particular saints, with whose images they toyed as children do with baubles; but it was to the sanctity of their clergy that they were indebted for so great celestial favour! How true the reflexion of 'Daniel Stern':—' L'homme voulait se faire semblable à Dieu. Les prêtres ont fait Dieu semblable à l'homme, et la vanité de l'espèce humaine s'est contentée.'

The sovereigns of Gouria lie interred beneath the slabs with which the church is paved, but there are few inscriptions to distinguish the occupants of the tombs. The Gouriels still enjoy the privilege of being buried inside the edifice, the small churchyard adjoining, being for the sole use of the monks.

To travel with post-horses in the Caucasus, it is necessary to obtain from the governor or chief of police of a town, a *padarójnaya*, 'order for horses,' to secure which document a passport must be produced. The *padarójnaya* is good only for the journey between two places named in it, and becomes worthless after that journey has been performed, when a new one must be procured; a small fee is charged for this paper. The tax is 2½ copecks for each horse per *verst*, and 12 copecks are paid at each station for the use of the *pereclodnáya*, 'travelling cart'; the *yemstchyck* changes with the horses, and receives a gratuity of 15 or 20 copecks.

Hampers were replenished, and post-horses ordered for midnight, the hour fixed for our departure being 2 A.M.

I received much attention at Ozourghety from Baron Heijking, officer of police, whose guest I became, and who afforded me every facility for going about. His quarters were at the military barracks, where 600 men are in garrison.

GEORGIAN CURRENCY.

Russian paper money, silver and copper coin, is in circulation all over the Caucasus; there is also the following old Georgian currency:

Schaour	. . .	5 copecks.
½ Abaz	. . . . .	10 ,,
Abaz [1]	. . . . .	20 ,,
2 Abaz	. . . . .	40 ,,

[1] Originally a Persian coin, named after Abaz the Great, 1585-1629.

THRONE OF THE METROPOLITAN; TCHEMOKMEDY. EIGHTEENTH CENTURY.

CHAPTER XIII.

NINETEENTH DAY.

Early departure—The fair of Gouria—The *Diospyrus lotus*—Women of Gouria—The wine country—Fair at Orpýry—Railway at Samtredy—Pass of Iyelagory—Numerous ruined churches—Their supposed origin—The Poti-Tiflis railroad—Souram—King Vakhtang—Arrival at Tiflis.

IT was a dark morning and heavy clouds were gathering from the west, as we started from Ozourghety in a *pereclodnáya* at 2 A.M. This early stir was a necessity, for I was anxious to reach Samtredy in time to meet the train from Poti to Tiflis. Our horses were fresh, and the clatter of their hoofs echoed again as they cantered over the hard stones in the now silent street of bazaars, and we soon cleared the little town, the dogs saluting us with savage barks from the courts in their keeping.

After crossing the Natonycba, we ascended the Nasykyryla pass, by the side of a ravine at the bottom of which is the Bah'by, and after fording some of the tributaries of the Soupsa, stopped at Nagomary to change horses. A great fair is held here annually on July 20, at which the entire population of Gouria may be said to assemble, for people flock to it from all parts to lay in their yearly supplies of stuffs, hardware, crockery, cattle, &c., there being no tradesmen in Gouria, and few shops, and this fair becomes the only mart in the province. 'You would see what fine cows and beautiful women we have,' said the *yemstchyck* winking, ' were you to come to our fair.'

In the broad valley of Pasoutchy was the first herd of cattle we had yet seen, and the *khourmà* (*Diospyrus lotus*), a kind of date plum, was growing luxuriantly; it is largely imported into Russia as a dry fruit, and a favourite spirit is made of it; maize was also growing, but there was a general appearance of abandonment and neglect. The tower seen on the right of the road, is all that remains of the residence of the *crystav* Mihail of the family of the Gouriel, who was assassinated a few years ago by his own peasantry, for oppressive practices. At Tchynataoúry, where we again changed horses, was the house and farm of the *crystav* David (Gouriel), and from this point the road ascends the well-wooded Pyatzwan, the enchanting scenery being enlivened by frequent falls of water and mountain streams, which find their way into the beautiful valley through which flows the Hebytz-tzkalys; on the opposite side of this valley is the Monastery of Gamatchnebouly, a favourite pilgrimage of the poverty-stricken mountaineers, who have few churches at which they can assemble. But what shall I say of the indigence of the peasantry in these highlands; of their tatters and scared looks as they flew off the road and hid themselves in the wood at our approach—not the males, but the females? And yet, if report be true, there are not many Lucretias in Gouria—

> . . . where, to love inclined,
> Each swain *is* blest, for every maid *is* kind.

The women in Gouria, to judge by the few we had the opportunity of seeing, are decidedly interesting; there is nothing characteristic in their costume, with the exception of the cotton shirt, which, drawn in at the waist, is worn in such a manner as to display to the utmost the contour of their charms.

We changed horses for the third time at Hebytzheby, a snug little village by the Hebytz-tzkalys on the southern slope of the Sodjavah', from the summit of which we enjoyed a most extensive view of the plains, and of the windings of the Rion. We were in a vine country, but none of the wine we called for was at all drinkable. On reaching the plain, we crossed the Rion, at the village of Orpýry, on board a barge propelled with paddle-wheels worked by hand. We had no small difficulty in pushing our way through the crowded streets where a fair was going on, for the goods were spread out on carpets on the ground, leaving barely sufficient space for a vehicle to pass; there was no shouting, no cries, no haggling, for men and women moved about lazily and noiselessly. Wools, cottons, and most of the fabrics offered for sale were of Russian manufacture; leather work, cutlery, and pottery were native. A few *versts* farther, and we were at Samtredy, in ample time for the train.[1]

The Rion is crossed for the last time just before reaching the Koutaïs railway station, and beyond Kvyryly the railway skirts the Tzheretely, on the banks of which is Byelagory, in the midst of wooded hills occasionally relieved by rich and bounteous pastures. The pass and rock of Byelagory offer some striking points, and as the traveller is borne along, he will notice the sharpness of the curves in the line of rails, many being at a radius of eight chains.

In this neighbourhood are the remains of numberless churches and castles that crown the peaks and summits, the latter reminding one of the *schlœsser* on the Rhine. The country

[1] For railway time-table, see Appendix IV.

people attribute to the great Queen Thamar the foundation of all the sacred edifices, and to the Genoese the erection of the fortresses, a ready method of clearing up all doubts as to their origin. The motive for the existence of so many churches, assigned in his quaint work by Chardin, a traveller of the seventeenth century, is likely to be the correct one. 'The Georgians, like the other Christians by whom they are bounded on the north and west, follow the strange custom of building the greater number of their churches on the tops of mountains in remote and inaccessible places. They are looked at and reverenced at the distance of three or four leagues, but they are seldom visited; indeed it is very certain that but few are opened even once in ten years. They are erected, and then abandoned to the elements and to the fowls of the air. I was never able to learn the reason for this foolish practice, all those of whom I inquired having ever made the same silly reply: "It is the custom." The Georgians are advised that whatever the nature of their transgressions, they ensure remission by building a small church. For my part, I believe that they erect them in such inaccessible places, to avoid the expense of decorating and endowing them.' [1]

On reaching Bejatouban we were transferred to a diligence, the working over the pass of Souram being suppressed for a time. The post-road keeps the railway pretty well in sight as it passes through the defile, on to the plateau, and down to Souram.

The railroad from Poti to Tiflis owes its existence to British capital and enterprise. The British engineers who surveyed the

[1] *Journal du voyage du Chev. Chardin en Perse et aux Indes Orientales*, &c., Amsterdam, 1711. Chardin's travels extended from 1664 to 1681.

[2] The altitudes above the sea in English feet, given in the margin, are from the Russian topographical map of Transcaucasia.

track recommended the boring of a tunnel through the hill; but the Russians shrank from so heavy an undertaking, and at a considerably less cost the railway was made to climb up one side, and run down the other, by gradients of 1 ft. in 22 ft. over a distance of about eight miles, throwing even the Bhore Ghaut into the shade as a matter of skill in engineering.

The station at Souram, a small and insignificant village inhabited by Armenians, was the temporary terminus, but accommodation for travellers was shamefully neglected. We had three hours to wait for the departure of the train, and improved the occasion by walking to the old fortress picturesquely situated on an eminence; a portion only of the walls, which are of considerable thickness and strength, are left standing on their solid foundation of rock. This fortress dates from the reign of Vakhtang, king of Georgia, 446-499, surnamed *Gourgasal*, 'wolf-lion,' from his habit of wearing a helmet of gold, having a wolf in front and a lion behind. It was restored and occupied by a Persian garrison in 1634, on the accession of Rustam to the throne.

At 6 P.M. the train proceeded through broad valleys increasing in sterility to the narrower valley of the Kour. As is the practice in Russia, the train made unnecessarily long halts at each station, and it was well-nigh midnight when we reached Tiflis. The terminus is fully two miles from the city, but good carriages are in waiting, and the traveller may be certain of being rendered every assistance by the polyglot guards, who are always very civil.

CART OF GOURIA.

CHAPTER XIV.

TWENTIETH DAY.

Foundation of Tiflis—Population—Climate—River Kour—Its fish—Water supply—Public buildings—Monastery of St. David—Gryboïedoff—His popularity—Fortifications at Tiflis—Botanic Gardens—Cemeteries—An exciting scene—The bazaars—Character of Georgians—A ball—Georgian ladies—National dance.

TIFLIS, the capital of Georgia—Tbylysys-Kalaky—was founded 1,350. by King Vakhtang, *Gourgasal*, who built the city in 469, where had stood the fortress of Tchourys-Tzykhè, erected by the Persian *crystav* as a bulwark against Mtzkhetha the capital of the kings, when Varaz-Bakar was on the throne of Karthly, 379-393; and the seat of government was removed to Tbylysys-Kalaky from Mtzkhetha, by Datchy, 34th king, who reigned 499-514. The city received its name from the hot mineral springs, so much in favour to this day, on the right bank of the river Kour in the Gyozyohety-oubany quarter; one is here reminded of Tœplitz in Hungary, celebrated for its thermal waters, and that *tyeplô* is the Russian word for warm. Tiflis has had to submit to conquest by the Mongols, Persians, Greeks and Turks; it was destroyed eight times, and completely sacked and the inhabitants massacred, first under Tamerlane in 1387 and 1393, and again by the vile Aga Mohammed Shah in 1795.

Next to the Georgians, the Armenians predominate in the population of Tiflis, which includes Persians, Tatars, some Jews, and a few French and Italians, and in its immediate neighbourhood is a thriving and orderly colony of Germans, descendants of emigrants from Würtemberg.[1] In summer the inhabitants are glad to fly to the hills and highlands to escape the excessive heats from June to September, when the thermometer averages 100° in the shade; in winter the weather is temperate,[2] snow falls at rare intervals and seldom lies for twenty-four hours. Some proof of the acknowledged mildness of the climate may be urged in the fact, that few families keep covered carriages, and there were but two closed conveyances for hire during the time we were at Tiflis.

The Kour, the ancient Cyrnus or Cyrus, on which the Georgian capital is built, is reputed to have salmon, but I never met with an assertion of the fact; the nearest approach to salmon is a large fish, the *oragouly* in Georgian, and *lassassyna* in Russian, which means 'flesh of salmon'; when salted it is excellent, and is then called *syómga*, 'salmon.' Other fish in the Kour are the *tomm*, 'scilurus,' called in Russian *ousatch*, 'one who wears a moustache,' from the barbules or wattles with which it is provided; the *loko*, and the *pytchouly* a small and delicate fish; while at the estuary of the Kour in the Caspian, is taken the great sturgeon called *byclouga*, or hansen, a specimen of which at the Tiflis Museum, measures 14 ft., and weighed 33 *pouds*; the weight, however, of this fish sometimes reaches 70 *pouds*; the roe is greatly esteemed. Ystachry, who travelled in the tenth century, states that 'fish of two sorts are taken in the Kour, the dorakine (?) and azap (?), which surpass all others in this country'; [3] and in the *Coll. Ramusio* is given the relation of a merchant, a traveller in Persia in 1500, who in allusion to the

---

[1] Population in the Government of Tiflis amounts to 635.315 (Census 1873).
[2] See meteorological table, Appendix V.
[3] *Der Brief des Landes*, Mormann, 1845.

morones, *barbus fluviatilis*, in the Kour, stated that they were 'migliori che la carne de' fagiani.'

The Kour is the only source for supplying the city with water, and, notwithstanding its polluted state, the Georgians have what may indeed be called a religious liking for it ; they love it as the St. Petersburgers love the water of the Neva, and drink of it as their fathers drank of it before them ; but then the stomach to receive it must be Georgian. The *toulouh'tchye*, 'carriers', lead their horses laden with two huge buffalo skins called *toulouh*', for the sale of water, which is delivered at people's houses and sold by the *vedro*,[1] the measures being slung across the animal's neck, and the vendor keeps his reckoning by notching scores on a short stick he carries at his belt.

Three bridges span the Kour, the largest being the Woronzoff bridge, which unites Kouky the left bank to the Georgian quarter ; near it is a statue of the late prince as Governor-General in the Caucasus ;[2] two other bridges, the Meteky and Nicolaïeffsky, unite the Armenian and Persian quarters in the direction of the bazaars.

After traversing the Woronzoff bridge *en route* from the railway terminus, the traveller passes the public gardens to the Galavynsky prospect, the principal street, and certainly one of the most promising in attractiveness in Russia ; turning to the left he will see the gymnasium, law courts, site for the new cathedral, and palace of the Governor-General of the Caucasus, the most important command in the empire, a post held at present by H.I.H. the Grand Duke Michael, brother to the Emperor ;

---

[1] The *vedro* is equal to 3¼ gallons.

[2] Prince Woronzoff is stated to have thrown up his command in the Caucasus during the late war, because he felt he could not rely upon the troops with which he was supplied for the defence of the country, and for the maintenance of order among the unsubdued and disaffected populations in his government.

the Grand Duke is also *namestnyk*, 'lieutenant,' of His Imperial Majesty.

The palace is an edifice which would have looked to better advantage had it stood on higher ground, or on a stereobate like the Palazzo Pitti at Florence. In front of the palace is the main guardhouse, with the lath and plaster Roman Doric colonnade, emblematic of military power and glory, so affected in Russia. Near it is the public library and museum; the former includes an excellent reading-room, not opened until noon, a great detriment to scholars. In the museum is a natural history and geological [1] collection conveniently classified; the archæological and ethnological departments are in some confusion, but the arrangement of the former will doubtlessly mend under the auspices of the Archæological Society lately founded at Tiflis.

In the shops in the Dvartzóvaya-oúlytza, 'palace street,' are exposed many European luxuries, including the latest *modes*, and beyond, is the Erivanskaya ploshtshad, 'Erivan square,' in the middle of which is the Tamamshoff Karavanserai, and Opera House. Three main streets lead out of this square—one to the 'European quarter,' where wealthy families live in well-built houses all differing in design, with balconies of elegant construction, and having gardens attached to them; another conducts to the Georgian, Armenian, and Persian bazaars; the third to the market-place and Russian bazaar, where a sort of fair is held every Sunday morning, at which it would appear that soldiers do the most business, in bartering and selling condemned uniforms and boots. In

---

[1] The geological collection has been formed chiefly by Mr. F. Baïern, whose property it is, during a lengthened residence in the Caucasus. Though zealous and enthusiastic in his studies and pursuits, Mr. B. is one of those men whose merits do not appear to have ever been recognised, and whom Russia can ill afford to treat with the indifference and neglect to which he has been subjected.

the Erivan square, frequent but inconsiderable sales by auction take place, notice of which is given by the loud blowing of a horn, when a motley group of idlers assemble.

There are two good hotels near the square; from the windows of the Hôtel d'Europe, an idle moment in the early morning may be amusingly spent in watching the hard driving at bargains for the purchase of charcoal and firewood, by the side of the scores of heavily-laden little donkeys (these poor animals are one of the specialities of Tiflis), and waggon-loads of timber.

The prices of the necessaries of life are moderate, the cost of the best beef never exceeding 12 copecks per pound: but provisions are bad, rents and wages high, as are all foreign goods, yet Tiflis is, notwithstanding, a favourite residence with many Russians.

The hills between which the capital of Georgia lies, are perfectly naked, being seen to some advantage only in the early spring, when they are brightly clad in green, which however is short-lived, owing to the merciless and withering heats of summer. Half-way up the heights on the river's right bank and overlooking the city, is the Monastery of M'ta Tzmynda, 'St. David,' first erected in 1318 over the site where lived the holy Syrian Father; within the present edifice, of more recent date, is the tomb of the saint the patron and protector of married women, who visit his shrine in the month of May. A monk assured us that the church, as we saw it, was constructed entirely of materials offered by barren females, who made repeated pilgrimages, carrying with them upon each occasion a brick, a stone, or some mortar, as an offering wherewith to propitiate the saint, that they might become blessed with a family.

Beneath the church, in a crypt open to the light of day, lie the remains of Gryboïedoff, the Envoy Extraordinary and Minister Plenipotentiary of Russia, who was sent to Persia in 1828. He was a gentleman of an honourable and upright disposition, and he was fully determined to uphold the dignity of, and to exact the rights due to, his imperial master. He was, perhaps, of too unbending a character to have qualified him for being a suitable representative to such a Court as that of Persia; but if this were a fault with which he might have been charged, he paid a heavy penalty for his firmness. On February 11, 1829, he and all the members of the Russian mission fell by the daggers of an infuriated populace encouraged to revolt by the chief *mujtched* or priest, who pronounced the legality of rescuing from the Russian embassy two Armenian women, whose delivery as Russian subjects had been insisted upon, and who were placed in the custody of the second chief eunuch of the royal harem at the time enjoying the protection of the Russian Government, which he had claimed as being a native of Erivan. The number of Russian subjects massacred is stated to have been thirty-five.[1] In his notes of trave, Poushkin relates that when near the fortress of Gherghery, he met an *áraba*[2] drawn by two oxen in charge of some Georgians. 'Where are you from?' he inquired. 'From Teheran.' 'What is it you are carrying?' 'Gryboyed!' was the reply. After having remained a spectacle to the Teheran mob during three days, the mutilated body of Gryboïedoff could be only identified by a pistol-shot wound which had been received years before in the hand.[3] The monument to Gryboïedoff was erected by his youthful widow, a princess of the house of Tchevtchavadze, who has since been interred at his side.

Alexander Sergueitch Gryboïedoff is the author of *Gorye ot*

---

[1] *History of Persia, &c.*, R. G. Watson, 1866, p. 247.
[2] Any kind of four-wheeled vehicle.   [3] *Zapysky Poushkyna*, v. p. 76.

oumá,[1] a biting satire on the state of society in his day and one of the most popular pieces of the Russian stage; it was written in 1824 and acted for the first time in 1832, since which year it has gone through 93 editions, and has been translated into English, French, German, Polish, and Georgian, having, however, in its original form, suffered severely at the hands of the censor. Gryboïedoff was implicated in the events of 1825, but a timely warning from his friend and patron Yermóloff, rescued him from the fate of the rest of the Decabrists.[2]

In the European quarter is gained the ascent to the Sololaky, from the summit of which is obtained a bird's-eye view of the city, and although no conspicuous objects, no palatial buildings, no towering cupolas attract the eye, yet there is an unmistakable individuality about the whole place, and one is invited to gaze on with pleasurable feeling at the decided novelty of the scene. Along the ridge of Sololaky are the ruins of the fortress of Narykalà, which was extensively restored by Moustapha Pasha in 1576, during Turkish occupation. The erection at the eastern extremity of the hill, is said to have been a temple of the Persians to their divinity Chur, the angel appointed by Ormuzd to watch over the disc of the sun. Below the Sololaky to the south, are the Botanic Gardens the creation of Prince Woronzoff, but now little cared for; they overlook a deep ravine through which flows the Tsavkyssy, a stream easily forded to the Persian burial-ground on the opposite rocky bluff. The monuments are quadrangular chambers of brick surmounted by a dome, and entered at a door on the north side, the usual alcove, the *almghrab*, being on the east; each place of sepulture encloses three graves, all of which had, in every instance,

---

[1] 'Grief from wit.'

[2] Name by which were distinguished the nobles implicated in the insurrection of December 1825, and afterwards exiled to Siberia and the Caucasus.

been desecrated; every vault, barely 3 feet deep, is of brick, with convex bottom plastered over, and covered with an arched top also of brick, a large slab being laid over all; pains had evidently been taken to protect the bodies from the earth. Near the Persian cemetery is that of the Tatars.

The only means of carriage communication between the gardens and the city, is through the most disreputable part of the capital, a very 'suburra';[1] it is a sad reflection upon those whose concern it is, not to have disposed elsewhere of so much glaring vice and immorality.

The busy scene encountered on clearing the precincts of wretchedness defies description. We entered narrow and tortuous streets crowded with strange-looking lightly laden carts forming into caravans on their return to Bakou, and strings of camels clumsily blocking up the way, with their huge bales of cotton and silk from Persia and Daghestan; there were *ysvostchycks* gesticulating violently, and screaming *kabadah*, sounding like *gardà*— 'Take care! look out!' as they sought to hasten their fares through the throng of pedlars and street vendors of fruit, fish, poultry, arms, rugs, beads and silks, with here and there a Georgian female wearing the *tchadra*, a white shroud enveloping the head and almost the whole body, and the *toulouh'tchye*, in constant peril of having his flabby water-skins jammed; there was also the *polytzeysky sloujeétyel*,[2] giving half a hundred orders in as many seconds to as many different people, and upon being violently expostulated with, he would give half a hundred other orders with the same despairing results. This was truly Asiatic; we were in old Tiflis, in the ancient part of Tbylysys, for the walls of Sololaky

---

[1] Hor. Book v. Ode v. [2] Policeman.

that we had just quitted, enclosed Tbylysys to the south and west, while to the north it was protected by the river and other defences.

At the bazaars of Tiflis, as in most Oriental towns, each trade has its separate quarter. The first we came to were the hat or bonnet makers; in tall shops kept by Armenians, the Georgian and Armenian *koudy*, the Kabardah and Ossety *papack* made of the prized black and grey Bokhara lamb-skins, and the Persian high sugar-loaf hat, were displayed on pegs overhead and around; the floors of these stalls are 3 feet above the street, and serve as counters, the salesman and workmen squatting on pieces of matting. We then passed the cookshops and the bakers, where the whole process of kneading and baking may be watched; the favourite substitute for bread eaten by the Georgians and Armenians is the *tchourekeby*, a large and flat piece of dough like a monstrous pancake. Beyond these eating-houses is the Tatarsky meydan, a square, where confusion seemed to be worse confounded—for bales and goods lay strewn about, adding considerably to the difficulty of locomotion; our progress here became even slower, but it answered our purpose, for it enabled us to witness strange sights and customs.

From the market-place we got to the wine shops, where the *bourdyouky*, great buffalo skins, and *tyky*, goat or sheep skins,[1] filled with the Kakhety wine, are laid on their backs and present the disagreeable appearance of carcases swollen after lengthened immersion in water. From the wine shops we passed on to the sandal and slipper makers, tea-dealers, chandlers, and foreign

---

[1] We read of skin vessels in the Odyssey vi. and Iliad iii., and in the Georgics, as also in Herod. ii.; and wine skins are in use in Spain at the present day. The largest *bourdyouk* usually contains 75 *vedros*; a *tyky* from three-quarters to one *vedro*.

goods stores, the boot, brass-work, wool and bedding bazaars, until we at length reached the arms bazaar, perhaps the most attractive of any.

The armourers' stalls, very small, crowded with every kind of weapon, and thrown wide open, are slightly above the footway; the artificers at work were shaping sword and dagger hilts in ivory, bone, or horn, fitting flints to locks, scabbards to sabres, and new stocks to gun-barrels. The connoisseur is certain of finding a prize for his armoury if he carefully examines the shelves and presses, although blades with an inscription in Roman letters, and there are many such, are offered as arms of the Crusaders or of the *Ghenouczsty*, the Genoese, when they are only too evidently recent importations from Hungary.

A genuine Andrea Ferrara I saw, had just been bought for one rouble! Native weapons are in abundance, such as the Lesghian pistol, Ossety rifle, Daghestan poignard, knife of Imeritia, Damascus sabre, and the blades of Persia of the boasted make of Mourza and of Hadgy Moustapha; but fabulous prices are set on a Kurd shield, a Bashkir's bow, a Hefsour shirt of mail, or a rich Persian breast-plate.

There is little inducement to loiter among the furriers and musical instrument makers with their poor stock in trade, when the silversmiths are so near in their quaint little stalls with glass fronts, where are displayed tempting silver ornaments in the favourite *niello*—such as dirks, tobacco boxes, belts, brooches, &c., and old Georgian drinking cups and flagons. The flagons called *koula*, peculiar to Georgia and Imeritia, are spherical with an upright silver spout, upon which is usually inscribed this couplet, 'Koula, thou art for wine, and for the delight of my spirits.' Other flagons have long spiral necks, single or double, that emit an exhilarating sound to the feaster as he pours the liquor down his throat ; for the Georgian is a great toper, three bottles of the wine of Kakhety being his ordinary allowance at dinner.[1] The Georgian is invariably in a merry mood, and rarely allows himself to be depressed by the troubles of life ; he loves wine and music, and ever seeks to drive away dull care :

> . . . . omne malum vino cantuque levato,
> Deformis ægrimoniæ ac dulcibus alloquiis.—HOR.

The process of working the *niello* ornaments at Tiflis is after the following manner :—A silver trinket or plate has a scroll, flower, or landscape deeply engraven on it ; into the design is poured a composition of silver, copper, and a small proportion of lead ; the ornament is then heated in the fire and rubbed over with borax, replaced in the fire for a short time, then withdrawn and left to cool ; when cold it is burnished to a smooth and bright surface.

Contrary to general custom in the East where bazaars are closed from sunset until broad daylight, work is continued at Tiflis after dusk, by the light of candles fixed in all manner of quaint contrivances for holding them.

In the evening we went to a ball at the *Kroujok*, 'club,' upon the introduction of a member and payment of a small fee. At 9 P.M. we entered a handsome suite of rooms, quite novel to us in their decorations of curious-looking cornices, brackets, and strange unnatural representations of birds and flowers painted on the walls ; while in one chamber, a myriad of small mirrors of every size and form, reflected numberless bright points from the lights in the suspended chandelier. The house had been built as a residence

[1] Notice on the wines of Transcaucasia. Appendix VI.

for himself by a wealthy Armenian, who specially engaged workmen from Persia to carry out his plans ; and was purchased by some gentlemen whose happy idea it was to convert the building into a club.

We found the gentlemen in uniform or in evening dress—this was *de rigueur*; but the ladies appeared in morning costume with remarkable trains, or in sensible short walking skirts, a few only being fashionably attired in *toilette de bal*; many, being Georgians, were in their national dress, which is still much worn. The *kába* is more frequently of bright green or blue silk, colours greatly favoured ; the skirt and short body are in one, the latter being open exposes the 'sweet chemisette,' called the *geulyssepyry*, and is encircled at the waist by the *sartquely*, a broad gaily-coloured ribbon, the ends of which reach in front almost to the feet. The *thav-sacravy*, 'head dress,' consists of a narrow black velvet band, stiffened, and worn round the brow like a coronet ; it is embroidered with gold or silk thread, and is sometimes ornamented with diamonds and other gems, the *letchaky*, a thin white veil cleverly arranged, falling from it in loose folds to below the shoulders. Married women are distinguished by having their hair dressed to the front in curls and plaits. This costume is the Georgian lady's attire for evening or morning wear, with some difference only in the quality of the materials. In summer a lace shawl is worn when out of doors, replaced in winter by the *katyba*, a kind of frock-coat lined with fur and trimmed with gold or silver lace ; it is a heavy-looking and unseemly garment. The *kosheby*, a half slipper with the toes turned up, is a cunning device for showing off a pretty little foot in a well-fitting stocking, but then it is only worn at home. To the appearance of the Georgian ladies may literally be applied the remarks made by Jean Jacques Rousseau, in his

THE LEZGHYNKA.

criticism of the Valaisanes:—'Des corps de robes si élevés qu'elles en paraissent bossues, et cela fait un effet singulier avec leur petite coiffure noire et le reste de leur ajustement, qui ne manque au contraire ni de simplicité ni d'élégance.'

The Georgian noble has the gold-laced *tchoha* or frock-coat, with *ourtmaghy*, split-up sleeves that hang from the shoulders; it fits over the *arhalouk*, an under-garment of silk tightened in at the waist with a rich belt at which various weapons, silver mounted and frequently jewelled, are carried.

In the course of the evening the *lezghynka*, the national dance, was performed by several couples. The movements of the lady were always very graceful as she glided along the floor, bashfully hiding her face with her hands and withdrawing from the advance of her pursuer, who moved onwards with a peculiar heel step, persisting in his suit. The music in quick time, but monotonous, is accompanied by the clapping of hands of all the company.

The etiquette of the ball-room at Tiflis is similar to that in Russia. A gentleman may not dance a second time with the same lady in the course of the evening; in a round dance, one, two, or more turns are taken, but if the dancers chance to stop, the gentleman must quit his partner, and without deeming it necessary to conduct her to a seat, he passes on to engage another. Under such a rule, a stranger with few acquaintances is necessarily excluded from the enjoyments of the evening.

But where are the beauties of Gourdjistan? Have the Georgians lost their claim to the empire of loveliness? They certainly have magnificent tresses, and

a Paphian pair
Of eyes which put out each surrounding gem,

but there is a marvellous sameness in the cast of their features; all have the same expressionless lip and nostril, and an equally passive air; while the seductive little dimple is unknown among them until they age, which they do at thirty, when it suddenly rushes into existence overgrown.

A TOULOUH'TCHYE.

CHAPTER XV.

TWENTY-FIRST DAY.

Reception by the Grand Duke Michael—Poor petitioners—The Grand Duchess Olga—Persian bazaars—The Bourka—The Great Prison—Nationalities of the inmates—Cathedral of Zion—St. Nina's Cross—Catholicos of Georgia—The Georgian and Russian churches—The Exarch—Prince Tzytzyanoff—A miraculous image—Sacred edifices—Nuns of St. Stephen—Evening concert—Purification.

AT an early hour I received a communication from the *Maître de la Cour*,[1] who informed me that His Imperial Highness the Governor-General would receive me at the general levée at one o'clock. On arriving at the palace, I was conducted up some stairs, passing on the way a goodly number of the working-class of both sexes, and ushered into the reception chamber, a large hall with life-size portraits on its walls of the several governors-general of the Caucasus. In it were assembled many officers in full dress, and a few gentlemen in plain clothes, all having their breasts liberally sprinkled with orders. The conversation was general and loud, until of a sudden the buzz ceased and the Grand Duke entered the room attended by an aide-de-camp. He is slight and of tall stature, with an agreeable expression of countenance, and courteous and easy in his manner; he was plainly attired in undress. He addressed a few words to each officer, and directed that I should be conducted to his *cabinet*,

[1] Prince Leoff Pavlovitch Ouroussoff.

where he would see me in a private interview; this I took as a compliment to my nationality and to the uniform I had the honour of appearing in. His Imperial Highness addressed me in English with tolerable fluency, and occasionally in French, and after conversing for twenty minutes dismissed me with much affability.

On returning to the hall, I found it occupied by the poor people I had seen on the landing, who were now pressing around the door leading to the private apartments, in their anxiety to present to the Grand Duke, on his appearing, their plaints and petitions, to all of which he would give a hearing; a wise indulgence in the centre of a vast and uncivilised territory, to a people not yet used to and unable to appreciate the establishment among them of courts of law and justice. The task imposed upon the Grand Duke on these occasions is eminently perplexing, for in some cases he is appealed to that sentences already passed by the law may be revoked, and in others he is besought to stretch out his hand to stay impending trials, and indeed to aid in the perpetration and encouragement of all manner of unfair dealing.

K—— had the honour of being received by Her Imperial Highness the Grand Duchess Olga, who has a thorough knowledge of the English language, and spoke of England with sentiments of great regard. Her Imperial Highness condescended to permit us the use of the 'Times' during our stay at Tiflis.

Besides the Armenian and Georgian bazaars already visited, there is the Persian bazaar on the left bank of the Kour in the Avlabar quarter, which is readily reached from the Tatarsky meydan by crossing the Sletcky bridge. The Persian bazaar is of peculiar construction, being a long, wide, but gloomy gallery with vaulted roof, the stalls upon either hand being lighted through small openings in the domes overhead. Carpets from Tabreez, and silks from Shemahà and Nouha, for shawls, sashes, divans, curtains, and bed covers, delight the eye; but here as elsewhere it is necessary to bargain to avoid being defrauded; the rule in making purchases, is to deduct a fourth part of the sum asked, when an offer of the balance is invariably accepted.

Near the Persian bazaar are the leather workers and *bourka* makers. The *bourka* is a cape of the coarsest felt, looking like a sheepskin from the long hairs outside; it is sometimes white, more frequently black, worn loosely at the neck chiefly by the mountaineers, and so contrived as to slue round the body for protection in front, at the back, or upon either side, according to circumstances, against cold winds and rain, and is of most service when the wearer is mounted. The best *bourkas* are made in Kabardah, and sold at Vladykavkaz.

High above the shops is the old fortress, which encloses the prison and the ancient Church of Metchsky, 'of the rupture,' said to have been founded at the same time as the city, and to have received its distinctive name on being restored by one of the kings of Georgia, who thus did penance for having unnecessarily gone to war. M. Brosset states in a note in one of his works, that he had been informed by a Georgian, in reference to the Church of Agarae which was the *métok* of Somkhety, that *métok* signified the residence of a vice-bishop; the transition from *métok* to *metchsky* is not great, and a more probable derivation of the title is obtained; this fortress church is considered a notable specimen of early Georgian architecture.

The fortifications of Tiflis in the seventeenth century have been thus described by an Eastern traveller: 'The fortress consists of two castles opposite to each other on the banks of the Kur, which separates the rocks on which they stand, and which are connected above by a bridge leading from one castle to the other. The great castle is on the south side of the Kur, and the small one on the north of it . . . . . . the circumference of the largest castle is 6,000 paces, the wall 60 cubits high, with 70 bulwarks and 3,000 battlements, but no ditch; the water tower which supplies water to the garrison in time of siege is situated on the Kur. In the castle are 600 houses terraced, some with and some without gardens, the palace of the Khan, a mosque, and a bath. The small castle was built by Yezdejerd Shah; it is of stone, in a square form, with only one gate at the head of the bridge, and has no Bezestan or Imaret. Three thousand watchmen light fires every night, and continually cry *khoda khob*—" all's well." Though it is a Persian town, yet its inhabitants are for the most part Sunnis and Hanefis, from the time of the Ottomans.'[1]

Permission to visit prisons is never given in Russia with good grace; application has to be made to the governor of the town, who takes some time to think about it. In describing the prison at Odessa, I endeavoured to point out its painful condition and baneful system, but I had not then seen the jail at Tiflis. I have visited the Turemny zamok, otherwise Litoffsky zamok, the great jail at St. Petersburg, where order, cleanliness, and other civilising influences are at work; but here, in one of the chief cities of a vast empire, where all the luxuries and many of the refinements of civilisation are to be obtained and enjoyed, are brutally *herded* together a mass of our fellow-creatures, not only

---

[1] *Travels in Europe, Asia, and Africa in the seventeenth century*, Evliya Effendi; translated from the Turkish by J. v. Hammer, London, 1846, ii. p. 172.

guarded by lofty walls and secure portals, but menaced at every step by the bayonets of a rude soldiery ; yet the necessity for humane treatment would rather suggest itself here, in the guardianship of a heterogeneous and semi-barbarous assemblage of men, many with scarcely a nationality, more without a home.

What the State allows for the maintenance of an ordinary prisoner, and what his cost actually amounts to, are two different matters ; there can be little doubt that at St. Petersburg the seven copecks allowed for his keep are invested for his benefit, both as regards quantity and quality. He has meat every day except on Wednesdays, Fridays, and fast-days (not a few in holy Russia) ; a loaf of good black bread weighing 10 lbs. is the daily ration for four men, and he has as much *kvass* as he can drink. How different at Tiflis, where, if quantity is a desideratum, quality is none! The price of provisions in the Caucasus is considerably less than at St. Petersburg ; it might therefore be expected that the prisoners would live at least equally well at Tiflis as they do at the northern capital ; but this is far from being the case, and the question therefore arises: What becomes of the balance ?

Scrupulous care is taken to keep Christians apart from those of other religious persuasions. The actually Christian provinces in the Caucasus are Georgia, Imeritia, Mingrelia, Gouria, and Armenia ; the nominally Christian are Abhase, Ossety, and Swannety ; and among the Mahomedan provinces are Daghestan, which includes the Tchentchen, Lesghians, Derbend and Koubash ; Bakou, Shirwan, Karabagh, Tchatalish, Lencoran, &c., &c.

Returning through the bazaars, we stopped to see the Georgian Cathedral of Zion, which dates from the fifth century, and was last restored in the early part of the eighteenth century. To the right of the 'holy doors' inside this church is a silver casket, which contains unquestionably the most precious relic in Georgia.

When St. Nina preached Christianity in Karthly at the beginning of the fourth century, she made for her own use a cross of vine-stems and bound it with her hair; it was the first cross raised in Karthly, over the spot on Mount Karthlos, whence, through the efficacy of her prayers, was overthrown Aramazt, the idol of the Karthlosides; that cross is now preserved in the casket. In 1811 it was offered to the Emperor Alexander, who accepted the gift, but instantly caused it to be returned to Georgia.

It is related that after Djelal-eddin, Sultan of Khorassan, had overrun the kingdom, 1225-30, and made the conquest of Tiflis, he destroyed the dome of this cathedral, and threw a bridge from his palace to its roof, that he might have the gratification of treading a Christian temple under his feet.

The Cathedral of Zion was the church of the Catholicos of Georgia. When that dignitary was resident at Mtzkhetha he was styled the spiritual king of the country, and was treated with honours similar to the monarchs. The Catholicos was elected by the bishops; he consecrated the king, the *mthwars*,[1] archbishops, metropolitans, and bishops, at the time that the Church of Svety-Tzk'hovely, 'pillar of life,' at Mtzkhetha, was the head of all other churches.[2]

It was towards the close of the fifth century that the Georgian and Armenian Churches separated, for the latter, being imbued with the ideas of Eutyches, rejected the decisions of the Council of Chalcedon; a century later, the Georgian and Russian Churches united.

The office of Catholicos of Georgia, now long suppressed,

---

[1] Or *erystavs*.   [2] Brosset, *Hist. de la Géorgie*, i. p. 229.

has been substituted by a Russian exarch who is resident at Tiflis, and is styled Exarch of Georgia and Archbishop of Karthlyny and Kakhety ; he is a member of the synod at St. Petersburg.

The Georgian Church may be considered in all respects identical with the Russian, but there are instances in which the exarchate tolerates the use of the old Georgian liturgy and some of its rites.

In front of the Cathedral of Zion is the belfry restored by Prince Tzytzyanoff, with contributions from prize-money received by the troops after the storming of the fortress of Hadjinsk. Tzytzyanoff, who has already been noticed in these pages, was Commander-in-Chief of the Russian forces, and had proceeded in 1806 to open negotiations with the chief of Bakou for the surrender of that fortress, when he was met with an act of treachery as flagrant as that to which he himself was about to invite the governor to commit ;[1] for he was assassinated on approaching the walls of the town to hold council, as pre-arranged, with the Khan; his head was immediately sent as a trophy to the Shah, and the remains were subsequently interred in the cathedral, by his successor the Marquis Paolucci.

When Aga Mohammed devastated Tiflis, he razed to the ground the palace of the kings of Georgia ; the site remains, and near it is the venerated Church of Antchyskatsky, where we saw another precious relic of much repute among the Georgians ; a miraculous image of great antiquity 'not made with hands,' and brought from the episcopal city of Antcha. The richly jewelled frame bears the following inscription : ' By command of the great Queen of Queens, Thamar, the crowned of God, who has made an offering of the materials, I, Ivané Antchel Renael, have

[1] Watson, *Hist. of Persia*, &c. : p. 151.

caused the frame of this mighty image to be made ; may it protect Her Majesty now and to eternity. It has been made by Beka. Christ have mercy upon him.'[1]

There are about fifty sacred edifices in Tiflis. The principal church of the Armenians is the Pasha Vank, a handsome building within a high-walled enclosure; an inscription below a window records that it was erected by Ghoulants Khodja Giorgi, in the reign of Vakhtang VI., 1719-24 ; the Georgians have given the name of Pasha Vank, because they say it was erected by a Turkish pasha who had embraced the Christian faith.

Full service is performed on Sunday mornings at the Church of St. Stephen by the nuns of the convent, who drawl out the prayers, but do not meddle with the sacraments; it is impossible to conceive a service more purely mechanical and unimpressive. The members of the community are ladies of birth and fortune, who bring with them a dowry for the benefit of the sisterhood ; their dresses in pearl grey, bright blue, deep violet, &c., are of damask and *moire*, fitting close to the neck, the head, including the chin, being bound up in black silk, while a large tulle veil falls down the back, covering the shoulders.

A concert was given in the evening by the Amateur Philharmonic Society, under the patronage of the Grand Duke and Grand Duchess, who honoured the performance with their presence. The Georgians pride themselves on the prolific musical talent that is born among them, and form the majority of the members of this society ; the music played was Russian, being selections from L'voff, Varlamoff, Glinka, and others ; but some Italian airs were sung with much effect by a gifted lady, the wife of an officer in the garrison.

In the course of the evening we observed a practice common

[1] Brosset, *Voy. Archéo.* Rapp. v. p. 30.

PURIFICATION.

enough in Russia, but the salubrity of which may be doubted. As in other parts of the Continent of Europe, the Russians are much given to sitting in close and ill-ventilated rooms; doors are kept shut, and windows fastened, even in fair weather, the necessity for a continual supply of oxygen being seldom recognised, and in lieu of a judicious purification of the atmosphere, recourse is had to the burning of incense, and agreeable odours are substituted for the needed fresh air.

GEORGIAN FEMALE WEARING THE TCHADRA.

CHAPTER XVI.

TWENTY-SECOND DAY.

A merry officer—The Bagration-Moukhranskys—A Georgian tradition—Town of Gori—Its defences—Churches—Clubs—A native saddle—Rock of Ouplytz-tzykhè—Excavated chambers and crypts—Their distribution—Origin—Crypts at Vardagh—Royal sepulchres—Arrival at M'zhett.

THERE are two localities of much interest within easy distance of Tiflis by rail: the one is M'zhett, the ancient capital and residence of the kings of Georgia; the other Ouplytz-tzykhè, a rock-cut town near the old fortress of Gori.

Accompanied by an Italian named Ferrari, engaged for a few days as interpreter, I took a ticket at the Tiflis terminus for the 10 A.M. train, which, however, did not start until 11 o'clock. In the same compartment were two Russian officers who spoke French with fluency, and it was an agreeable surprise to me when I learnt that they were proceeding to Gori expressly to visit *la ville des cavernes*. We arranged to go together, and believing that with such desirable companions the interpreter might be dispensed with, I instructed Ferrari to leave the train at M'zhett and engage a room at the post-house, where I should pass the night on my return from Gori.

Matters, however, did not work quite smoothly. One of the gentlemen, of a peculiarly sociable and mirthful disposition, amused himself at each station when the train stopped for a few moments, by partaking largely of *vodka*, and generously insisting upon treating everybody he chanced to see to a glass; in this he was not beset by difficulties, nor had he to exert his powers of persuasion with many. By the time we reached Gori, our jovial friend had become so unsteady and irresponsible, that his brother in arms, offering many apologies, begged I would excuse *la mauvaise plaisanterie*, and expressed his deep concern at being unable to accompany me as he had purposed. I now regretted having left Ferrari behind, but there was no help for it, so I walked into the town, and with the aid of an Armenian gentleman a horse and guide to Ouplytz-tzykhè were soon obtained.

But I must return to the third railway station from Tiflis, to call attention to an old castle of the Bagrations, perched like an eagle's eyrie on the peak of a rock to the right of the road, where the Ksanka, a tributary, joins the river Kour. The rock, which rises perpendicularly, has three of its sides laved by these streams, and on the land-side is inaccessible and secure from assault.

The Princess Bagration-Moukhransky,[1] to whose family the castle belongs, and whose acquaintance I had the pleasure of making at St. Petersburg, related the tradition that when the Persians had overrun Georgia, this fastness, the last to fall, sustained a lengthened siege. The enemy summoned the Georgians to surrender; in reply, the Georgian chief mocked the invaders by causing a

---

[1] The Bagration-Moukhranskys, who took precedence in Georgia immediately after the Royal house, are descended from Bagrat, son of Constantine king of Karthly. Bagrat's brother, George IX., reigned from 1525 to 1534, and Bagrat received in appanage the domain of Moukhran, which lies to the north of the Kour, between the rivers Aragva and Ksanka, and is so called from *moukha*, 'the oak,' of which there are great forests. At the extinction of the direct line in 1649, the Moukhrans were called to the throne, but their succession ceased in 1744, when the kingdoms of Karthly and Kakhety became united under the Bagrations, or Bagratides, of Kakhety.

magnificent salmon to be sent to the Persian commander, with the intimation that so long as he could get fresh fish and fresh water he should continue to hold out. The subway, by which communication was at that time maintained with the river, no longer exists.

There are few places more picturesquely situated than is Gori. It has been a matter of regret with the Russian Government, that upon the annexation of Transcaucasia, the fertile and more suitable district of Gori was not selected for the site of the chief town, in preference to the dreary valley where lies Tiflis. Dubois asserts this fact, and alludes to the disappointment of General Yermóloff at seeing Gori when too late, Tiflis having already been fixed upon for the capital.

Gori lies at the limits of a glorious plain, where two streams, the Bleejah'va and Medjoura, unite and fall into the Kour. The city, which, according to M. Brosset, takes its name from a neighbouring hill, was founded by David II. in the tenth century, and is built at the foot of an isolated eminence upon which is a considerable fortification that encloses a church of antiquity. The fortress in its present form was constructed in the reign of Rustam, 1634–58, and destroyed by Nadir Shah. It is asserted on local tradition, that the Emperor Heraclius kept his treasures in the fort, whereby the hill became named 'the Golden Mountain.'

In the Ouspenye, 'Church of the Assumption,' at Gori, is preserved an image that was the gift of the Emperor Justinian. There is also a church of the seventeenth century, erected by some Capuchin friars who were sent from Rome on missionary duties.

The inhabitants of Gori are principally Armenians. There are no inns, but travellers may rely upon obtaining a bed at one or the other of two clubs in the town, on presenting their cards to a member. The majority are Armenians, a people invariably well disposed and ready to be of service to Englishmen.

Quitting the town for the crypts, the road traverses a large cemetery, where are several small chapels, and passes thence over a succession of plateaux divided by small ravines. I unhappily rode a native saddle, a simple and ingenious instrument of torture. The very hard seat sloping *à dos d'âne*, is fully eight inches above the horse's back; short stirrup leathers, not made to lengthen, raise the knees to a level above the waist, and stirrups barely three inches wide complete the diabolical contrivance. Any more effective plan for checking all circulation can scarcely be imagined. I impatiently awaited the moment when I should be relieved from my uncomfortable position, and had determined on walking back, the distance being only eight miles.

No *cicerone* was needed to call attention to the strange-looking cliff of considerable extent that we were nearing, with its irregular and serrated summit, and having on the face of it innumerable crypts and caverns. At the foot of the cliff is the hamlet of Ouplytz-tzykhè, where some good-looking Armenian youths offered to be our guides; I told them I wanted to see the little chapel in their hamlet, a building of great antiquity, but the priest was absent and had taken the key with him.

To mount the cliff, we walked up a narrow trench hewn in the rock along the south approach, and by a gradual winding ascent entered what appeared to be a street with small, very small habitations, now roofless, arranged terrace-like the one beyond the other upon either side. At the end of it, near the summit, is a large vaulted chamber open to the south, hollowed out of a conspicuously high piece of rock. The ceiling is artistically and tastefully sculptured with designs in regular octagon, and about the front are the remains of exterior decorations, such as pillars, &c., but the hand of time has committed sad havoc. This chamber, unique in itself, which communicates with others of smaller size and of a distinct kind, measures 13 feet by 13 feet, and is about 18 feet at the highest part of the vault. In its front, from whence is obtained a commanding view, the rock has been ex-

VAULTED CHAMBER, OUTLYTZ IZYKUÉ.

cavated to leave an open space and a breast wall at the edge of the cliff. Had this been a royal residence or a fane?

In another direction is a large rectangular apartment that also calls for special notice; it is 24 feet by 22 feet, and 16 feet in height, faces the east, and is the finest example of several excavations that approach it in style. It is ornamented with mouldings in relief along the walls and ceiling, which had been supported beneath an imitation beam by two central pillars with ornamented bases; the roof at the front, which is completely open, projects slightly, but does not appear ever to have been supported. This chamber also communicates with others, all being provided with apertures for light, with seats, reclining places, recesses, and deep receptacles in the floors for the conservation of supplies. The rock of Ouplytz-tzykhé is everywhere perforated with caverns

RECTANGULAR CHAMBER, OUPLYTZ-TZYKHÉ.

and crypts of various dimensions, but all are of lesser pretensions than the two that have been described. In none has one stone been laid above another, be it rough or hewn; no bricks, no fragments of rock, have been employed for the purpose of erecting, roofing, partitioning, or paving. Ouplytz-tzykhé is a town — there can be no other designation for it — consisting of public edifices, if such a term may be employed, of large habitations presumably for the great, smaller dwellings for others, each being conveniently divided, and having doorways, openings for light, and partitions, while many are ornamented with cornices, mouldings, beams and pillars. The groups are separated by streets and lanes, where steps have been cut for facilitating ascent and descent, and grooves, unquestionably intended for water-courses. There are likewise open spaces or squares, and yet the whole has been entirely hewn and shaped out of the solid rock, demonstrating, in the general distribution and economy of space and material, the rarest ability in engineering and architectural skill; *credat Judæus*. A deep and steep hollow in the lower part of the rock, is believed to have been a subway of communication with the river Kour.

Ouplytz-tzykhè, 'fortress of Ouphlis,' called by the natives 'the fortress of the Lord,' is stated in the annals to have been projected and completed by Ouphlis, son of Mtzkhethos and grandson of Karthlos, after whom Georgia was first named Karthly;[1] Karthlos was the son of Thargamos, who was the great-grandson of Japhet, the son of Noah! We read, however, in Genesis x. iii., that Togarmah was the son of Gomer, who was the son of Japhet. M. Brosset observes, that it is not known upon what authority these statements of the Georgians are founded, except that they have partly quoted them from the earliest Armenian writers, who are believed to have received the traditions from the Georgians.

Ouplytz-tzykhè is also mentioned in the annals as having been a fortress in the time of Alexander of Macedon; that it was enlarged by king Arshag, 20 B.C., besieged and taken by Constan-

---

[1] Karthlos, the patriarch of the Iberians and Georgians, is stated to have first settled in that part of the country where is now the rivulet Karthly, near M'zhett. Karthly or Georgia was called Djorgian by the Arabs in the seventh century, and Gourdjistan by the Persians in the tenth century. The name Georgia is probably after the Giorgi, one of the Caspian nations mentioned by Pliny, although the clergy affirm that their country was called Georgia in honour of St. George the Cappadocian martyr, who is its protector and tutelary saint.

tine, king of Abhase, 881-923, and that it was an inhabited city up to the domination of Bagrat III., 980-1014.

Whatever the earliest history of this remarkable place, one cannot be inclined to concede that, like most rude crypts, it constituted, as we now see it, the refuge of a barbarous or oppressed race; the methodical distribution and internal ornamentations, with the provision made to meet domestic requirements, proclaim it to have been rather the abode of delight during the oppressive heats of summer, of a significant and advanced people in comparatively late times, after 'the caves, the high places and pits,'[1] had undergone extensive alterations to make them habitable.

On the river's left bank, and opposite to Ouplytz-tzykhè, are other crypts near Myndory.

The grottoes and excavations at Vardsy or Vardagh,[2] in the province of Ahal-tzykhè, are in some respects similar to the crypts of Ouplytz-tzykhè, but they are fewer in number and devoid of any architectural ornamentation. They were commenced by George III., 1156-84, and are supposed to have been completed by the great Queen Thamar, his daughter. Some of the sovereigns of Georgia were interred at Vardsy, which disputes with Ghelath the burial-place of Thamar.

As I was hastening on my way back to Gori, for the shades of evening had put an end to further exploration, I met my fellow-travellers of the morning on their way to the *cavernes*; the bacchic soldier had recovered from the effects of the fluid which confounds

                      the chemic labour of the blood,
       And tickling the brute brain within the man's
       Makes havoc among those tender cells, and checks
       His power to shape —

[1] 1 Sam. xiii. 6.   [2] Anciently Vard-tzykhè.

and sat his horse steadily enough. I subsequently learnt that they passed the night at the hamlet, spending the following day in 'the fortress of the Lord.'

There is a fair refreshment-room at the Gori railway station. The train from Poti did not arrive until 7.30 P.M., considerably after the hour that it was due; and at 9.30 I was in my room at the post-station of M'zhett, an apartment specially furnished 'for the use of generals,' and therefore the best in the house; for generals *jouent un grand rôle* in Russia, and particularly in the Caucasus.

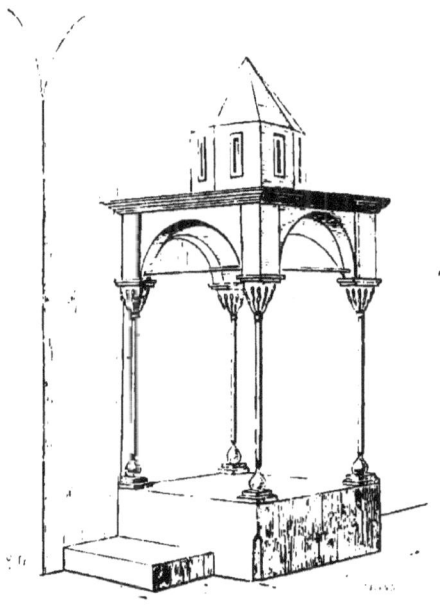

CANOPY OVER THE THRONE OF THE KINGS OF GEORGIA AT MIZKHETHA.
SEVENTEENTH CENTURY.

CHAPTER XVII.

TWENTY-THIRD DAY.

An Imperial hand-basin—Russian Ablutions—Mtzkhetha, the capital of Karthly—Kings of ancient Georgia—Georgian alphabets—Conversion of the Karthlosides—The Cathedral at M'zhett—Relics and Miracles—Tombs of Kings—Annexation of Georgia to Russia—Chapel of St. Nina—Disturbed graves—Lermontoff the poet—The Iron Castle—The Orbeliani family—Presbyter John.

WHEN the *stóroj*[1] was directed this morning to bring in some washing utensils, that domestic re-entered the room with a slop basin of brown ware and a kitchen clout; the latter I could dispense with, for I had my own linen, but I maintained that as I was occupying 'a general's room,' I was entitled to a general's wash-hand basin. The *stóroj* insisted that there was nothing else. Ferrari, a useful man upon such occasions, then applied to the station-master, who himself appeared and supported the statement of the *stóroj*. Showing some official papers with which I had been provided, I again asked for a general's washing gear. 'The generals have nothing better when they come here—this is all I have for them.' 'Well,' I replied, 'I may be more particular than your generals, but pray let me have something cleaner and larger.' Here the station-master seemed to lose all patience, for he crossed himself and spat, and cried out: 'But if I tell you that Mihail

---

[1] 'Watchman' at post stations, who attends to the wants of travellers.

Nicolaevitch has been satisfied with this!' 'What! the Grand Duke!' 'Certainly,' he replied. The impudence of the old fellow was admirable, and as I felt the wind taken out of my sails, I was under the necessity of submitting, and performing my ablutions *à la Russe*. The Russian washes himself thus: an attendant pours out as much water as will fill the palms of both hands, and the palms, so filled, are carried up to the face rapidly several times, until it is completely wetted. The *monjyk*[1] needs no attendant, for he fills his mouth with water, and squirts it in small quantities at a time into his hands. Both processes are very simple if not quite effective!

The city of Medzkhitha, Mtzkhetha, or Mychete, the Μεστλῆτα of Ptolemy,[2] and now called M'zhett, was founded by Mtzkethos, the eldest of the giant sons of Karthlos, whose dominion extended from the river Aragva, on which the city was built, to the Sper, 'Black Sea.' Its wealth and power ensured it the precedence over all other cities, and acquired for it the name of Dedak'halak'hy, 'the mother city.'

The first king of Karthly was Pharnawaz, 302–237 B.C., who fixed his residence at Mtzkhetha, the seat, previous to his reign, of the ruler of Karthly, whose title was *mamasaklysy*, 'head' or 'lord of the house.' Pharnawaz caused a great idol to be set up over the grave of Karthlos, and called it after himself Aramazt, his name in Persian. The idol was on the hill of Karthly, where had stood a fortress erected by Karthlos, on the right bank of the Kour to the west of Mtzkhetha, and which afterwards was called Armazt-tzykhè, 'fortress of Armazt,' probably the Harmozica on the Cyrus, 18 stadia from Seusamora,[3] afterwards the fortress of Samthavro. Pliny calls it the strong city of Harmastis.[4]

[1] 'Peasant.'   [2] Ptol. *Geog.* V. ii.   [3] Strabo XI. iii. 5.   [4] Pliny VI. x.

Pharnawaz, who was a man of genius as well as a bold soldier, originated the orthography of the Georgian language. The Georgians have two different alphabets, the military or vulgar, and the ecclesiastic, and it would be interesting to know which of the two was invented by Pharnawaz. According to the traditions of the Georgians, it was the military alphabet, doubtlessly so entitled because the people were exclusively addicted to warlike pursuits. Some of the military letters, from their rounded and graceful forms, much assimilate the Zend alphabet, as has been shown by the learned Anquetil-Duperron,[1] and others bear a striking resemblance to the Sanscrit.[2] With regard to the ecclesiastical alphabet, it appears to have been introduced by Mesrob from Armenia in the early part of the fifth century.

Mtzkhetha continued to be the residence of the monarchs of Karthly until the reign of Datchy, who removed the capital to the new city of Tbylysys-Kalaky, founded by his father Vakhtang, as already noticed. From that period Mtzkhetha declined, but it continued to be the seat of the patriarchs.

It was in 322-24 that the King Miriam, and his subjects, became converted to Christianity by Nouny or St. Nina, who, according to some accounts, had escaped the persecutions of Tiridates when Rhipsime and other martyrs suffered death. Through the interposition of her prayers the pagan altars were overturned, after which she prevailed upon the people of Karthly to desist from offering human victims as sacrifices.

M'zhett at present consists of a few cottages and *doukanns* irregularly scattered, the villagers being engaged in an extensive trade in coarse pottery. In their midst is a high battlemented

---

[1] *Mém. de l'Acad. des Insir. et Bell. Lettres*, xxxi. p. 339.
[2] Brosset, *Hist. de la Géorgie*, i. p. 43.

wall, which encloses the cathedral and some insignificant buildings for the accommodation of the clergy. This church, probably the handsomest in the Caucasus, stands over the site of a sanctuary erected by King Mirian upon his conversion, wherein to deposit the seamless garment of our Saviour, which had fallen by lot to the Jews of Mtzkhetha, and was brought hither by one Elioz. The sanctuary, consecrated to the twelve Apostles, was replaced by Mirdat III., 364-379, with a larger edifice in stone, named Svety Tzk'hovely, 'pillar of life,' and in the fifth century it became the see of a bishop. George VI. afterwards rebuilt the cathedral, which, having been destroyed by Tamerlane in the fourteenth century, was restored by Alexander in 1656, and a cupola was added by Rustam. It was finally embellished in the early part of the eighteenth century by Vakhtang V.

We applied for permission to see the church, when the *decanos*, arch-priest, firmly but most courteously insisted upon accompanying us; he was replete with the traditions and legends of Georgian chroniclers.

The edifice has a handsome porch, and is ornamented on the exterior with œillets, mullions, and sculptured crosses; the interior is cruciform and illuminated by a great dome. In this church were crowned and lie buried many of the sovereigns of Georgia, and not a few of the patriarchs; the throne of the latter, gaudily painted, is to the right under the dome, and in the south transept is a small raised platform with marble canopy, under which the kings sat. In the body of the church is a lofty tabernacle, the *samyrone*, 'place whence issues sacred oil,' covered with frescoes illustrating the life of St. Nina. Beneath this monument was buried the seamless garment of our Saviour, the handiwork of the Virgin Mary, from which came the supply of 'the sacred oil.' When the

Persians invaded Georgia, the priceless relic was sent for safe custody to Moscow, where it has since remained. Another relic, formerly the property of this church, was the habit of the prophet Elias, which used to be kept inside a railing in the south aisle.

In front of the *ykonostass* are two marble sarcophagi, over the remains of the two last kings of Georgia, Heraclius and George. The inscription in Russian on the tomb of the latter runs thus :—

'Here rests the Tzar George, who was born in 1750. He ascended the throne of Georgia in 1798, and desiring, from love for the welfare of his subjects, to secure to them for ever their well-being, ceded Georgia to the Russian Empire in 1799. He died in 1800. With the view of preserving to future generations the memory of the last Georgian Tzar, the Marquis Paolucci, Commander-in-Chief, caused this monument to be placed here, in the name of His Majesty the Emperor Alexander, in the year 1812.'

The renunciation of his crown in favour of the Emperor of Russia by the Tzar George XII.,[1] in the name of himself and of his successors, we are told drew down upon him the hatred and curses of the nobles of his country. His queen was ashamed of the pusillanimity which had induced her timid husband to yield compliance to the insidious demands of the agents of Russia, and when it was wished to arrest her person in order that she might be conveyed to Moscow, the indignant princess drew her dagger and wounded the Russian officer [2] who had attempted

---

[1] This sovereign is styled George XIII. by the Georgians, George XI. having reigned twice.

[2] The wounded officer, General Ivan Petrovitch Lazareff, expired immediately.

to seize her.[1] Prince Alexander, the younger brother of George, was not disposed to see the crown thus pass from his father's family without making an effort to secure it for himself. He used his utmost endeavours to raise a general revolution, but the chiefs of the country saw the hopelessness of attempting to throw off the Russian yoke, unless they could obtain the armed support either of Persia or of Turkey. His schemes became known at Tiflis in time to admit of measures being concerted to thwart them, and General Lazareff gained a decisive victory over the hardy followers of the Georgian prince on the banks of the Iora.

After the annexation of Georgia to Russia, the Emperor Alexander issued a proclamation to the Georgian nation, dated September 12, 1801, of which the following is an extract. 'Ce n'est pas pour accroître nos forces, ce n'est pas dans des vues d'intérêt ou pour étendre les limites d'un empire déjà si vaste, que nous acceptons le fardeau du trône de Géorgie ; le sentiment de notre dignité, l'honneur, l'humanité, seuls nous ont imposé le devoir sacré de ne pas résister aux cris de souffrance partis de votre sein, de détourner de vos têtes les maux qui vous affligent, et d'introduire en Géorgie un gouvernement fort, capable d'administrer la justice avec équité, de protéger la vie et les biens de chacun, et d'étendre sur tous l'égide de la loi.'[2]

The graves of the sovereigns of Georgia and of the patriarchs are simply overlaid with a slab, the inscriptions they bore having become generally illegible. Over one tomb is inscribed in Georgian letters:—

'I Mariam, queen of Georgia, daughter of Dadian, have taken

---

[1] When Queen Maria was being conveyed to Russia by General Toulchkoff in 1803, an attempt at rescue was made in the pass of Darial by the Ossets.

[2] Watson, *Hist. of Persia*, &c., p. 142.

possession of this little tomb. You who look upon it, for the love of Christ pray for me. In the year of Jesus Christ, 1680.'

On another tomb in Arabic :—

'Whilst reigning over my royal states, in the fifth cycle of my reign, the world visited us with an untimely and afflicting death, for our consort the Queen Thamar was hidden from our eyes. In our desolation we brought her to this sepulchre, which is our own, and we caused this slab to be placed over the coffin. All you who read this, recite a prayer. Should any person through violence or cupidity, be he king or dydébouly,[1] destroy or injure this tomb, may he be judged for our sins, upon the great day of judgment. In 7192 from Adam, in the paschal year 372–1684.'[2]

We asked to see the thesaurus, but the *decanos* assured us that there were no jewels, plate, or MSS. at M'zhett, a statement which scarcely agrees with the report made by M. Brosset in his *Voyage Archéologique*. We were shown one relic only, a *plashtchenjtza*,[3] which produced such a murrain and so much disease in Tamerlane's camp after that chieftain had converted it into a saddle-cloth for his own use, that it was immediately restored to save his forces from utter destruction.

At a short distance from the cathedral, in a westerly direction, is the convent and church of Sampth'avrok, also founded by Miriam, and since subjected to the same destinies as the mother church. One of the sisters readily offered to conduct us, and pointed out within the court a small chapel where had stood the hut of St. Nina when she first arrived at Mtzkhetha in 318, and in which she prayed

---

[1] Grandee the highest rank of nobility in the kingdom of Georgia.

[2] Brosset, *Voy. Archéo.* Rapp. I.

[3] The pall that covers a sepulchre of Christ in Passion week ; it is usually of rich velvet gorgeously embroidered in gold, and having upon it a figure, also embroidered, of the dead Saviour.

with her cross of vine-stems. We were also shown the foundations of the palace of Vakhtang *Gourgasal*. In a northerly direction above the post-road is a small eminence, on which are the ruins of the fort Natgh'k'hour, 'place where has been a citadel,' which was probably one of the defences of the ancient city.

In the spring of 1871, when the new road from Tiflis to Vlady-kavkaz was being constructed, a cutting was made through a slightly elevated piece of land, a ploughed field at the foot of Natgh'k'-hour, and close above the old road on the right bank of the Aragva. In clearing away the soil many graves were disturbed, the form and contents of which were of a nature to induce the Government to employ M. Baïern, of Tiflis, to prosecute researches in the summers of 1871-72-73, when that gentleman laid open upwards of 200 tombs.[1] Similar burial-places have since been discovered to the east under the Zedadjeny ridge on the left bank of the Aragva, by which it may be inferred that the old city extended in that direction. On the hill above the junction of the two rivers, are the ruins of the Djouarys Sagdary, 'church of the cross'; it is also called Djouary Patyosany, 'the venerable cross.' It was here that St. Nina replaced an idol with the cross, and hither came some of the Syrian fathers to live and preach. In holy times invisible means of communication existed between the tower of this church and the cupola of the cathedral, of which the saints in both sanctuaries availed when they desired to confer speedily and unseen! The 'church of the cross' dates from the seventh century, having been constructed by Prince Dimitri, son of the dynaste Stephanos I.; it is covered with inscriptions in Georgian. Lermontoff,[2] the gifted

---

[1] See Appendix VII. for a description of six graves opened on this site.

[2] Mihail Youryevitch Lermontoff, born 1814, died 1842, claimed descent from Thomas the Rhymer, Lermont or Learmont of Ercildoune, a village on the Leader, two miles above its junction with the Tweed. See *Contributions to Minstrelsy of the Scottish Border*

THE CRIMEA AND TRANSCAUCASIA.

Norma lateralis.

Norma capitalis.

MACROCEPHALOUS SKULL, M'ZHETT

Russian poet, has made this 'holy place' the scene of his beautiful poem Mtzyry, 'the novice.'

Near the post-station, the road winds at the foot of a hill whereon had stood the city of Sarkhynè, 'iron castle,' which, if the annals of Georgia are to be believed, was besieged by the forces of Alexander of Macedon during the space of twelve months. Sarkhynè was founded by a Turanian people from that part of Asia which lies between China and the Oural, who came to Karthly in the reign of Cyrus, and offering to the Karthlosides their alliance against the oppression of the Persians, were invited to establish themselves near Medzkhitha, the capital.

To the princes of the family of Djenkapour, of the royal race of Djenesdan, who were the chiefs of these Turanians, was given for a residence the fortress of Orpeth, or Orbise, situated on the river Kram, and the Djenkapour thereafter became known as the Orboulk or Orbethetsik, from the custom in Karthly of calling princes by the names of their possessions. In return for the friendly reception accorded them, the Orboulk united with the Karthlosides, and aided them in throwing off the Persian yoke, a service which obtained for the chief Orboulk the rank of *sbasalar*, or generalissimo of the forces.

During the reign of Pharnawaz, the Orboulk were in high favour, and took precedence next to the sovereign. In course of time, the head of the house became the *crystav of crystavs*, the

in the poetical works of Walter Scott. Lermontoff's ancestor Lermont, whose name was subsequently Russianised to Lermontoff, left Scotland in 1621 or 1633, and went to Poland. He removed to Russia, where he entered the army in the reign of Mihail Feódorovitch. The poet was an ardent admirer of Byron, whose style he frequently sought to imitate. Bielinsky, a contemporary critic, says : 'Lermontoff produced little, far less than might have emanated from his prodigious talent. His carelessness, impressionable disposition, and mode of life distracted his attention from study and meditation, the loves of the Muses.'

highest of court dignities, and enjoyed, with other prerogatives and privileges, the special honour of placing the crown on the head of the monarch. The *sbasalar* had twelve banners, under each of which marched 1,000 men; while the banner of the king was red and his pennon white, the banner of the Orboulk was white and his pennon red. At entertainments he sat upon a cushion apart and higher than did the *dydébouly*, and ate bread off a silver dish. The Orboulk formed matrimonial alliances with the royal house, and bore a distinguished part during many reigns in the histories of Georgia and Armenia.

The first of the Orboulk, or Orpeliani, who is individualised in the annals of Georgia, is Liparit, a warrior in the time of Bagrat I. and David I., 875-900; and among the more remarkable of the race was Ivané, who in 1123 delivered the country from Tiflis to Ani out of the hands of the infidels. A second Ivané,[1] who died in 1145, was the conqueror of Tmanis, or Toumanis, on the frontiers of Georgia; and a third Ivané overthrew Shah-Armen (Sokman II.) in a great battle near Ani in 1161,[2] after that city had

[1] With this prince of the house of Orpeliani, Professor Bruun identifies the mysterious personage known as Prester John, first brought to European notice by the Bishop of Gabala, *Jebbel* in Syria, in a communication made to Pope Eugene III., as shown in the history of Bishop Otto of Freising, and in the continuation *Ann. Admutensium*, see Pertz, Mon. Germ. Sc. ix. p. 580. In a work he is preparing for the press, the learned Professor goes on to state that the brother-kings of the Medes and Persians, the *Samiardi fratres*, are not to be looked for in Sanjar himself and the son of his sister, as Oppert has it in his work *Der Presbyter Johannes in Sagen. Geschichte*, &c., Berlin, 1864; for they were the Sultan Masoud, the nephew of Sanjar by his brother, and Masoud's own nephew Daud, David, who reigned over Armenia, Arran, and Aderbaidjan. Oppert discovers Presbyter John in the person of the Gour Khan of Karacathay, who obtained a signal victory over Sanjar in 1141.

[2] This Ivané is another Prester John, according to Professor Bruun, *A Strán-stvovanyah' Tzarya Presytera Ioanna* V. *Zapysky Imp. Ounov.*: 1874, the same who corresponded with several potentates in Europe, *Recueil* iv. p. 548, and the receiver of the letter addressed by Pope Alexander III. in 1177, *Indorum regi sacerdotum sanctissimo*, *Recueil* iv. p. 549. The Professor quotes numerous authorities to prove that

been taken by his sovereign. This powerful prince, Ivané, having excited the envy and suspicion of the usurper George III., then on the throne, was arrested through the treachery of the king, had his eyes put out, and was otherwise mutilated. All who bore his name, with the exception of two who happened to be abroad, were exterminated, and their property confiscated, and thus was it that in 1177 the Orpeliani, 'whose immense possessions comprised more than the half of Georgia,' fell from power and from the exalted position they had held for centuries, their dignities and territory being bestowed on the Mkhargrdzélidze,[1] princes of Kurdish origin, who had the good fortune to succeed to the royal favour.

some portions of Transcaucasia were included under the name of India. The novel idea of the Professor is fairly supported by more facts than one. The Orpeliani, as *shasalars*, were invested with the priestly office of placing the crown on the head of the king; on the advance to the siege of Ani, Ivané Orpelian, *shasalar*, received from the hands of the king the fragment of the true cross, with which to lead his armies to battle; Brosset, *Hist. de la Géorgie*, i. p. 390; and in the chronicles of Ibn-Alathir, *Journ. Asiat.* 4me. série, xiii. p. 491, it is recorded that in the year 1155-56 (a date, however, that does not accord with that given in the Armenian chronicles) the city of Ani was taken from the Emir Cheddad, *by the priests of Armenia*.

[1] In the atabek Ivané Mkhargrdzélidze mentioned by the Bishop of Acre, Professor Bruun sees the Prester John of 1219, entitled King of the Indians (Caucasus) by Piano di Carpino, and called *Joannes rex Georgianorum*, by Sanudo, III. v. p. 13, the melik Ivané of Oriental writers, among whom is Ibn-Alathir, who alludes to him as king of the Georgians. In his letter to the pontiff Honorius III., this Ivané styles himself *comestabulus totius Bratice* (Georgia) *sive Armenie*; Brosset, *Additions*, p. 304. In 1247, another Prester John appears, viz., Taïyang Khan, the father-in-law of the Khan Ogotaï; he was the Prince Naïman, as Wylie has it, and not the prince of Karacathay of Oppert, or Keraïte of l'autier, *Le livre de Marco Polo*, &c., Paris, 1865. The Prince George of Marco Polo, and of Giovanni de Montecorvino, was a descendant of Taïyang Khan, as was also Koushlouk, who on this account was called Presbyter John by the Nestorians, and not because he became the Gour Khan of Karacathay after having dethroned his father Tchih-lou-kou, as stated by Oppert.

There is evidence of the existence of a Prester John in the early part of the fifteenth century. Among the archives at Königsberg are two letters, dated January 20, 1407, addressed by Conrad of Jungingen, Grand Master of the Teutonic Order, *Regi Iba via* (of Abhase, and certainly not of Abyssinia) *sive presbytero Johanni*. Karamsin iii. p. 388.

In his narrative of Marvels, 1332, Sir John Mandeville, knight, tells us (*Voyages and Travels*, &c., London, 1670) that the 'Emperor Prester John is christened, and a great part of his land also . . . . . they believe well in the Father, the Son, and the Holy

Among the princes of the Caucasus who served Russia with loyalty upon the cession of the crown of Georgia to that empire, were Demetrius and John, descendants of the Orpeliani[1] who escaped the general massacre in 1177.

We returned to Tiflis by the night train.

Ghost. . . . The Emperor Prester John when he goeth to Battel hath no banner born before him, but he hath born before him three Crosses of fine Gold, large and great, and richly set with precious stones . . . and when he hath no battel, but rideth to take the air, then hath he born before him but a cross of a Tree . . . Prester lived in a city called Suse.'

[1] Now Orbeliani.

THRONE OF THE CATHOLICOS AT MTZKHETHA.
SEVENTEENTH CENTURY.

CHAPTER XVIII.

TWENTY-FOURTH AND TWENTY-FIFTH DAYS.

Departure for Armenia — Comfortable travelling — Armed shepherds — Droves of camels — Abdoullah — The *Tchapars* — Their organisation and duties — The telegraph — Tatar noble and suite — Supply of horses — Human warrens — Novo Akstafa — Post-stations — Russian soldiers — Delyjann — A heavy supper — The sect of the Malakany — A copper mine — Endurance of camels — The Goktcha lake — Ancient monastery — Armenian mountaineers — Abdoullah again — Feats of horsemanship — Mount Ararat — Obsidian — Arrival at Erivan — Accommodation for travellers.

I RECEIVED an invitation from the Governor of the province of Erivan,[1] to accompany him upon his return journey into Armenia, and be his guest during my stay in the chief town of his government. To be the travelling companion of a Governor in the Caucasus, is a piece of good luck that does not fall to the lot of many travellers, and I eagerly accepted the kind invitation, declaring myself ready to start at a moment's notice.

At 9.30 A.M. his Excellency and I left the city in a carriage and four post-horses,[2] the General's servant Abdoullah, a Lesghian, being on the box. In a second carriage was an officer of the General's staff, Panah Khan a native prince, and another officer whose leave of absence had expired. The day was fine and bright, but a high north-west wind raised such a dust that now and again we felt wellnigh blinded.

[1] His Excellency General Nicholas N. Karmaline.
[2] For the hire of carriages, see Chap. XXV.

The two first stages include Saganlough and Yagloudjynsk, eight miles apart, and these were got over by eleven o'clock. The advantage of travelling with an officer of rank was soon experienced, for the rapidity with which horses were changed was marvellous, previous notice having been sent to fix the probable time of the General's arrival at each station. The obsequiousness of the station-masters was exceedingly comic, and the *yemstchycks* put on the air of couriers who brooked no delay.

When near the third post-house, we passed large flocks of sheep moving leisurely and grazing, the shepherds being clad in their *bourkas* and armed with a *kynjāl*,[1] 'dagger,' and pistol at the waist, and a rifle slung across the back. They seemed to have little enough trouble with their charge, for a stately buck, mindful of his importance, attended by scarcely less spirited he-goats, took the lead, and the sheep followed readily enough. A little farther on some scores of camels in single file were steadily wending their way towards the capital, travelling at the rate of forty miles a day under their burdens of cotton and silk in pressed and, unpressed bales, the handsomest of them, led by the *tcharvadarr*, being at the head of the column, gaily adorned about the head and neck with parti-coloured tufts and tassels; he carries a weighty bell,[2] but his burden is lighter than that of the others, which averages from 5 cwt. to 6 cwt.[3] The last camel in the line is also adorned, but not so lavishly as the leader.

The movements of these patient but vicious animals are

[1] *Khantchar*, in Turkish.

[2] A similar custom prevails in the Alps, where the finest cow takes the lead with a heavy bell suspended at her neck, when she is called Heerde-kuh, 'the cow of the herd.' Similar instincts appear to guide the cow and the camel, for we are assured that each would contest the attempt to give precedence over itself to a rival.

[3] The maximum charge for carriage between Erivan and Tiflis (171 miles), is fifty copecks per thirty-six English pounds.

directed by certain cries, given quickly when the beasts are required to go faster, and pronounced slowly to slacken their pace ; a kick behind the knee makes the animal sit. The caravans travel all day, and at the night encampment the goods are piled together, camels and drivers forming a circle around.

At noon we reached Novo-Alghetka after some little uphill work, when the breeze had freshened and disturbed the dust even more than hitherto, and we were forced to envelop our heads in rugs to avoid being choked by it. Far away to the left, the clouds that were blown off the roads in Kakhety, hid from view to their very summits the mountains of the great range.

At Novo-Alghetka we stopped to lunch, and here Abdoullah, with good-natured zeal, commenced a course of officiousness that well-nigh paralysed every attempt at self-comfort. We had scarcely alighted than he pounced upon the General, dragged the pelisse off his back, placed a chair before him, and looked displeased because his chief did not immediately avail himself of it. He then turned towards me, prepared for a similar assault, but I had fortunately already divested myself of my overcoat. Abdoullah then seized the hampers, and turned out their contents in a twinkling ; pickle and mustard bottles had their corks drawn, and the Lesghian would have opened every wine bottle and have probably proceeded to tear asunder the cold turkey, had we not, with a kind of intuitive presentiment, forestalled him by laying hands on the various articles.

At this station we were joined by an escort of two mounted guards, *tchapars*. These wild horsemen are not likely to be of service against an attack of robbers, indeed they have been known to sneak off on such occasions ; but they are useful in clearing the way of obstructions caused by caravans, and are a substitute for a courier, by hastening with the *padarójnaya* on nearing a post-house, to give notice that a fresh relay of horses is needed instantly. The *tchapars* expect no remuneration, nor is it customary to give any except for some personal service on the road. The *tchapar* stations are six miles apart; at each is a detachment of six men, who are housed in the hilly districts in a small rude habitation, where men and horses live together; on the plains they live in a burrow underground, and are provided with a look-out platform, 15 feet to 20 feet above the steppe, whence the eye can scan the flat country over a considerable distance. The *tchapars* are firstrate horsemen, whose duty it is to scour the plains and roads for the protection of travellers. They enter the service and quit it as they think proper; their uniforms are as varied as their features, for they are the *báshy-bézouks* of the Caucasus, but they are all armed alike, that is to say, with a rifle, pistol, sabre, and *kynjàl*. Each man receives ten roubles monthly, and for this consideration he has to find his own horse and forage, arms, clothing, and victuals; he has no responsible chief, and as he cannot make both ends meet on such small wages, he is frequently in league with the Tatars, his co-religionists, by whom depredations and highway robberies are chiefly committed. As a protective measure these guards are scarcely needed, and travelling in the Caucasus may be considered comparatively safe, if the general advice not to travel at night, and especially across country, be followed.

The neat iron stanchions of the Indo-European Telegraph Company, and the roughly dubbed posts of the Russian telegraphs, appear side by side on this road. The former line, after crossing the Strait of Kertch from Yeny-Kaleh to Temrouk, passes through Yekatery nadar to Touapse, Soukhoum-Kaleh, and Otchentchýry on the coast, whence, striking inland through Sougdydy and Orpyry, it meets the railroad near Samtredy, and following it to Tiflis, lines the post-road thence to Erivan and Teheran.

As we were traversing the Karayass, a desolate steppe like the Ukraine, but without the luxuriant pasture of the latter, we encountered a *moursa*, Tatar 'noble,' mounted on a beautiful Arab, a breed seldom seen in the Caucasus. He was seated on a handsome saddle with gorgeous saddle-cloth, and had at his waist-belt numerous weapons, richly ornamented in silver; his attendants, who were armed to the teeth, rode tall powerful horses with huge heads and long legs, which we learnt were of the genuine Turcoman race. The vast table-land in Transcaucasia does not enjoy a reputation for horseflesh, and the Russian Government looks rather to the south east steppes, where the Cossacks of the Ukraine and of the Don, the Circassians, Calmucks, and Kirghiz supply the best horses for military purposes. The Crown, however, has studs for brood mares at Hranovaya, Byelovodsk, Orenburg, and Yanoff, and there are more than 3,000 private studs in Russia. An official return made within the last two years, shows that in European Russia there are close upon 20,000,000 horses, half a million of which are sold or bartered yearly. The horses in the Caucasus are small, hardy, and enduring; the *tchapar's* costs from 40 to 50 roubles.

The tall tombstones that mark the graves of Mussulmen, present a strange appearance on this steppe; the largest, of a single slab fully 7 feet in height, are sculptured with more or less artistic taste and care; they are the tombs, in scattered clusters, of the Kyzyl-bash, 'red heads,' whose dwellings are burrows under ground, formed in the following manner. A hollow being excavated, four uprights of poplar, and sometimes a fifth in the centre, are firmly set in the ground, and across them are irregularly placed other timbers which support the bramble and mud roof. This dwelling is divided into two compartments by a mud wall, the first being lit from an opening in the roof, but it is perfectly dark in the next, whither the females retreat upon the intrusion of a stranger. These underground habitations might be passed unnoticed but for the hay-ricks, which stand on scaffoldings of sufficient height to secure the provender from the reach of cattle. It was amusing to watch the agility with which the women hurried off the road at our approach; we happened to overtake one of these creatures, who coyly looked askance at us as we passed, and if she was a specimen of her sisterhood, we felt how confidently we could sympathize with them in their anxiety not to be seen! The Kyzyl-bash are nomads, who quit their warrens in the early spring to wander over great distances until the return of winter.

The Kram, a tributary of the Kour, is spanned by the Krasnoy-most, 'red bridge,'[1] of solid structure, built originally by the Persians, and restored, in 1653, by king Rustam. In Chardin's time, there was a village near it named Koupzikent; and refreshment rooms for travellers were fitted up between the arches of the bridge.

Beyond the Kram, we passed a considerable underground village named Shyhylou, and changed horses at Salaogly, and again at Zohr-arh or Zar-ah-sou, where the stables are underground; within a dozen yards, the semi-devoured carcass of a horse lay where the beast had fallen and perished. A little way beyond, the land is irrigated by small streams that unite with the Akstafa, and it was cheering to look upon bright verdure such as we had not seen since leaving Byelagory. On approaching

[1] The Armenians call it Kotratz kamourtch; it is the 'ruined bridge,' Katoglyly klydy in Georgian, and Syreck kyupry in Tatar.

some woodland, a flock of starlings flew across the road—the only feathered creatures we had seen since the morning, except the grey crow. At 5.20 P.M. we stopped at Novo-Akstafá to dine, Abdoullah again setting to work, and producing some excellent *shtchy* served hot, that had been brought in bottles; a plan to be strongly commended.

A body of 600 soldiers, who had completed eight years' service, were halting at this station; they were under the command

SHVHYLOV.

of officers, were receiving pay and rations, and would be under military discipline up to the day on which they were dropped at their homes. It struck me that there was some good stuff among them.

Novo-Akstafá is decidedly the best station on this road, but travellers would do well not to arrange for passing a night here, as they might meet with disappointment. It is a centre whence roads branch off to Tiflis, Erivan, Alexandropol, Elysavetpol and Bakou, and the accommodation is consequently in great demand. As a rule, the rooms in these post-houses are furnished scantily enough, there being little in them but a deal table, one or two wood-bottomed chairs, and a wooden bed-frame, all needing repair sadly; wind and rain have free ingress at the doors and windows; they have no carpets, window blinds, or curtains; a rusty *samovar*, a few dirty plates, and knives that will not cut, complete the *ménage*.

From Akstafa we proceeded rapidly over an excellent road
1,674 through Ouzountaly, 'long valley,' and the valley of the river
2,312 Akstafa to Karavansaraï, whence the ascent towards the pass of
2,816 Delyjann becomes very perceptible, especially after leaving Tarstchaï station; but it was the steep ascent of Kazak beghy, where we entered the snow limit, that necessitated increased exertions on the part of our laboured horses.

4,200 At 0.45 A.M. we pulled up at the post-house of Delyjann where I exposed my thermometer for half-an-hour, and was surprised to find the mercury at freezing point only, for we had begun to feel the cold most sensibly. The village of Delyjann is situated at the foot of the pass that bears its name and divides Georgia from Karabagh; it is a military station with a garrison of 400 men, under the command of a colonel, who, as late captain of the Emperor's company in the regiment of grenadiers of Erivan, had become entitled to the honour of being nominated an aide-de-camp to His Majesty.

At Delyjann we were about to enter the limits of the General's command, and here, as elsewhere, everybody was up and awaiting him. An officer, by birth an Armenian, received the Governor as his guest, and entertained us to a supper that consisted of a great many good things, to which, I believe, we did full justice after our chilly drive. Our host was unremitting in his attentions, and solicitous after our comfort. So far as I was concerned, I found I was expected to drink copiously of London stout, 'because all Englishmen live on porter.' The assertion was qualified, fortunately with success. Ditto—*in re* sherry. I was then required to take wine of the Caucasus, and especially that of Armenia, because a stranger was bound to taste the produce of the country— point argued—which ended in a compromise, and all this irrespective of the established *vodka* at *zakoúska*, and the concluding *petit verre* of excellent Chartreuse! Verily, Russian officers do not spare their guests. Our host showed us some handsome antique Russian and Georgian flagons in silver, which would have excited the envy of many a connoisseur; the former were not unlike the old English drinking flagons of the sixteenth century; the latter were in repoussé.

We took leave of this most hospitable gentleman at three in the morning, exchanging his comfortable quarters for the raw air and deep snow. On passing Golovyn, one of the earliest Malakan[1] settlements in the Caucasus, the road turns suddenly to the left, and the toilsome ascent of the pass commences; one is greatly struck, when on the rising zig-zag road, at the contrast offered by the northern slopes, well wooded and covered with snow, to the southern slopes, that exhibit a barren and bare surface.

At a mile from the village of Delyjann, is the forest of that name; through it courses the Shamlou, on the right bank of which, and within 200 yards of the road, are two veins of copper pyrite, the

---

[1] The Malakany who call themselves 'the real Christians in the spirit,' assimilate the Douhobortsy (see page 112) in many of their tenets; the Malakany distinguish all other sects by the name of *myr lyje*, 'the worldly.'

one being 40 ft. above the other; the fusion of this pyrite has produced one-tenth part of good copper.¹

7,124 At 16 *versts* from Delyjann, is the highest point of the pass, where the thermometer, with a gentle northerly air, was at 30°. While changing horses at Semyónovka or Seménovka, a caravan of camels went by on its way to Tiflis. It seems an anomaly to meet these quadrupeds in a mountainous district under circumstances presumably contrary to their nature of endurance, for are we not habituated from childhood to associate the 'ships of the desert' with parched, sandy plains, under an unendurably hot sun? But Sir Samuel Baker tells us, that the peculiarly spongy formation of the foot renders the camel exceedingly sure, although it is usual to believe that it is only adapted for flat sandy plains. This capability however is not shared generally by the race, but by a breed belonging to the Hadendown Arabs, between the Red Sea and Taka. Sir Samuel further states that there is quite as great a variety in the breed of camels as of horses.²

Another caravan we passed on this day's journey numbered 115 camels, all laden; they blocked up the road completely, and the *tchapars*, who are of considerable service upon such occasions, had hard work to clear the way. The little concern with which our horses met and rubbed against these animals, suggests how unavailing would have proved the stratagem of Cyrus who placed camels mounted by horsemen in front of his forces, had the Lydian warriors fought on chargers such as ours were.³ I believe that the Turks have availed themselves of a similar cunning device.⁴

¹ For list of mines in Transcaucasia, see Appendix VIII.
² *The Albert Nyanza, great basin of the Nile, &c.*; Sir Sam. W. Baker, M.A., F.R.G.S.
³ Herod I.
⁴ In the *Narrative of the Embassy from the King of Castille and Leon to the Court of*

Beyond Semyónovka we sighted the Goktcha, or Sevan lake, 6,340 and kept along its shore to the next station, Elénovka, an extensive 6,370 fish mart, where we purchased some of the fine trout for which the lake has been celebrated from all time; this fish, uncommonly like the great lake trout, *salmo ferox*, is salted and sent over the country.

Marco Polo thus wrote of a great lake near a certain convent of nuns, called St. Leonards, which Colonel Yule believes to apply to the lake Sevan: '..... there is a great lake at the foot of a mountain, and in this lake are found no fish, great or small, throughout the year, till Lent comes. On the first day of Lent they find in it the finest fish in the world, and great store too thereof; and these continue to be found till Easter-eve. After that, they are found no more till Lent comes round again; and so 'tis every year. 'Tis really a passing great miracle!'[1] Times, however, have changed, for the trout now bite at other seasons as well as during Lent. Three centuries and a half later, Chardin wrote:— 'On y prend de neuf sortes de poissons. Les belles truites et les belles carpes de trois pieds qu'on apporte à Erivan, viennent de là.'

From the road between Semyónovka and Elénovka, is seen a

Timour, in 1403-6, Ruy Gonzales de Clavijo relates, that at a battle fought at Delhi between Timour Beg and the lord of India, the latter 'collected a great force, and had fifty armed elephants; and in the first battle the lord of India defeated Timour Beg by means of his elephants. On the following day they renewed the contest, and Timour took many camels, and loaded them with dry grass, placing them in front of the elephants. When the battle began, he caused the grass to be set on fire, and when the elephants saw the burning straw upon the camels they fled. They say that the elephants are much afraid of fire, because they have small eyes; and thus the lord of India was defeated.' Translated for the first time by C. R. Markham, F. R. G. S., and printed for the Hakluyt Society, 1859.

[1] *The Book of Sir Marco Polo, the Venetian*; translated by Col. Hy. Yule, C.B., 1875; (2nd edition) i. p. 53.

small island on the lake, upon which is the monastery of Sevan, renowned for its sanctity in the ninth and tenth centuries. It was constructed over the foundations of a fortress destroyed by Mervan, governor of Armenia in 742.¹ Matthew of Edessus, an Armenian chronicler of the twelfth century, shows the monastery of Sevan to be of great antiquity, by making mention of Stephen III. as having succeeded Vahan in the Patriarchate of Armenia, from the place of Superior of the convent of The Twelve Apostles on the island of Sevan, in the year 432 of the Armenian era.²

This lake, probably the Lychnites of Ptolemy,³ is about 43 miles in length, and 20 miles at its widest part; it is known to the Persians and Turks by the names of Kouktcheh-darya or Kouktcheh-denghyz, i.e 'blue sea,' Goktcha being the Russian name; in ancient times it was the lake of Kegham, so called after a king of Armenia. Of the three great lakes in Armenia, the water of the Goktcha only is fresh; in the lakes Ourmiah and Vann, it is saline.

5,687 At Nygny-Acty, the country changes to complete desolation and wretchedness. In this Armenian village the people live in rudely constructed stone huts, with strange-looking conical erections of mud adjoining them, which are the stoves wherewith the hovels are heated; fuel is scarce in this stony and sterile region, but a ready substitute is found in a preparation of cow-dung made into cakes and sun-dried; it is called *bok*, or *argols* by the Tatars, and *kyrpytch* by the Russians

13,436 Two great mountains now appear, Mount Alaghez to the right,
11,711 and the summit of Ak-dagh far away to the left, but their altitudes can scarcely be appreciated in consequence of the great elevation of

---

¹ *Mémoires Hist. et Géog. sur l'Arménie*: M. J. Saint Martin, Paris 1818; i. p. 148.
² The Armenian era introduced by the catholicos Moses, commences in the year of our Lord 552: the year 1876 therefore corresponds to the Armenian date 1325.
³ Ptol: *Geog.* v. 13.

the road itself. At Souhaya Fantanka, where we stopped to breakfast, Abdoullah was again to the fore, bustling about, taking complete charge of the small post-house and its large stable-yard, confounding the station-master and his belongings, and setting at nought the *storoj*, that he might regale us with a dish of Goktcha trout, *padjár-jnnaya*, i.e. 'broiled.'

Near Fantanka, a detachment of *tchapars* was drawn up on the road-side under the command of an officer of police, who had been despatched from Erivan to meet his Excellency. As we came up with them they shouted, *Sdravy'ye jelaïem*,[1] the usual military salutation in Russia to a superior officer, and formed in rear of the carriage, when suddenly some of those dashing horsemen galloped ahead, going through a series of break-neck evolutions, such as throwing the body completely over to the right with the left heel resting on the horse's hind quarter and firing off their rifles to the rear, or turning clean round and sitting astride, facing the horse's tail, and keeping up a rapid fire; they would also throw their fur hats, or rifles, to the ground, wheel and pick them up going at full speed.

As I was watching these novel exercises, Abdoullah startled us by jumping up and crying out, *Vott, vott, Ararat!* 'There, there, Ararat!' The *yemstchyck* stopped the horses, and we gazed for some moments in silence on the superb landscape spread before us, the morning being bright and clear, with not a cloud, not a haze to dim the picture. From this elevation is probably obtained the best view of great and little Ararat; for at a distance of 30 to 40 miles the eye enjoys a wide range, and the lordly Ararat is taken in at its true proportions.

There is abundant cause for enthusiasm at the sight of this mag-

[1] We wish you health.

nificent mountain, peerless among the mighty works of the Creator; but there is equally good cause for doubt in the predominant belief, that it was on this very mountain Noah went forth from the ark. Saint Martin gives copious evidence from the writings of the holy fathers and of other commentators, that the mountains of Armenia in general, but more especially those in the Taurus chain, were anciently known by the name of Ararat.[1] St. Jerome, the monk of Chalcis and author of the Vulgate, who spent a long life in the study of dialects in the East (he died in 420), is very explicit on this point. In the Bible, we read that ' the ark rested in the seventh month, on the seventeenth day of the month upon the mountains of Ararat,'[2] but if we examine further, we shall find it said of the descendants of Noah, that ' it came to pass, as they journeyed from the east,[3] they found a plain in the land of Shinar, and they dwelt there '; which clearly shows that they got to the plain on the banks of the Euphrates, where afterwards was Babylon, which is to the south of the Ararat of our days.

A few *versts* beyond Fantanka, where the country has been disturbed by volcanic action, the ground is covered with pieces of black and grey obsidian, which is taken to Tiflis, and worked up into effective personal and other ornaments by a lapidary on the Kouky side of the Kour. When polished, the lights reflected on the surface resemble those of the cat's eye, or chrysoberyl.

Between Ailyar, the last station, where the heads of the departments in the city had assembled to welcome back the governor, and Erivan, which lies in a hollow, we passed over one of the vilest of roads overspread with large pieces of lava, that sorely tried the springs of the vehicles. We entered the town, first

---

[1] Saint Martin, *Mém. sur l'Arménie*; i. p. 260. [2] Gen. viii. 4.
[3] 'Or eastwards.' See reference, Gen. xi. 2.

through narrow lanes between high stone walls with few doors and fewer windows, then through streets of houses with an upper story, but a general absence of windows; and at 1.30 P.M. we alighted at the residence of the governor, having done the distance from Tiflis, 171 miles, in 28 hours.

His Excellency soon made me feel at home by enjoining that I should consider myself perfectly independent in the distribution of my time and movements, promising every assistance in his power.

I received a gratifying welcome from her Excellency, and the evening was spent in music, an accomplishment in which Madame excels. This was a luxurious close to a day which had been entered upon by crushing snow on the top of mountains seven thousand feet above the sea, and spent in driving through stony valleys and over broken ground and lava roads in the highlands.

There are no hotels at Erivan; the post-house accommodation is abominable, but a bed may be sometimes had at the club, pronounced *clou-oub*, on presenting a visiting card to any of the members, who are chiefly Armenians. The rooms at the club, however, are in great demand, and frequently engaged; in which case, it would be necessary to fall back upon the new karavansarai near the bazaars, the intention to pass the night there being communicated to the *Vspravnyk*, 'head of the police.' Meals and wines may be obtained without any difficulty at the club, where there is a good dining-room, and a bar well supplied with *zakoúskas*.

The new karavansarai is a spacious building, of a size to accommodate several hundred travellers. Around its large court numerous small chambers in tiers are prepared for their reception, those on the ground floor, of a larger size, being at their disposal as goods stores and show rooms for the transaction of business wholesale. The place is frequented entirely by Mahomedans of various nationalities, who never make themselves in the least degree obnoxious, although they dislike the intrusion of Christians.

TCHAPAR STATION ON THE STEPPE.

CHAPTER XIX.

TWENTY-SIXTH DAY.

Foundation of Erivan—The fortress—Sardar's palace—Mosque—The 'Blue Mosque'—A strange custom—A passion play—The bazaars—Armenian churches—Rites—The Persian quarter—Persian women—Education of Christian children.

THE city of Erivan, called by the Persians Rewan, is on the left bank of the Zanga, or Zenghy, the Hrastan of the Armenians. It was a considerable town in the seventh century, and became a strong city during the reigns of the last kings of Persia, who fortified it. According to some traditions, Erivan was called Erovantavan, which means 'place of the defeat of Erovant,' because it was built on the field where Erovant II., king of Armenia, was vanquished in the first century, by a Persian army which had accomplished the restoration to the throne of Ardaces, who had been deprived of his inheritance.[1] Other and older traditions assert, that after the deluge when 'the waters were dried up from all the earth,' Noah seeing before him a delightfully attractive country, cried out, Erevan! 'it has shown itself,'[2] and the name has remained to this day. By another account we learn that in the year 810 (1407), Khoja Khan Lejehani, a rich merchant of Timour's suite, settled here with all his family and servants, cultivating plantations of rice, by which means a great *kent*[3]

---

[1] Saint Martin: *Mém. sur l'Arménie*; i. p. 116.
[2] *Erevil*, v. to see.   [3] A town.

was formed. Five years later, Shah Ismail gave to Revan Kul, one of the Khans, an order to build a castle here, which being finished in seven years, was named after him Rewan, or Erevan.[1]

In the course of the forenoon I handed Madame to her carriage, and we traversed the *meydan*, an open space crowded with small dealers in harness, crockery, and secondhand wares, and where a number of camels were reposing, to visit the old fortress which we entered after passing three lines of defence built of earth and clay, and separated by ditches. This fortress was erected in its present form, or nearly so, by the Turks in the sixteenth century; it was taken by the Persians in the reign of Shah Abbas, lost to the Turks, and reconquered by the Persians under Nadir Shah, 1726-47; the king of Georgia, Heracleus, besieged it in 1780, and it was unsuccessfully attacked by Prince Tzytzyanoff in 1804, upon which occasion the Russian army was almost annihilated; the Russians, however, finally carried it by assault in 1827, and Prince Paskievitch, the commander-in-chief of the forces in the field, had the title of Count of Erivan conferred upon him. The cession of the province of Erivan to Russia, was included in the treaty of Turkmantchaï in 1828.

Of the palace of the Sardars[2] in this fortress, one apartment only remains to attest its former splendour; it is a large chamber gaily painted in the Persian style, and decorated with varied designs in glass. On its walls are life-size portraits of Abbas-Mirza, of Houssein and his brother Rassam, and of the legendary heroes of Persia, such as Zal, and Roustam whose strength equalled that of 120 elephants.[3] Over the door of entrance is a large painting which represents Abbas Mirza hunting the boar; and facing it is another painting illustrating Nadir Shah's

---

[1] Evliya Effendi: *Travels, &c.*   [2] Viceroys.   [3] Moses Chor. p. 96.

progress in Affghanistan. The apartment is entirely open on one side to a court, where two pillars covered with reflectors support the ceiling; on the opposite side is an alcove of oriental lattice, fitted with panes of variegated glass and decorated with paintings similarly to the apartment; in its centre is a small marble fountain.

From this gorgeous chamber we passed into the court of the harem, bisected lengthways by a watercourse at one time lined with white marble, in which the fair inmates were wont to bathe. The apartments, entirely stripped of their ornamentations, and now, alas! coarsely whitewashed, have long since been appropriated by the authorities for military purposes.

Leaving the court of the harem we crossed the *haraparack*, 'esplanade,' to a spacious quadrangular enclosure, having at the south side a large mosque open to the north, and on the north side a smaller mosque open to the south. The former, in which the faithful assembled to pray in the summer season, had been beautifully faced within and without with glazed tiles in brilliant colours, bearing floral and other designs, and texts from the Koran. This handsome edifice, said to have been constructed by the Persians in the early part of the seventeenth century, and its dome covered with bright blue tiles, have equally suffered, first from Paskievitch's artillery, and since, at the hands of antiquarians and collectors. For many years the Russians employed the enclosure as an arsenal, and if now abandoned, the mosque is not deserted, for true believers from afar never fail to visit it and curse the fate that consigned it to destruction by the unbelievers. There was a second mosque in the fortress of still more ancient date; but it has been razed to give place to an Orthodox church with the usual whitewashed walls and green domes.

Hussein Ali Khan is the great mosque of the city of Erivan. Like the fortress mosque it is a handsome building cased with the bright blue tiles that have given it the name by which it is best known, the 'Blue Mosque.' The cells around the court were occupied by pilgrims, and in the *meh'teb*, 'school house,' were many youths undergoing instruction.

A strange custom is observed at Erivan by the Mahommedans for raising funds to bury a pauper. The corpse is laid on the ground at the entrance to the court of the 'Blue Mosque,' each passer-by being expected to contribute towards defraying the expense of burial, and when sufficient money is found in the cap of the deceased, placed for the purpose by the side of the body, the dead person is carried away for interment. Should decomposition set in before enough has been collected, the police interfere, and the expenses fall upon the Imaums, 'leaders in prayer.'

At a smaller, but more ancient mosque, the Zaal Khan, a curious dramatic performance of three days' duration, a sort of passion play, takes place yearly, to which the Governor and officials are invited; the representations given being various episodes in the assassination of Hussein, the son of Ali and grandson to the Prophet, by the followers of his rival Yezid.

The bazaars are near the 'Blue Mosque,' in long narrow alleys rudely roofed over, where it is melancholy to see the rows of stalls that remain closed and the little animation there is even in the busiest quarters; for Erivan, once a Persian city, is now only an insignificant Russian frontier town. Persian goods are scarce and not of a good quality; and when we asked to be shown some native manufactures, inferior French silks, and Manchester and Bradford cottons were unrolled before us. The stalls are two or three feet above the ground, and have their doors, which work on hinges overhead, triced up in the day, and being fitted with hooks and other contrivances, fancy articles are suspended from them to tempt customers. Dealers in personal ornaments, antiques, gems unset, and coins, are ambulatory, and must be looked for hanging about the arms bazaar, where curious bell-mouthed pistols, *karabyne*, peculiar to Armenia, are to be purchased. But the most interesting part of the bazaar is where the blacksmiths are at work ; I watched five men hammering at a bar of iron, the one stroke following the other with astonishing regularity, as if the arms that wielded the blows were worked by machinery ; at a grunt from the master-smith, every arm was raised high, and the bar returned to the furnace. We also saw the bakers shaping doughy pancakes, like the *tchourekeby* at Tiflis, but of larger proportions, and here called *lavash*.

The Armenian episcopal church at Erivan is that of Sourp Sarghis, 'St. Sergius,' to which is annexed a seminary lately established by Father Stepanè, one of the two monks of the Gregorian Church, who have obtained university degrees in Russia. There are five other churches, among them the Zorrahvohr, 'The All Powerful,' in which St. Ananias is buried. We asked the priest who accompanied us—he was a handsome man of forty—what was the date of its foundation, for it is said to be of great antiquity ; he naïvely replied, 'I do not know ; it is a very old church ; I was not here when it was built !'

Armenian churches are cruciform in their construction, the altar being at the east end. There is no *ykonostass*,[1] as in the Russian Church, but an image, that is to say, a painting on canvas or panel, for graven images are not tolerated, is over the altar in the middle of the *pem*, a narrow raised course in the centre aisle,

[1] Altar screen.

covered with carpeting, silk, silver or gold cloth, on which are laid candlesticks, the censer, and a Bible resting on a piece of silk, for the priest does not touch the book with his hands. There is no baptismal font, which is substituted by a basin in the lower sill of a recess in the north wall. Baptism is more frequently held at the house of the parents, and consists of immersion three times, as emblematic of Christ's burial during three days ; after which the infant receives unction with myron,[1] and the eucharist, which is administered by the priest, who rubs the infant's lips with his finger after having dipped it in the chalice. From the priest, who was officiating as we chanced to enter a church, we learnt that the *sacrament* of baptism is termed by the mild name of Haghortouthyoum! A lamp is found for ever burning before some image, more frequently that of the Virgin Mary and Child, as in the Orthodox and Roman Catholic churches, and so remains unheeded the exception taken by the 'Christian Cicero' to the custom of the Romans, who lit candles to the Deity as though he were ever in the dark![2]

In the old Persian quarter of the town, we strolled in narrow, crooked lanes between high walls which mask the dwellings within like the defences of a fortress, with the object of screening the fair sex and debarring it from communication with the outer world. The modern part of Erivan is laid out in long, uninteresting streets, very dusty and ill-paved *à la Russe*; a dull enough town, but for the agreeable resort in the new gardens near the *meydan*, a happy thought of the governor.

A great variety of costumes are seen in the bazaars, that of the Persians being more easily recognised by the sugar-loaf hat. The

---

[1] Sacred oil, employed also at the consecration of priests, bishops, the patriarch, &c.
[2] Lactantius. *Inst.* VI. 2

Persians form a large proportion of the population, and dispute with the Tatars, numerical superiority over the Armenians; there are also many Greeks from Nahitchevan, who are builders, masons, and road-makers.[1]

The uncomely dress of the Persian women consists of a blue cotton mantle which envelopes the head and the body to below the knees, where it meets loose pantaloons of the same material, tightened in at the ankles and of one piece with the socks, while the face is completely covered with a thick *tchadra*, having small eyelet-holes in front of the eyes; the feet are thrust into high-heeled slippers half their length, which give the wearers an awkward gait as they drag their uncouth figures along, with their arms motionless and constantly in one position.

The Russian language is taught at all schools, where the appreciable qualities were discipline and cleanliness. Girls are instructed in lace-making, embroidery, and drawing, but the great hindrance to education complained of by those in charge is the practice of giving daughters in marriage at an early age.

[1] The population in the government of Erivan amounts to 466,168 (Census 1873).

PERSIAN WOMAN.

CHAPTER XX.

TWENTY-SEVENTH AND TWENTY-EIGHTH DAYS.

Rough road to Ghergarr—Fierce dogs—Reception at the monastery—Its history—The 'holy lance'—The church and rock-cut sanctuaries—Inscriptions—Legend of Rousoukna—Bash-Gharny—Magnificent ruins—Throne of Tiridates—Basalt—Artaxata—Coins and antiquities—Return to Erivan.

I WAS fortunate in making the acquaintance at the governor's residence, of a gentleman[1] who, like the majority of educated Armenians, is an accomplished linguist. Having arranged with him for an excursion to Bash-Gharny and the monastery of Ghergarr, we left Erivan at mid-day in a *calèche* and six post-horses, accompanied by a most intelligent officer of police[2] who was mounted on a handsome grey charger. It had snowed heavily during the night, but the morning was clear and mild; thermometer 37°.

For the first three miles we had a repetition of the detestable Aïlyar road, the carriage supporting the excitement amazingly well while the battle of the springs and rocks lasted. As we jogged over the desert and stony tract, we passed two miserable-looking villages, Dyervez and Ochtchapert, the cliffs near the latter being perforated with crypts, and at four o'clock we alighted at Bash-Gharny at the cottage of the Emperor's forester, where,

[1] M. Gustav A. Kalantaroff.   [2] M. Valère N. Chagoubatoff.

thanks to his Excellency's kind forethought, we found a good dinner awaiting us.

Being desirous of getting to the monastery of Ghergarr before night, we engaged horses in the village, and at six o'clock proceeded by a bridle path over a succession of arid downs. Daylight was waning, and as we passed Bardouk where large numbers of sheep are folded, the shepherds' dogs flew at us like a pack of fierce wolves, barking and snarling in the most ferocious manner. Our guides, who were on foot, placed themselves for protection between the horses, and the *tchapars* of our party even drew their sabres to keep them at a distance.

On reaching the monastery, we dismounted in the little court illuminated by the flames from half-a-dozen grease pots held up at arm's length by the young seminarists; at the same moment a door opened at the opposite end of the court, and from it issued the tall figure of an aged monk, clad in black and wearing the *verharr*, conical 'cowl.' He advanced with slow and stately step as we approached to meet him, with his hands folded in front, a large jewelled cross suspended on his breast glittering in the uncertain light. He was attended by another monk, and had come out in the cold night air and deep snow to offer us a welcome and hospitality. The first salutations being over, he conducted us to apartments where preparations had been made for our expected arrival. When tea was served, the archimandrite Raphael and the monk Petros squatted on some carpeting, and with the assistance of the gentlemen who were with me, I learnt from the reverend father all he could tell us about this secluded nook.

'Many, many years ago, the holy lance that pierced the side of our Saviour was removed to this monastery; and so long as it was preserved here, the revenue, proceeding from the gifts and offerings of worshippers at its shrine, was considerable; but when the holy lance was restored to Edzhmiadzin, the pilgrimages were discontinued and the prosperity of Keghart [1] ceased; it is a very poor place now. We have some land that yields 6 halvar (19 bushels) of corn yearly; to this should be added the offerings of the people who come once a year on the day of the Transfiguration, and in this way we make up an income of about five hundred roubles.'

Yet Father Raphael has saved enough money to enable him to erect a small building within the walls, as a seminary for young aspirants to the clergy; there are five of these youths, two deacons, and an old blind and friendless man, a recipient of charity; these, with the archimandrite and monk make up a community of ten persons, who are fed and clothed on 70l. a year.

The reverend gentleman looked somewhat incredulous, when, in reply to his enquiries, I stated that Protestants believed in the Trinity, and in the divinity of the Lord Jesus Christ.

At nine o'clock our hosts withdrew, and I was glad to roll myself up in a clean sheet and on a comfortable bed, in the room assigned to visitors.

The monastery in which we had passed the night was the seat of one of the earliest bishoprics founded by St. Gregory the first patriarch of Armenia, and therefore dates from the third century. It became known by the name of Aïrits vank, 'monastery of the crypt,' which was changed to Keghart, after the holy lance, one of the most precious relics now preserved at the patriarchial church of Edchmiadzin, had been removed to it for safety.[2] It rejoices in a third name, Gor-gaetch, 'see and fly,' for tradition asserts that when the Persians despatched a force to pillage the monastery,

---

[1] *Keghart*, Arm. 'a lance.' Marked Ghergarr on the Russian maps.
[2] Saint Martin, *Mém. sur l'Arménie*, ii. p. 421, 461.

the infidels were no sooner in sight of the church, than myriads of armed angels appeared on the adjoining heights, and the enemy turned and fled. Indeed the possession of the holy lance was always believed to ensure the victory to them who guarded it.[1]

Having been fearfully disturbed by insects during the night, I greeted daylight and spent the early morning in surveying the situation of this retreat. Keghart is indeed a solitude and a choice refuge for the recluse. The monastery is situated on the north side of a wild and naked glen up the Goktcha valley, the walls overlooking a jagged precipice at the bottom of which flows the Gharny-tchaï; above and around are bold, projecting grey rocks that rise high in the air, each threatening to roll over and carry all before it. There is no vegetation, not a shrub; nothing but a little herbage on the banks of the stream; perfect stillness reigns, disturbed only by the periodical bell summoning to prayers.

When it sounded at 7 A.M. for the *Aravodjvajam*, the first morning service, I went to the church and found it conducted in a very hurried and matter-of-fact style by the Monk Petros and the young seminarists; it was the flesh warring against the spirit, for the interior was cold and miserably damp, and our guides, who alone formed the congregation, very soon followed my example and left it.

The church, extensively restored in 1136 by a prince Bhrosch during the patriarchate of Gregory III., is a small cruciform edifice built under the ledge of a rock; the arched entrance is richly sculptured, and the interior, lighted solely from the dome supported on large pilasters, has several inscriptions on its walls, which serve as records of its history.

On the north wall within the church, is the following: –

---

[1] *Hist. Hierosol. Baldrici Archiep.* Bongars edition, 1611. ii.

'By the grace of God, I prince Bhrosch [1] son of Vasag, of the race of Gagnakoff, have purchased, with my own money, this holy place (of pilgrimage), with fields, mountains, and all its appurtenances, of the rulers of this world, and . . . much gold and silver has been expended by me in the erection of crosses, for censers, and sacramental fans.[2] I built the church and set up the holy images . . . in the tombs which are for me, and for my family for ever. And I have given for the good of the church, the villages that I have bought, Vohtyhabert, Bertag, and eleven thousand . . . if any of my kindred or friends attempt to lay hands upon, under whatsoever pretext, this home of saints bought with my gold . . . that one.'

On the south wall :—

'By the grace of God, I, Hasan, son of Vakhtang, grandson of the great Sembat of the royal race . . . entered the service of this holy place, and made a gift of a beautiful gospel . . . and calendar. And they who serve have promised ten masses annually at Easter, five for myself, three for my mother Nana, two for Rousoukla, my helpmate. Whosoever transgresses, let him be damned by the three hundred and eighteen patriarchs.'[3]

On the south wall outside the church, and on the west side of the arched entrance :—

'Of the Kingly race, the Lord of the universe, ruler, atabeck Ivanè, consanguineous relative of the vanquisher of the world

---

[1] Prince Bhrosch was the son of Vasag Khatchenetsi, the scion of an ancient family and governor of the castle of Vaïotsdsor in the province of Siounik'h ; one of his descendants is mentioned in a letter dated April 19, 1699, that was addressed by the *melyks*, 'princes' of Armenia to Pope Clement XI. Saint-Martin, *Mém. sur l'Arménie* ii. p. 257, iii. 479. See also *Additions et éclaircissements à l'Hist. de la Géor.*: Brosset ; 1851. p. 321.

[2] Fans were anciently employed in the Armenian churches, for brushing away flies from the priest while he was officiating ; fans with little bells attached to them are now sometimes in use as ornaments.

[3] The 318 patriarchs of the council of Nicea.

Za . . . [1] of the elder Sarkis, viceroy and commander-in-chief, and his son Avak and Shahnshah who vanquished the Kaïem and the Kantzan as far as Akana . . . and as far as Nahutchevan, and thence as far as Kamsaran . . . and afterwards made a pilgrimage to the holy place Aïritsvank . . . to the churches and to the sacred relics, and it was agreeable to me to leave the remembrance of my name on an inscription, and I have given . . . fortress . . . salt of the transplendent church. Let him who opposes himself to me be covered with shame, and damned by the three councils.'

Over the entrance is a representation, in relief, of a lion devouring an ox ; above it is inscribed :—

'By the will of God, I, Selgord Taganetz, of Tiflis, have restored the cupola of this church as a memorial of my own self, for Taga, the sultan and wife Daredjana, and my son Stepanè, my brothers Zal and Sograb . . . in the year 804 ' (1355).

Beneath is the following :—

'By the will of God, I, Tytors . . . to this holy place one hundred daëkans [2] and am promised five services.'

After the early mass, we were taken over the monastery by the monk Petros, not a particularly intelligent man, but most good-natured and polite. We first ascended to the roof of the church, where the flags are marked with the names and initials of

---

[1] This name, only partly legible, is evidently intended for Zakharè, who was named *emir shasalar* of Georgia, or commander-in-chief of her forces, by queen Thamar after the fall of the Orbeliani (see page 185). He vanquished the Persians in many battles, and conquered all their country between the Kour and Araxes. At the death of Zakharè in 1212, his brother Ivanè (see page 185, note 1), the consanguineous relative mentioned in the above inscription, received the title of *atabek* from the same sovereign ; he died in 1227 : Saint Martin, *Mém. sur l'Arménie*, ii. c. v. and Brosset *Additions, &c.* p. 266 *et seq.* Zakharè and Ivanè were the sons of Sarkis of the Mkhargrdzélidze family, now represented in the Russian empire by the Arghoutinsky-Dolgorouky ; Dolgorouky, or *Long-armed*, being the exact signification of the name Mkhargrdzélidze.

[2] The gold daekan was worth 4 . 3d., the silver daekan, 5d. to 6d.

monks and pilgrims of all times, who have also erected massive monuments of red porphyry called *kavank khar* by the natives, and excavated the rock in many places for chapels and hermitages, in which dedicatory and memorial inscriptions and a great variety of crosses are hewn. These crypt-chapels and cells extend from the church in a westerly direction, to the number, it is said, of forty, the farthest from the church, which is the largest, having a prodigiously long inscription on the rock at the entrance. We got

THE ROUSOUKNA SANCTUARY, KEGHART.

thus far, and then retraced our steps to the monastery enclosure, and passing through an excavated gallery, entered the sanctuary known as that of Rousoukna, which is entirely hewn out of the solid rock. It is illumined by a large dome, supported on four great pillars with huge capitals and bases, and is adorned like the smaller chapels, with numerous crosses in *stacciato*, or very low relief, the floor being paved with sepulchral slabs.

The dimensions are as follows :—

Length .	14 paces
Width .	11 ,,
Height .	49 feet
Extreme height to centre of dome	91 ,,

An inscription on the south-east pillar is to the following effect :—

'With the help of God, I, Papack the son of Bhrosch and my wife Rousoukna have excavated this house of prayer out of one natural rock to the memory of our souls, and as an everlasting monument to ourselves, with our honest (-ly possessed) revenues. This has taken place during the eparchiate of Father Markar, 737'[1] (1288).

On the south-east pillar, is inscribed in verse, without any date :—

    Divine symbol
    To Simeon monk
    Be protector
    Be his soul's guardian
    His sin's redemption
    Who gave an unchangeable gift
    To the holy church of Keghart
    The abiding place of saints
    The miracle working
    Adorned by God's word
    As an ineffaceable remembrance

It is related that this sanctuary was entirely excavated by Papack unaided, while Rousoukna sat at the opening above, and with her long and beautiful hair pulled up the baskets as fast as Papack could fill them with dust and stones. The work was

[1] This inscription is reproduced by Dubois, iii. p. 397, and Brosset, *Additions, &c.*, p. 321, in both works with some variations.

commenced at the opening and proceeded with downwards; when completed, the place of entrance was selected and the doorway begun; the implements that were left at the unfinished work, on retiring for the night, were found in the morning removed to another part; this being repeated a second and a third night, the hint was taken, the old doorway abandoned, and the entrance effected where it remains to this day. The original spot fixed upon for the entrance, and given up, is pointed out as a proof of the miraculous intervention.

From the Rousoukna we went to another large sanctuary, constructed upon three sides of large square blocks of grey freestone, the fourth, the north side, being the solid rock. The lofty dome, handsomely sculptured in Arabian lattice work, is supported, like the sanctuary of Rousoukna, by four massive pillars, the ceilings in the aisles being carefully finished in a variety of tasteful designs; on its walls are some beautifully sculptured crosses.

Over the entrance is inscribed:—

'In the time of Zakharè (of) my brother Ivanè of the royal race and their children Shahnshah [1] and Avak [2] during the eparchiate of Barseg the solitary, with the aid of my brother I erected this Cathedral Church with great luxury—the year 664' (1215).

The dimensions of this Chapel are:—

Length	18 paces
Width	22 ,,
Height	58 feet

On the north side two openings lead into several excavations

[1] Shahnshah, d. 1261, the son and successor of Zakharè, was the noble Sahenna visited in 1252 by Rubruquis when on his return from seeing the great Khan:—Saint Martin, *Mém. sur l'Arménie*, ii. p. 258.

[2] Avak succeeded his father Ivanè as *atabeck*, and died, 1250.

in the rock. In one is a spring commended for its sanctifying and hygienic properties; in the others are small chapels having domes with moresque ornamentations, and two arched recesses with curious sculptures over them are believed to have been the burial-places of persons of distinction.

On the south side of one of the small chapels is repeated the inscription we read on the north wall of the church:—'By the

WALL SCULPTURES OVER ARCHED RECESSES, KEGHART.

grace of God, I, prince Bhrosch son of Varsag, &c., &c.'; and at the end is added:

'I have hewn this house of God in the rock, as a memorial of myself, for my children, my wife Hatyne Hatoun.'

Over the entrance to it, are two inscriptions:

I. 'I, Zakharé, in 706 (1257), restored the church of the

Astvazatzyn [1] with my honestly possessed revenues. I bought the land Demary for twenty daëkans and the place Arnezaï Gavanagh in which to keep pigs, for twenty daëkans, and have gifted them to the holy Astvazatzyn, and they who serve the Church have promised two services, one for me. . . . Mankanagh. . . . whoever deprives the Church of these possessions, let him be damned by the 318 patriarchs.'

II. 'In 630 (1181), I, Father Stepanè, patriarch of Aghuance, entered the service of this monastery at the time of the rule of Father Gregory, and have gifted the relics of the Apostle St. Andrew, and the image of the birth of John; and they who serve this place have promised to hold a service in all the churches on the day of the Transfiguration.'

On the north side of the same entrance are the three following inscriptions:—

I. '626 (1177), I, Stepanè Kourkya, give to the holy places the land of Karapoghotz which I inherited during the eparchiate of Gregory [2] . . . one for Stepanè . . . two services for sister Saremtro, to father and mother. . . .'

II. 'In the year *49 the Christ loving prince Zakharè and Ivanè restored the water Amarnamataky; the dwellers in the holy places have promised to perform services at the principal shrine on Thursdays and Fridays throughout the year.'

III. 'I, Aziz, reared in the house of Houtlou Hanum and Bhrosch, have given twenty daëkans. They who serve in this place have promised one service annually. Whoever transgresses let him answer for it.' [3]

---

[1] The Holy Virgin, literally, 'She who has given birth to God.'

[2] Gregory IV., surnamed *Pzgha*, the 'infant.'

[3] I am indebted to M. Gustave A. Kalantaroff of Erivan for the literal translation into Russian, from the Armenian, of the original inscriptions; they have been reproduced in English by K.

To reproduce every inscription at Keghart would fill a volume; the most interesting and important are here given for the first time, I believe, in a European language; they are the registers of the arduous and laborious nature of oblations offered in the persuasion of justification by works, and in complete ignorance or repudiation of the words of the Apostle, 'the just shall live by faith,' and 'they being ignorant of God's righteousness and going about to establish their own righteousness, have not submitted themselves unto the righteousness of God.'

I felt greatly inclined to linger about this interesting solitude, but the day was half spent, and ground had yet to be got over; we therefore took leave of our attentive hosts after contributing something for the benefit of the monastery. The old archimandrite and his subordinates accompanied us to the gate showering blessings on our heads, and soon Ghergarr was lost to view. We returned to Gharny by the same road as that on which we had travelled the previous evening, not caring to try the old and now abandoned bridle path at the bottom of the valley.

Two thousand years before the birth of Christ, so say the Armenian chroniclers, a prince founded a city which he named Keghamè, after himself; the name was afterwards changed by Kharnig, the grandson of Keghamè, to Kharny, and is now Gharny, or Bash-Gharny, 'upper Gharny,' a small and indigent village inhabited by herdsmen and woodcutters employed in the forests of Kyzyl-dagh, where they say wild boar are plentiful.

To get to the ruins of Kharny, which are to the south-west of the village, I passed under an arch of comparatively modern construction to the venerable remains that mark the limits of the 'fortress,' a ponderous wall of massive squares of grey lava, rent asunder and displaced in a singular manner from its foundation, by some violent disturbance of nature. Following a track that leads to the left, we saw some large capitals and other remains lying about, and farther on came to an imposing but melancholy sight —a large heap of hewn and sculptured grey porphyry piled in utter confusion; a sore spectacle indeed, and as complete a chaos as it is possible to conceive. Moses Chorenses, the Armenian chronicler of the fifth century, relates that Tiridates king of Armenia, who constructed the fortress of Kharny which became his favourite residence, caused a handsome palace to be erected within it for his sister Khosrovitoukhd, and that an inscription in Greek characters recorded the dedication.[1] But it is a temple rather than a palace that is indicated by these superb remains; and their Grecian style of architecture may have been due to a desire on the part of the monarch to introduce a taste for higher art among his people, after his return from a lengthened residence abroad. The edifice, which had its front to the south, probably inclined towards the east in its fall; and although the structure would appear to have collapsed within the limits of its own foundation, each fragment lies far removed from its original annex, for portions of the entablature, of the pediment, of cornices, the bases, &c., lie tumbled in marvellous disorder; destruction of which there is no record, and that could only have been effected by an earthquake. The fortress, or some part of it, probably existed in the ninth century, for in allusion to the death of the patriarch Machtots, A.D. 897, an Armenian historian of the thirteenth century states that he was

---

[1] 'Per id tempus Tiridates castelli Garnii ædificationem absolvit, quod quadratis et cæsis lapidibus, ferro et plumbo compagmentatis construxit, atque ibi umbraculum statuit et monumentum mirifica arte cælatum, pro sorore sua Chosroiduchta, in eoque memoriam sui Græcis literis inscripsit.—Moses, Chor. p. 224.

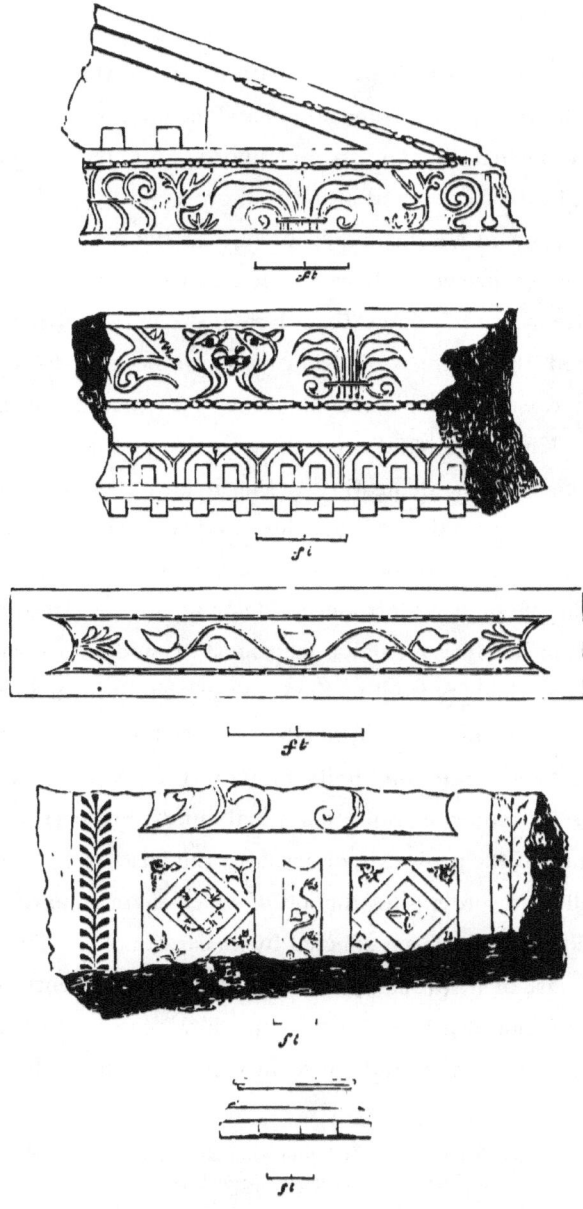

interred in the cemetery of Kharny, *in front of the marvellous throne of Tiridates.*[1]

Some twenty yards beyond the ruins is the brink of a precipice, another limit to the fortress; at a depth of several hundred feet, on its course to swell the Araxes, is the Gharny-tchaï, between tiers of columnar basalt superb in their regularity, like mighty sheets of corrugated iron. On the banks of this stream, known in bygone ages as the Azad, or Medzamor, stood in ancient times the city of Tovin founded by Chosroes II. 316–325, the capital of Armenia during six centuries, and the seat of the patriarchs from 452 to 924. It was at Tovin, called Dewyn in the annals of Armenia, that the Council was held in 551; the decay of this city dates from the time of its conquest by the Mongols. At the confluent of the Azad was the celebrated city of Ardaschad, or Artaxata, founded by Artaxias, 189–159 B.C., governor and afterwards sovereign of Armenia; but according to Strabo, Artaxata was built by Hannibal on a peninsular elbow of land on the Araxes, in a situation eminently fitted for defence.[2] In the first century Artaxata was devastated and burnt by the Roman general Corbullon, and afterwards rebuilt by Tiridates, who named it Neronia as a compliment to his protector the Roman Emperor. Ardaces II. subsequently called the city after himself, and Ardashad became the capital of Armenia during several epochs up to the year 798.[3] In 1514 it was the scene of the victory of Selim I. over the Persians under the Sophy Ismaïl. The sites of Tovin and of Ardashad are both within easy distance of Erivan.

[1] Kiracos de Gantzag: XIIIme siècle *Hist. d'Arménie*, trans. by M. Brosset; St. Petersburg, 1870, p. 43.
[2] Strabo, XI., xiv. 6.
[3] Saint Martin: *Mém. sur l'Arménie*, i. p. 117.

At Bash-Gharny, I secured some Georgian coins of the reigns of Queen Thamar, 1184; Thamar and David, 1193; Queen Roussoudan, 1223; George IV., 1212, and Demetrius II., 1273, all in good preservation; and among other relics found by the peasants, a copper vessel bearing in relief the words *Myrzah Khany vohrty Petros*, 'Peter the son of Mirza Khan.' In 1772, Mirzah Khan was *melyk* of a principality in the province of Artsakh, the ancient Katchen, styled by Constantine Porphyrogenitus, Ἄρχων τοῦ Χατζιένης,[1] and now known as Karabagh. The title of *melyk* was assumed by petty princes in Armenia, many of whom paid tribute to the Persians; but there were others who preserved their independence.

A regulation which forbids the detention of horses over a certain length of time, compelled our return to Erivan. We dined at the ranger's cottage, and started soon after four o'clock, our object being to save daylight over the bad roads.

ANCIENT KING OF ARMENIA.

CHAPTER XXI.

TWENTY-NINTH DAY.

Vision of St. Gregory—Road to Edchmiadzin—Wines of the district—The monastery—Reception by the Patriarch—The library—Printing office—The patriarchal church—Consecration of bishops—The treasury—Relics—Letter to the Saviour—His reply—The three churches—The college—Conversion of Tiridates—A present from the Patriarch.

SCHOGHAGHATH! Edchmiadzin! To a vision of St. Gregory, *Lousarovitch* 'the Enlightener,'[1] is ascribed the origin of these names, and the story is thus related:—St. Gregory saw the heavens open, and a ray of light descend, preceded by a host of angels and a human figure holding a hammer. This vision appeared in the direction of Vagharshabad.[2] Soon the hammer struck the earth, which opened, the mountains trembled, and out of the bowels of the earth there issued a frightful and hellish clamour. Then there arose near the palace[3] a golden pedestal in the form of an altar, from which there issued a pillar of fire surmounted by a canopy of clouds, and above them shone a cross; a spring from beneath the altar, watered a large tract of land. Around this edifice were

---

[1] In Armenia, conversion to Christianity is called 'enlightenment'; he who converts is an 'enlightener'; and in Georgia to baptize and to be baptized, is 'to give light,' and 'to receive light.' Ouhtanes d'Ourha, Xme. siècle. *Histoire en trois parties*, trans. by M. Brosset, St. Petersburg, 1870, p. 266. 'Enlightenment' or baptism, see Heb. vi. 4.

[2] Or Viashatabau, ancient capital and residence of the kings of Armenia.

[3] Of Tiridates; reigned 259-314.

four pillars, three of which stood over the remains of the holy martyrs,[1] and a glorious light in the form of a cross illuminated the whole. An angel then appeared to Gregory and interpreted to him the vision. 'The human form,' he said, 'is the Lord's; the edifice surmounted by a cross signifies the universal church placed under the protection of the cross, for it is on the cross that the Son of God has died; this spot must become the place of prayer; the pillar of fire and the spring are symbolic of Divine baptism, which flows from the church universal for the regeneration of mankind; therefore prostrate thyself,' the angel added, 'at the sign of grace which God has made manifest to thee, and erect here a church.'[2]

The site where St. Gregory had this vision was thenceforth called Schoghaghath, that is to say, 'diffusion of light,' and the spot where the Lord descended was named Edeh, 'came down' Miadzin 'the Only-begotten'; a tabernacle beneath the dome in the cathedral marks the consecrated place. Edchmiadzin became the seat of the Armenian patriarchs, of whom St. Gregory was the first, for a century and a half from 302, the year of its foundation; it was then removed to Tovin, and after various changes was finally established at Edchmiadzin, in 1441. The first Christian church was built in 309, where had stood a temple dedicated by the ancient Armenians to their goddess Anahid, 'Venus,' and the monastery dates from the patriarchate of Narses II, 524-533.

Edchmiadzin, the cradle of the Gregorian church,[3] is 18 *versts* from Erivan; the first part of the road traverses barren and stony land covered with large blocks of lava, on all of which it is curious to notice

---

[1] St. Rhipsime, St. Guiane, and others.

[2] *Histoire, dogmes, traditions, et liturgie de l'Église Arménienne orientale*:—Dulaurier, Paris, 1855.

[3] St. Gregory established the church in Armenia in 289. He was consecrated bishop of the Armenians by Leontius, bishop of Cappadocia.

a thin calcareous deposit. Near the hamlet of Djafarabad is a circular brick erection like a tower, said to be the remains of a monument raised by the Persians to commemorate a victory; another hamlet called Shyrabatt, is a medley of mud huts.

The first thing that strikes a stranger on entering the village of Edchmiadzin is its dull and deserted appearance, yet material prosperity belongs to it; the land is productive and valuable, and seldom to be purchased at less than six hundred roubles the *desyatína*,[1] the whole district being wine-producing. We alighted at the quarters of the chief of police, whose lengthened residence in the country enabled him to give the following information on the wines of this locality.

There are ten sorts of wine at Etchmiadzin;[2] of the best qualities, one is quite colourless like water, dry and strong; two other wines having the same properties are of a rose colour, and somewhat sweet in flavour. These three wines contain on an average 16 per cent. of alcohol by weight, and are sold at six copecks the bottle, other wines being even cheaper; but none leave the province, the supply being unequal to the demand. Eight hundred *desyatjns* of land are laid out in vineyards, which yield 10,000 *karas* of wine annually, each *kara* being equal to 250 bottles. The Patriarch engaged a French vine-dresser a few years ago, who produced a very fair sparkling wine, but the undertaking not proving remunerative, it was abandoned. The strongest wine is obtained from vines grown on chalky soil.

On arriving at the Monastery, I was informed that the Patriarch's[3] hours of reception were over. His Holiness dines at one, enjoys a *siesta* until four, after which he gives no audience. In

---

[1] One *desyatjna* = 2·86 acres.   [2] The name is so pronounced by the Russians.
[4] The title of Patriarch is applied throughout, in distinction from the Catholicos at Sis, in Cilicia.

the present instance he made an exception in favour of a guest of the Governor, and sent word that he would receive me forthwith.

The residence of His Holiness is entered from a court adjoining that in which the church stands. I was first conducted to a small and negligently furnished chamber, and after a few moments ushered into a long, narrow apartment, richly carpeted but with very little furniture, and having suspended on its walls a series of portraits of kings and warriors, a sea-piece by the marine painter Aïvazoffsky, and a portrait of the Emperor, &c. As I reached the middle of the room, His Holiness rose from his seat at the opposite end and held out his hand in a salutatory manner, but I followed the custom of the country, and raised it towards my lips, upon which he invited me to be seated.

The Patriarch of Armenia is a heavy-looking man of about sixty; he was attired in the *lodeck*, a black satin garment lined with violet satin, worn over the *paregélte*, a black vest and skirt. To a gold chain around his neck was suspended the *panaghè*, a large medallion bearing a representation in enamel of the Virgin and Child; it was set in brilliants, and surmounted by a cross in brilliants and rubies. His Holiness also wore the *kamelavka* of violet velvet, a hat introduced into the Armenian from the Russian Church, since the annexation of Armenia to the Empire.

The Patriarch asked whether I had come from England, Scotland, or Ireland, and hoped that I had travelled in Russia with comfort; he said it afforded him great pleasure to welcome a stranger from a distant land; that the Church of Armenia received the dead as readily as the living, witness the remains of an Englishman [1] who lies interred beneath the church walls, by the side of the most distinguished Patriarchs.

[1] Sir John Macdonald; this is a noteworthy instance of religious toleration.

His Holiness requested me to write my name and address in full, and invited me to pass the night at the Monastery, giving instant directions that my wants should be attended to; he also gave orders that I should be taken to the library and treasury.

I was impatient to enter the world-renowned library of Etchmiadzin; my thoughts had been dwelling upon the reputation it enjoys of possessing the most interesting and rarest of MSS., the envy of nations and scholars, jealously guarded and inaccessible for many generations, all attempts at research being rendered futile by the monks! Had not every effort to cause the publication of a catalogue failed, until the learned M. Brosset announced in 1840, the fact of there being at Etchmiadzin 635 works, of which 462 were in the Armenian tongue? The Professor's catalogue, now out of print, has been succeeded by another, of which I obtained one of the few copies that are for sale. The richest collection of MSS. of the literature of Armenia, which dates from the fourth century, is, however, more probably in the possession of the Mechitarists at their monastery on the islet of St. Lazarus at Venice.

In the ante-room of the library are the portraits and diplomas of the Patriarchs. The Patriarch is chosen by the votes of the Armenian bishops of all lands, who come for the purpose to Etchmiadzin where the election takes place, after which he is *appointed* by the Emperor of Russia.

According to the statement of the monk librarian, there are now at the library from 1,700 to 1,800 volumes, we were shown some of the more remarkable Bibles and devotional works, but not the charters, which are never exhibited under any circumstances; the books we saw were thus described:—

1. Testament of the tenth century, beautifully illuminated,

in a massive carved ivory binding. 2. Bible of the thirteenth century, in leather binding—had belonged to Aytoun II., king of Armenia. 3. Bible of the thirteenth century, illuminated with portraits of the Evangelists; in a modern binding of questionable taste. 4. Bible of the thirteenth century. 5. Bible of the fourteenth century—artistically illuminated. 6. Bible of the seventeenth century—with the seal of the Patriarch Nahabied--- (1691-95) illuminated with arabesques and figures.[1]

The librarian said that there were books of many languages and of every period, some being in the English tongue, but when I requested to be shown the latter, he replied that they were all dreadfully old and could not be of the least interest to anybody!

From the library we went to the printing-offices, where 25 men were at work, in the type foundry, at printing, and bookbinding; we also saw the dormitories and apartments for pilgrims and visitors, and two refectories, long vaulted chambers in a very untidy condition; in each is a canopy under which the Patriarch presides when he assists at a repast, and there is also the reading-desk at which chapters from the Scriptures are read during meals, a custom similar to that observed in Russo-Greek and Papal monasteries. There were at Etchmiadzin—

Archbishops and Bishops .	5
Archimandrites and Monks .	20
Novices . . .	25

but these numbers frequently vary.

The cathedral has a large tower over the west end, with the usual conical steeple, and an open tower of six pillars, with similar

---

[1] For a list of the principal MSS. and works in the library at Etchmiadzin, see Brosset, *Voy. Archéo.* Rapp. iii. p. 23.

steeple, is above each transept wing ; the latter were erected in 1691 by the Patriarch Eghiazar, and the porch of red porphyry, prolifically sculptured, dates from 1633-55. . To the right on entering is a white marble monument over the grave of Sir John Macdonald, British envoy to the Court of Persia, who died in 1830; it is by the side of the Patriarchs Alexander I., 1714 ; Alexander II., 1755 ; Daniel, 1806 ; and Nerses, 1857 ; all remarkable men.

The interior of the church is gloomy, ineffective, and entirely deficient in any fascinating touches of architectural force and decoration ; the walls are covered with heavy designs in *fresco* of purely Oriental taste, representing flowers, birds, and arabesque ornamentations.

On the *pem*, faced with the white alabaster of Erivan, are painted the figures of the Apostles, the Virgin and Child being in the middle, St. Philip and St. Stephen at either end. In the transept chapels are represented the Prophets, and under the dome between those chapels is the tabernacle already mentioned that marks the sacred spot where 'the Only-begotten descended.' Portions of the nave are railed off for the exclusive use of the clergy, as may be noticed in all Armenian churches. Near the high altar are two thrones ; one, of handsomely carved walnut wood was presented to the Patriarch James IV. by Pope Innocent XI., 1676-89 ; the other, a beautiful work of art in tortoise-shell and mother-o'-pearl, was a gift from the Armenians at Smyrna to the Patriarch Asdovadzadour, 1715-26.

At the sanctuary in the south transept monks prepare for the episcopate. When the day for consecration arrives, the Patriarch takes his place on a throne in the north transept chapel, at the top of seven steps, and the bishop-elect has to move across the church on his knees from the south to the north transept, and still upon his knees ascend the seven steps, typical of the seven grades in the Church ;[1] having reached the top step, where the Patriarch is seated, the ceremony of consecration is proceeded with.

The present Patriarch, Gevork (George) IV., has of late years added to the cathedral by extending it at the east end behind the altar; the new erection is in exquisitely bad taste, for it is totally at variance architecturally with the church itself, the decorative style of which has been so affected and maintained in the periodical repairs. This new building, entered from the vestry, is to be henceforth the treasury, to which strangers will not be admitted except by permission of the Patriarch. In it are ecclesiastical vestments and mitres that have been preserved for centuries, and pastoral staffs in gold and silver, ivory and ebony, many being richly jewelled ; there is also a large collection of jewelled ornaments and church plate.

One important relic in a glass case is the 'holy lance,' which had been preserved for many years at Keghart. It was brought into Armenia in the year 34[2] by the Apostle Thaddeus, who came in the first place to Edessus, one of the capitals, to which city he was sent by the Apostle Thomas, as commanded by the Saviour, for the purpose of healing Abgar the king ; for it is asserted by the Armenian chronicles that the king had written to our Lord, praying

---

[1] The seven grades in the Armenian Church are these :—

    1. Oupranapanoutioan . . . Door-opener.
    2. Sargavakoutioun . . . Deacon.
    3. Avaksargavakoutioun . . . Archdeacon.
    4. Khahanaoutioun . . . Priest.
    5. Vartabedoutioun . . . Archimandrite.
    6. Episcoposoutioun . . . Bishop.
    7. Epi-copossapitoutioun . . . Archbishop.

[2] In 1421, the 'holy spear-head' was among the precious relics of the Emperor at Constantinople ! *Voyages et ambassades de Guillebert de Lannoy*, 1399-1450, Mons. 1840, p. 43

that he might be delivered of a malady. Whilst at Edessus, Thaddeus founded the first Christian church, consecrated several bishops, and then came into greater Armenia. Here he converted the King Sanadrang and many of his subjects, but that prince returned to idolatry, and Thaddeus was put to death, suffering martyrdom in the year 52.[1]

The letter of Abgarus to the Saviour:—[2]

'Abgar Chamatsy, Prince of the country, to you Christ the Saviour, who have appeared (in the countries) at Jerusalem, greeting.

'I have heard of you and of the cures which you perform without applying remedies, without using herbs; it is said that you restore sight to the blind, cleanse the lepers, and cast out unclean spirits; that you restore to health people afflicted with old maladies, and that you raise the dead. Having heard all this about you, I have come to the conclusion that you are either God himself descended from heaven for the purpose, or that you are the Son of God. I therefore write to implore you to come and relieve me of an illness that afflicts me. I have also heard that the Jews murmur against you, and seek to ill-treat you. Although small, my city is sufficiently large to contain us both; come, that we may live together.'

The bearers of this letter met Jesus at Jerusalem, as is attested by the words of the Gospel, where it is stated that some pagans approached Jesus, and not daring to speak to him, addressed themselves to Philip and to Andrew. Philip spoke to our Saviour, who did not accept the invitation, but directed the following reply to be sent.

Reply to the letter of Abgarus, written by the Apostle Thomas, as was commanded by the Saviour:

---

[1] Dulaurier, *Histoire*, &c.
[2] This letter and the reply were translated from the Syriac by Eusebius. *Acc. Ch. hist.*, lib. i. cap. 14.

'Blessed is he, who, not having seen me, believeth in me; for it is written of me, that they who have seen me have not believed, but that they who have believed without seeing me, shall live. As you have written to ask me to come to you, I must accomplish that for which I was sent, which, having accomplished, I will ascend towards Him who sent me. I will send to you after my ascension one of my disciples, who will cure you of your disease, and will give you life, as he will likewise to them that are with you.'

This letter was carried by the messengers of Abgarus, together with the image of our Saviour, which was an impression taken from life, and exists to this day in the city of Edessus.[1]

Cedrenus,[2] a monk who wrote in the thirteenth century, states that the letter of the Saviour escaped the plunder of the Saracens on their invasion of Mesopotamia (1032), and was sent to Constantinople by Maniaces, the Governor of Lower Media. The portrait was also taken to the Byzantine capital, after its recovery from the hands of the infidels by the celebrated General Korkas in the tenth century.

The next precious relic at Etchmiadzin is the hand of St. Gregory in a silver-gilt case, kept tied and sealed to secure the sacred contents from being surreptitiously extracted when the relic is carried about, for the purpose of healing the sick and performing other miracles; the Patriarchs are consecrated with this hand. There are also the hands and heads of other saints and martyrs, all in silver cases, a fragment of the ark, and a piece of the true cross. The only profane relic in the collection is a heavy coronet in gold, said to have been worn by Tiridates.

Some thirty years ago, during the patriarchate of Nerses, a marble statue adorned with a golden wreath was brought to the

---

[1] Oukhtanes d'Ourka, p. 230. [2] Ced. *Comp. Hist.* 731.

Monastery by some Kurds, who had found it in a tomb (?) on the banks of the Západny Arpa-tchaï, 'Western Arpa-tchaï,' at the Russo-Turkish frontier. What had become of it? None could tell.

The monks who crowded about us were painfully ignorant of the history of the various relics in their treasury, and few of them knew the fables by which those relics are sanctified. I was accompanied by Father Vahan, of the church of St. Guiane, an intelligent and well-bred man, who speaks French, and gave me much information. Father Vahan, and Father Stepanè of Erivan, are promising members of the Armenian clergy, who, being competent to raise the tone of clerical education, will certainly advance the interests of the Church, if called upon to fill positions of trust and authority.

To the south of the Monastery buildings is a large reservoir, filled from the K'hasagh, and rendered available for purposes of irrigation; this water supply and the wood beyond, with many other improvements, will be lasting memorials of the beneficial patriarchate of the lamented Nerses, a man of progress and of infinite merit. In the same direction is the cemetery in which monks have been interred for ages, and where the tombstones peculiar to Armenia are seen in every variety; from this direction is viewed, to its greatest advantage, the Monastery of Etchmiadzin, enclosed by high battlemented walls with turrets, and having the appearance of a vast fortress.

The Churches of St. Rhipsime and of St. Guiane, both near the Monastery,[1] are believed to have been founded by Tiridates. In the latter are interred those Patriarchs whose lives may not have earned for them the distinction of receiving burial at the cathedral. Their merits are discussed by the Synod at Etchmiadzin, the

---

[1] The Turks called Etchmiadzin, Outch Kylyssè, 'The three churches.'

organisation of which, as at present constituted, dates from the year 1836, and is formed of four bishops and four archimandrites, who are selected by the Patriarch, subject to the Emperor's approval. The sittings of this Synod, at which the Patriarch presides, are permanent, and are always attended by an officer appointed by the Crown.

To the east of the Monastery is the new college and seminary supported out of the revenues of the church, which amount, it is said, to 80,000 roubles per annum. The yearly allowance of His Holiness is 10,000 roubles; and of the balance, one half is expended in the most necessitous requirements, which include the maintenance of the community, and the remainder is reserved for repairs and building purposes.

The bazaar, the property of the monks, is within a high-walled enclosure to the west; it is chiefly a mart for corn and hay.

I did not see a vestige of ancient remains, nor could I learn of any about the neighbourhood. Vagharshapat, named in remote times, Ardimet K'haghak'h, 'City of Diana,' was founded by Erovant I. in the sixth century B.C. In the second century of the Christian era, King Vagharsch surrounded the city with walls, and named it after himself; it continued to be the capital until 344, during which period Dertad Medz, 'Tiridates the Great,'

. . . . . the priest and king, with laurel crown'd,

having persecuted and delivered to the executioners, Rhipsime, Guiane, and other Christians, was smitten by the Lord as was Nebuchadnezzar, losing his reason and becoming like a beast of the field.

Khosrovitoukhd, however, the sister of the king, who at this time was living in strict seclusion, had a vision and heard the voice

A PRESENT FROM THE PATRIARCH.

of an angel say to her, that Gregory alone was able to heal her brother; Gregory having accordingly been sent for from the pit in which he was confined restored to Tiridates his reason. The pagan king being suddenly inspired with the spirit of truth, fell at the feet of the apostle, who promised him pardon from heaven!

Tiridates was afterwards baptized with 400 myriads of human beings on Mount Nimrod, N'pat, the Niphates of the ancients,[1] so called because of the snow with which it was covered.

Before returning to Erivan, I had the pleasure of a visit from Father Vahan, who brought to me a portrait with autograph, as a present from His Holiness.

[1] Νιφάτης ἀπὸ τῆς νιφάδος.

ARMENIAN MONK.

CHAPTER XXII.

THIRTIETH AND THIRTY-FIRST DAYS.

Excursion to the plairs—Church of St. George—Burial in Armenia—Mourning—Poplar plantations—Armenian cottages—Murder—Civic government in the Caucasus—A patient—Monastery of Khorvyrab—Martyrdom of St. Gregory— A wedding procession—Armenian nuptials—Seclusion of Armenian women—Turcoman gipsies—The River Araxes -Aralyk--A Mahomedan colonel—The Kabardines—Ride to Ararat—The Kurris—Arkhoury—St. James, *Myzpynsk*—A piece of the Ark—Ascensions of Mount Ararat—Cossack dances—A pleasant evening.

AN ever clear sky and even temperature, though it was the month of January, made the weather enjoyable and exactly suited for excursions so full of interest; I had encouraging and most attentive hosts in their Excellencies, and an intelligent companion in the officer of police—what more could traveller or tourist sigh for!

At eleven o'clock the *calèche* and four post-horses with an escort was reported ready, and we at once started, clearing the town by an equally bad road with the others we had gone over, for similar rocky and uneven ground had to be overcome. At a distance of 5 *versts* from Ervan the face of the country changes, and irrigation commences at the village of Shynkavyt. At Norokvyt, another village on the road, is a small church inside high walls, for all churches and monasteries in Armenia were thus protected against the assaults of infidel invaders. The natives have much pride in showing this little Church of St. George and the grave of Sourp

Gevork[1] who is buried in it. We found a corpse in a shell in front of the altar; it was wrapped in cotton and silks, looking like a mummy, the arms being crossed over the chest, whereon lay a Bible, and would be buried without the coffin, which was for temporary use only. People in most countries seek in some manner to save a body from being pressed or mangled at its burial, and it is not often that we hear of the earth itself being heaped over a corpse, even when a coffin is not employed. The Mussulman populations in the Caucasus and the Crimea invariably excavate a side niche at the bottom of the grave, into which the body is laid; the niche is blocked up with stones, and the grave filled in. We have seen the manner of the Persian tombs at Tiflis. The Arabs on the river Sobat dig a hole similar in shape to a European grave; an extra trench is formed at the bottom of the vault, about a foot wide; the body is laid upon its side within this trench, and covered with bricks made of clay, which are laid across.[2]

The ancient manner of mourning for the dead is still observed in these parts by the Armenians; the women, demonstrative only in such hours of sadness, for they are seldom seen or heard at other times, allow their hair to fall loosely about the shoulders, covering the head with a black kerchief; the men bare and beat their breasts.[3] One of their superstitions in regard to the dead is, that they appear before the living; but they are changed, for their heels are seen in front, and the toes are where the heels were in life!

The land in this part of the country is good, yielding corn and oats plentifully, and a sufficiency of tobacco for local consump-

---

[1] St. George. [2] Baker, *The Albert Nyanza*, &c., i p. 54.
[3] We read of the practice of beating the body when mourning in Jeremiah xxxi. 19, and Ezekiel xxi. 12.

tion; there are few trees except poplars, which grow in plantations carefully walled in, mud being freely employed in the construction of these enclosures, for we have left all the stones behind. The poplar is never allowed to reach an unwieldy size; when hewn down, it is cut into certain lengths and sold for the framing of mud huts. In most of the villages these huts are enclosed within walls, with a court in which cattle and poultry roam at will; the outer chamber receives its light from the doorway; another chamber, the largest, is lit by a *louvre* in the roof, and an inner room is used for storing lumber. The family lives day and night in the large room, which is spread with matting and carpeting; but there is no furniture, and recesses in the wall serve the purposes of shelves. In one cottage I observed a simple substitute for a seat, where in a corner stood a small loom over a square hole in the ground, on one side of which the weaver sat with her feet in the hollow. There is an attempt at tidiness in these dwellings, but the inmates are very dirty.

We met four prisoners in charge of the *starshyná*, 'elder,'[1] of a village where a murder had been committed a day or two previously, and of which crime these men stood accused; the body of the victim was found pierced with thirty-two dagger wounds. One of the prisoners had his eye bandaged, and one arm in a sling, and on his shirt were blood-stains; my companion informed me that on two occasions this miscreant had got off criminal charges laid against him, for, in the Caucasus as in Russia, circumstantial evidence does not suffice to convict.

The provinces or governments in the Caucasus are divided into

---

[1] In Tatar villages he is called the *kent-houder*, by the Armenians *tanouter*, and *mamarabbyer*, literally 'father, lord, or head of the house,' by the Georgians.

ouyesdy, 'districts,' which are under a *natchálnyk*,[1] and his *pamóshtchnyky*,[1] 'aids'; next to the *natchálnyk*, is the *priestav*,[1] local superior of the district, or *chef des sergents*. Each district is divided into *sélskye óbstchestva*, 'rural communes,' which consist of one or more *derévny*, 'villages,' that are under a *starshyná*,[2] 'elder,' who wears a heavy brass chain and badge of office; under the *starshyná* are the *pamóshtchnyky*,[2] his 'aids,' who are the chiefs of the villages, and wear brass badges on their breasts. There are also the *sélskye soúdya*,[2] 'rural judges,' who may not exceed twelve in number in each district; it is their duty to investigate all complaints and settle disputes, subject to the approval of the *starshyná*; the *candydaty* (candidats, Fr.) replace the *sélskye soúdya* in their functions, should necessity arise; and there are, finally, the *dobro-sóvestny'ye*,[2] who are appraisers in case of trespass or destruction of property.

Every tenth man in a village takes his turn at being a *desyátnyck*, 'tenth man,' whose duty it is to assist the *starshyná* and his *pamóshtchnyky* in the preservation of order, and who may be employed, when occasion arises, as messenger or guard, being even required to use force to further the ends of justice; in this manner the law is maintained in rural districts after a fashion, at no expense and with very little trouble to the authorities.

Since the emancipation, a *myravóy pasryádnyck*, 'peace maker,' has been appointed to each district, for the purpose of inquiring into and deciding the claims of the peasants against their former proprietors. The *myravóy pasryádnyck* is subordinate only to the governor of the province, to whom he makes his reports, and the decision of a special but permanent council, of which the governor is president, is final.

The villages in this fertile district are numerous. At a place

---

[1] Appointed by the Crown.   [2] Appointed on election.

called Houddaklòu we entered the vine country, where the plants, some of which appeared to be of great size, are earthed up in winter. At Kamarloù, where we stopped to change horses, I found a poor lad lying on some matting by the road-side, prostrated with fever; I immediately administered some quinine, giving a little at the same time to his friends with directions to repeat the dose until medical aid could be obtained, and had the satisfaction before we started of seeing the boy open his eyes and turn himself over, apparently fortified; some of the people bowed very low, and a few crossed themselves as we drove off.

It is necessary at this station to make arrangements with the post-master for proceeding to the Monastery of Khorvyrab, it being contrary to the regulations to employ post-horses off the post-roads, except in special cases. There is seldom any difficulty in concluding such an arrangement, but should the station-master prove intractable, saddle-horses may be procured, and they would be preferable when working against time, because the distance from Khorvyrab to Aralyk Bash-kent by bridle-path is only five miles, whereas with post-horses it is necessary to return and change them at Kamarloù, before quitting the road *en route* to Aralyk, and to do this it would be equally necessary to win the good graces of the station-master; it is therefore advisable, when pressed for time, to leave the carriage at Kamarloù, and engage horses there, which are to be obtained at two roubles the day, for the journey to Khorvyrab, Aralyk, Arkhoúry and back; the owners of the horses would be the guides, and will carry any small articles of luggage.

Six *versts* beyond Kamarloù we turned off the post-road on the whip hand, driving over swampy ground encrusted with salt, until we reached an isolated hill on the plain, at the top of which is the old

MONASTERY OF KHORVYRAB.

Monastery of Khorvyrab surrounded by a wall, and looking very much like some old feudal castle. The church is of modern construction, but the object of interest is a small ancient chapel dedicated to St. Gregory *Lousarovitch*, built over the well in which the saint was confined during the space of fifteen years, whence the name of Khorvyrab, 'dry well'; the pit, renovated in 640-660, is descended by a ladder 30 feet long.

When Gregory refused to worship the idol which Tiridates set

MONASTERY OF KHORVYRAB.

up, the servile courtiers excited the wrath of the king, who commanded that he should be bound hand and foot and taken to the province of Ararat, there to be kept in the fortress of the town of Ardashat, where he should be thrown into a pit, and left until he died. The pit in which they had cast the saint was a hole of stinking mud, used only for malefactors, and therefore filled with snakes and other venomous reptiles, the mention alone of which filled everyone with terror; for when a malefactor happened to be thrown into it, he died that same day from the stench of the place, because of the filth and mire, and of the snakes and other creeping things that lived therein. But, by the grace of God, the saint was kept from all harm.[1]

At the bottom of the pit we were gravely shown the crevices and openings through which the reptiles crept in and out,[2] also a well-worn stone on which the saint used to lean when he prayed throughout his long confinement for the conversion of heathens. The well is perfectly dry and clean, and was probably constructed at the same time as the church in which the body of the saint reposed for many years, until it was taken up to be *divided* among *Christian* communities in various parts!

We found one solitary monk at this Monastery, an archimandrite, who in the Armenian Church may perform the functions of a bishop or archbishop; he lives in a miserable dwelling near the church, and receives pilgrims and benighted travellers who chance to pass his way, which, however, does not often occur; while the savage dogs kept for the purpose prevent evil-disposed persons from invading the premises during the night. From the walls he pointed to the village of Shykyar or Shyklou, which he told us was called by the natives Takht Dertad, 'throne of Tiridates,' but upon what grounds he could not say.

We left Khorvyrab at 3.45 P.M., and were upon our return to Kamarloû when we passed an Armenian bridal procession, accompanied by a crowd of the male sex. The bride was seated on a horse led by four men, astride an enormous cushion of bright yellow silk; she was followed by her father, also mounted, with a

[1] *Life and Times of St. Gregory the Illuminator*, trans. by Rev. S. C. Malan, M.A. 1868.
[2] This legend is probably founded on the customs to which allusion is made in Zechariah ix. 11; Isaiah li. 14, &c.

youthful son behind him, and the rear was brought up by musicians playing upon the *zournà*, a short fife which emits a most unmusical sound, and beating the *naharà*,[1] a drum, by way of accompaniment; there was no attempt at melody, for the players blew and beat their hardest without any intermission. There were no demonstrations of joy, no semblance of a gathering bent on festivity, for the cavalcade moved silently and at so extremely slow a pace that it might almost have been mistaken for a funeral party, until our *tchapars* rode ahead to clear the way, when a faint effort was made to get up a cheer. Half a mile farther on we came to a road crossing, where the bridegroom, who was attended by his male friends, was awaiting the approach of the bride, to accompany her to the church.

After the wedding ceremony, the newly-married couple proceed to the bridegroom's house, where the bride's mother and other relatives await them, and are the first guests entertained by the mistress of the new household; as he steps across his own threshold the bridegroom breaks a plate, and thenceforth becomes the lord and master. The celebration of the marriage, however, is not completed, for the priest has attached a ribbon around the neck of the bride and bridegroom securing each with wax; these ribbons they are bidden to wear for three days and three nights, and they are exhorted to occupy separate apartments during that time, notwithstanding that they have become man and wife and live under the same roof; at the expiration of the term, they present

---

[1] The musical instruments among the people of the Caucasus, are, 1. The *zournà*, a small fife; 2. *tiry*, a large guitar; 3. *balabàyen*, a smaller guitar, usually of some sort of metal; 4. *tchongoury*, a kind of zither; 5. *tsancary*, a fiddle, with a long sounding bar which is rested on the knee; 6. *daera*, the tambourine; and 7. *dybylbyda* or *naharà*, a kettledrum, sometimes made of wood, but more frequently of baked clay. The various nationalities about the Caucasus have become so mixed up ethnologically, that it is difficult to trace the origin of some of these instruments.

themselves before the priest, who removes the ribbons by cutting them, and commends the pair for their obedience and chastity.[1]

Armenian women are rarely seen. During Mussulman occupation, when females were forcibly abducted to supply the harems of their conquerors, the people of this country were driven to the necessity of observing the very custom of their oppressors in concealing the fairest of the sex, and what was at first a precaution, became a practice which has continued to the present day. For several years after marriage, women remain confined in an inner chamber, and seldom see males, not excepting even their own fathers and brothers. This is in keeping with the practice in Persia as related by Herodotus, in his account of the manner in which Phædyma communicated with her father, Otanes.[2]

From Kamarloù we again passed through a wretched settlement, called Tchydamly, where the Moutroupp,[3] a tribe of Turcoman gipsies, a wild-looking and filthy people, live in mud hovels which they occupy in winter, and quit in the early spring on their maraudings; we did not see any of the women. In their burial-ground near the village, some graves had black patches over them, which on nearer inspection we found to be the remains of fires that had been kindled the night of burial, for the purpose, as they themselves informed us, of lighting the soul of the deceased to Paradise!

We soon turned off the post-road to cross the plain, this time to the left, and reached the ferry at the Araxes at six o'clock; the river, five feet in depth at this part, is very rapid,

. . . proud Araxes whom no bridge could bind;

but the ferry-boat was easily hauled across by one of the Cossack

---

[1] See the 'Song of the New Bride,' and 'A Song on the Bridegroom,' in Appendix IX.
[2] Herod. iii.   [3] Name given by the Armenians.

piquet stationed to guard it ; it is a large railed platform landed on two barges to which it is braced, and was of a size to receive our carriage, horses, and escort.

An hour's drive over sloppy ground brought us to the Shtab-kvartyra, the military station of Aralyk, 2 *versts* from the village of 2,602 Aralyk Bash-kent, and the head-quarters of the corps of Cossacks doing duty on the plains. The colonel in command [1] received us in the most hospitable manner, and the evening was very agreeably spent, thanks to my companion, the most patient of interpreters. Without knowing a sound of the English language, the colonel is an enthusiastic admirer of English literature and history; his ideal of a hero is Cromwell ; his delight, the study of Shakspeare and Buckle. His quarters are furnished with comfort, and he luxuriates in book-shelves well filled with translations from the English and the works of Russian authors. He loves his profession, is a loyal soldier, and seemed marvellously happy in his isolation, for he enjoyed no society, the only officer in his corps being a man of tastes and habits quite foreign to his own.

The colonel is a Mahomedan and native of Kabardah, a province to the north of the great mountain range and on the west side of the Terek. The Kabardines who are ' the blood ' of the Caucasus, the most advanced and once the wealthiest of all its nations, were the first to come to terms with Russia ; their sovereign claimed his descent from Sem, the son of Noah,[2] and the *ptche*, ' princes,' were powerful nobles. The Kabardines are famed horsemen, but their country is no longer celebrated for breed ; they now rear cattle and find the culture of bees profitable. Every Kabar-

---

[1] Colonel Temirhann Aktolovitch Shipsheff.
[2] *Voyages dans les steps d'Astrakhan et du Caucase*, &c. Comte J. Potocki. Paris 1829, i. p. 155.

dine wears in all weathers his *bourka*, of which he is very proud; he is much attached to his home, where the females of the family are treated with every consideration, and never leaves it except through compulsion. The Kabardines are hospitable and respectful to strangers, and have only of late years abandoned the custom of holding the stirrup while a guest mounted or dismounted.

The following morning the colonel kindly provided us with horses, and at ten o'clock we rode straight for Mount Ararat, up a gradual and perceptible incline, over ground covered with pieces of bright yellow, brown, grey, and dark-red lava and trachyte; here and there stood a huge black or grey rock, and some small patches of arable land lay fallow. There was nothing growing, no sign of vegetable life except a species of the *Euphorbia*.

We met a Kurd who was taking to the colonel a splendid wild goat, the *Ægoceros ægagrus*,[1] which he had shot on the mountain a few hours previously; the colonel sent it to the governor, who subsequently gave me the skin and horns. There was a settlement of Kurds in the direction of little Ararat, where we could see the smoke of their fires, but it was too far out of our way for us to visit.

As a rule, these Kurds avoid towns and villages, and shun observation; those we met on various occasions about the plains of the Araxes were men of middle stature, broad-shouldered, with gaunt faces and tawny complexions, and wandering restless eyes; they are men of few words and resolute in manner. The Kurds are nomads, who wander about the hills in summer with their herds and flocks, and resort to the plains in winter in search of pasture. They are the Mahomedans of Armenia, looking upon Armenia in

---

[1] The Georgians call it the *bodcha*. See Dubois iv. p. 281 (on the authority of Güldenstadt).

Russia as being a part of their country, and are to be found in numbers between Mount Ararat and Synack to the west. They are not more troublesome to the Russian authorities than are other vagrants, except that they stand accused of frontier smuggling. The Kurds wear an untidy sort of turban, a short jacket, a broad heavy sash around the waist, inside which they carry their pistols and daggers, short tight trowsers, the legs below the knees being swathed, and sandals or small shoes; they are fond of carrying at the waist a round shield studded with nail-heads or brass coins, and a rifle is slung across the shoulders; their language is chiefly Persian, but there are many who speak Turkish only.

After a two hours' ride we dismounted within the snowy limit of the mountain, which in summer is at an altitude above the sea of 13,700 feet. We scrambled up a rocky ridge, whence we saw to the east far below us an old cemetery on some very rough ground, with tombstones of red porphyry sculptured with crosses and other ornamentations; few inscriptions are legible, the one best preserved being in these words: 'Remember me, Minas, 942' (1493). To the west a deep ravine separated us from the village of Arkhoury.

What a painful stillness reigned around! Turning away from Ararat, the eye wanders over the immense plains where the bounties of Nature are lost in space, and where Nature itself seems gone to decay, leaving nothing but Mother Earth. The heavens were cloudless, and the sun had extended its rays and given light; but nothing had awoke to life, neither beasts of the field nor fowls of the air.

At one o'clock I placed my thermometer on a rock 12 feet above the snow, when the mercury stood at 48°.

We proceeded across the ravine to Arkhoury, a small level dotted with mud huts, above a rivulet of its name. The Armenians hold Arkhoury in special veneration, for Noah planted here the first vine, after he had go:e forth from the ark, from which circumstance is derived the name, *cark'h*, has planted, *ouh'rig*, the vine. The few people we saw crowded round and pressed us in a friendly manner to dismount and enter a hut; I was anxious to get to the Monastery of St. James, *Myzpynsk*, about eight *versts* farther on, and was not a little disappointed on being informed of the impossibility of reaching it for the next 'three moons,' on account of the depth of snow. When Dubois visited the church of Arkhoury in 1834, he found an inscription of the year 404=955 A.D. and at the Monastery of St. James, which is built of black lava, were inscriptions of the thirteenth and fourteenth centuries.[1] The church of the monastery owes its foundation and sanctity to the following incident.

A monk from Edchmiadzin, named James, had determined upon ascending Mount Ararat for the purpose of seeing the ark, supposed to have remained undisturbed since the Flood. After praying very fervently he commenced his task, walking all day and resting at night, but every morning on awaking he found himself at the same place from which he had started twenty-four hours previously. He prayed and persevered during the space of seven years, until at length an angel appeared who told him to desist from fatiguing himself unnecessarily; he commended James's piety and rewarded his faith by giving him that piece of the ark which is now preserved at Etchmiadzin, and a church was subsequently erected where the angel appeared to the monk.

Mount Ararat has been known to the Armenians by the name of Masis from the earliest ages, and was so called after Amassis, their chronicles state, who was an uncle of Haig the

---

[1] Dubois i. p. 408; iii. p. 463.

first king of Armenia. The Tatars call it Parmàk-dagh, 'finger
mountain,' and Aghyr-dagh, 'heavy mountain.' The Armenians in
general are unwilling to admit that the top has ever been reached,
although it is well known that Parrot,[1] Aftonomoff, Behrens,
Abich, Seymour, Tchodsko, Khanyloff, Stuart,[2] C. C. Tucker,[3] and
others, have either stood on the actual summit, or at a height
within a few hundred feet of it. The mountain is sacred, say the
Armenians, and no mortal shall overcome it. *Super Massis, nullus
debet ascendere, quia est mater mundi.*

We returned to Aralyk at five o'clock.

Our gallant host who desired to proceed to Erivan to pay his
respects to the Governor, had fixed upon the morrow for his visit,
and promised to accompany us if we would accept his hospitality
until the morning. As I should have missed the daylight drive
and arrived at the palace at a late hour had I proceeded to Erivan on
returning from the mountain, I accepted the invitation, and as it
proved, to my advantage, for the Colonel prepared a surprise.
After a dinner that would have done honour to the most efficient *chef*,
the Cossacks were mustered to sing and perform some dances of
perplexing figures in which from ten to twenty men took part,
showing off in a heel and hip step and doing a vast amount of
noisy shuffling. Of the songs all sung in chorus, some were wild,
others martial, without any melody, but probably much humour in
the words, judging by the shouts of laughter that burst from time
to time from all present.

---

[1] Parrot attained the extreme summit of Mount Ararat, Sept. 27, 1829. *Reise um Ararat*, Berlin, 1834, i. p. 159.

[2] See Appendix X.

[3] *Travels in the Central Caucasus and Bashan, including visits to Ararat and Tabreez, and ascents of Kazbek and Elbruz*, by Douglas W. Freshfield, 1869.

Our excellent host finished the evening by making a pleasant little speech, as a soldier in the service of His Imperial Majesty who was addressing a sailor of the Queen of England. We toasted their Majesties of Great Britain and Russia with honours, and thus brought to a close a day full of deep interest.

A MUSICAL PARTY.

CHAPTER XXIII.

THIRTY-SECOND DAY.

Lesser Ararat—The Persian frontier—A break-down—The Araxes—Its supposed ancient course—Return to Erivan—The Armenians—Their good qualities—Characteristics—Population—Religion—Patriotism—Sufferings—Road to Nahitchevan—Cosmetic waters there—Routes to Tiflis—Situation of Ani.

I NEED not keep secret the childish feeling of delight with which I gazed upon the mighty Ararat, the last thing at night, and again in the morning immediately upon rising. I gazed with earnest admiration, for it is in truth a noble and graceful mountain, almost symmetrical in its outlines, the lesser Ararat, perhaps because of its own conical form, looking almost dwarfed by the side of its great neighbour.   12,840

The Persian frontier is within ten miles of Aralyk, at Bouralan, a Cossack station near the Karà-sou or Karasynka, a small tributary of the Araxes. Persian territory is within pistol-shot of Bouralan, but a traveller proceeding to Persia would prefer the post-road which passes through Nahitchevan and Marhand to Tabreez.

As arranged the preceding evening, the Colonel took his seat in our carriage and we left Aralyk at 11 o'clock A.M. We had scarcely gone four miles when the *calèche* collapsed in the gentlest manner, and we fell tenderly into each other's arms; the break-down fortunately occurred near efficient aid, and I congratulated myself upon having stayed the night at the garrison, for such an accident after dark would have been exceedingly unpleasant. The Colonel instantly despatched a trooper to head-quarters for his own conveyance, and the other Cossacks, having dismounted, assisted the *yemstchyck* to detach the horses, and secure the two parts of the vehicle.

While this was being done we were treated to a little excitement, for three horses that had been tethered to each other gave the slip to the Cossack who was leading them, and galloped away over the plain, playing and frolicking in seeming enjoyment of their freedom; they kept increasing their distance, so as to preclude all hope of recapturing them immediately, when they suddenly wheeled and made straight for the barracks. The Colonel's carriage was soon with us, and at one o'clock we crossed the ferry of the Araxes.

This river, from 500 to 700 miles in its entire length, courses past Bouralan and along the Russo-Persian frontier to Karadoun, thence through the Mougan steppe until it unites with the Kour at Djevatt. The inference to be drawn on reading the account of Strabo is that the waters of the Araxes, a river well known to the geographer, discharged themselves into the Caspian Sea at a mouth other than that of the Kour; and in a paper[1] published some years ago at St. Petersburg, Professor Baer sought to demonstrate the probability of the fact, by tracing a supposed ancient course of the Araxes to the sea.

When on a journey from Lenkoran to Saljann, the Professor discovered what he presumed to have been a large river-bed on the steppe between the post-station of Pryshyb and Djeyran-bergska; he learnt from the natives that this river-bed, which they called a

---

[1] *Der alte Lauf des Armenischen Araxes*, von K. v. Baer. 19 Juin. 1857. *Bulletin de la classe des sciences hist. phil. et. pol. de l'Acad. Imp. de St. Pétersbourg.* Tome XIV. Nos. 20, 21, 22.

canal, goes straight to the sea, and that it commences near the lake Intcha, into which a stream of the same name falls, and he believes this canal to have communicated with the Araxes by junction with another canal called the Hardjy, which lies between the river Bolgary-tchaï and the Araxes, and crosses the frontier of Persia.

The Persians call the Araxes, Aras; its Armenian name is Eraskh, after Erasd, a descendant of Armenaz, the son of the first king of Armenia, 2107 B.C., who was the son of the patriarch Togarmah.[1]

We changed horses at Ahamzalou, and reached the town of Erivan at 4 P.M.

I may here appropriately observe, that during my intercourse with the Armenians in the Caucasus I found them at all times courteous and obliging, intelligent, and invariably good linguists; they are a laborious people whom nothing daunts, and their singular success in trade and commercial pursuits would appear to excite the envy of the populations among which they happen to live. They are more especially unpopular among the Turks and Tatars, who have a saying that it takes two Greeks to outwit a Jew, and three Jews to outwit an Armenian, while the Russians assimilate them to the Jews because of their penuriousness and love of money. An Armenian nobleman observed to me one day: 'My countrymen may assimilate the Jews, but they are wiser than the Jews, and therefore superior to them; for the Armenians are sensible of the advantages of a good education, and they avail themselves of opportunities for having their children brought up in conformity with the exigencies of the times, whereas our Jews quite ignore the necessity for education.' That of twenty-four successful

---

[1] Saint Martin, *Mém. sur l'Arménie*, i. p. 38, 207.

candidates at the University of Moscow for official appointments in 1873, thirteen were Armenians, is a fact that reflects no small credit on their proportion of the population of the Russian Empire.

The Armenians are a good-looking people, of fair complexion, with dark eyes and an abundance of black hair; they are in general of short stature, and disposed to obesity at a comparatively early age, the result in all probability of their inactive habits; it is said, however, that the mountaineers are a tall and robust race.

The Armenians wear a dress in many respects similar to that of the Georgians—viz., the high and tapering fur hat, garments of black material with loose sleeves, and the leather belt at the waist.

Their national appellation, according to the traditions of the country, is of the greatest antiquity, having descended to them from Aram, 1827 B.C., who was the fourth king; but Strabo relates that the country was so called after Armenus, a Thessalian, and one of the companions of Jason.

The following is the distribution of this industrious and thriving people:—

Turkish dominions	2,500,000 [1]
Russia	1,500,000
Persia	34,000
Austria	15,000
England; India and other British possessions	15,000
Roumania	8,000
Egypt	8,000
Other countries	120,000
	4,200,000 [2]

There are good reasons for believing that a few Armenians, but only a few, are Jacobites, a community so named after an obscure

---

[1] Estimated number at Constantinople, 200,000.
[2] *The Universal Year Book*, Mr. Hassarossian, Constantinople, 1873.

monk, but an earnest man, named Jacob Albardai, surnamed Baradæus or Zanzalus, who revived the sect of the Monophysites, and died Bishop of Edessus in 588. Now who were the Monophysites? They were also termed Eutychians, after Eutyches the abbot of a convent at Constantinople in 448, and pretended author of the doctrine which teaches that the divine nature of Christ had absorbed the human, and that therefore there was but one nature in Him—viz., the divine.[1] The Armenian Church, however, accepts the doctrine of Christ's manhood, and rejects with horror the doctrine of the Nestorians by which Mary is termed the mother of Christ; for in the Armenian Church, Mary is *Deipara*, the mother of God; and Mary, 'whose lowly spirit rejoiced in God her Saviour,' is made to take precedence of all saints. The Armenian Church is completely independent of every other, and has been so ever since the fourth General Council at Chalcedon in 451, when the absence of its bishops who were prevented from attending, produced an alienation that developed itself a century later into open rupture with other Christian churches.

No people are more deeply attached to their National Church than the Armenians, whose 'zeal under the rod of oppression is fervent and intrepid, and who have often preferred the crown of martyrdom to the white turban of Mahomet'; but this remarkable race has never succeeded in attaining a prominent position among nations in consequence of the warlike incursions and foreign occupations by which it has been troubled. It is the tenacity with which the Armenians have clung to their ancient traditions that has enabled them to preserve their nationality and language through centuries of terrible persecution and suffering without a

---

[1] *Ecclesiastical History*, &c., J. L. Mosheim, trans. by Arch. Maclaine, London, 1844.

parallel in history. During the Persian wars Armenia was invariably subject to Persia, until it was conquered by the Macedonians, 328 B.C. After the defeat of Antiochus, Armenia, which for a time became independent, was broken up into two kingdoms, those of Minor and Major Armenia, and when Armenia Minor became subject to Rome, Armenia Major was the theatre of war between the Romans and Parthians. Then came the oppression of the kings of the Sassanide dynasty, succeeded by the cruelty of the Osdigans, governors imposed on the Armenians by the Khalifs of Bagdad and Damascus; and in later times their unhappy country became the battle-field of the Turks and Persians, and they themselves the victims of the fanaticism and misrule of those Powers.

Since the final destruction of the city of Ani and the miserable termination to their attempt to form an independent kingdom under the house of Lusignan,[1] both of which events occurred in the fourteenth century, the Armenians have not hesitated to quit their country for foreign lands in the peaceful pursuit of commerce, and they are now distributed in many parts of the globe. In leaving their homes they have carried with them their literature, of which they are justly proud, for it dates from the fourth century, and they have thus never lost sight of their mother tongue,[2] even when colonising in small numbers. Their communities in various parts of Turkey, in Poland, at Amsterdam, Leipzic, Marseilles, and in British India all have printing-presses, and at Jerusalem the Armenians were the first to introduce printing.

Within easy distance of Erivan is Nahitchevan,[3] one of the

---

[1] Leon, the last king of Armenia, died at Paris in 1393. It is said that he sought the aid of Richard II., king of England, against the Turks.

[2] The Armenian language is Iranic, of the Aryan family.

[3] The cession of the Khanate of Nahitchevan to Russia was included in the treaty of Turkmantchai, 1828.

most ancient cities of Armenia. A day's journey on the post-road takes the traveller to Kyvrah or Hyrvah, the rest of the distance being accomplished on the morning of the second day. Nak'hdjavan means literally 'first descent,' a name given to the place because it was the first abode of Noah, after he came forth from the ark ;[1] it is also believed that the patriarch was buried there, and his tomb is shown to this day!

In the earliest Christian times, Nahitchevan was peopled by Jews until the fourth century, when it was ravaged by the Persians who destroyed 2,000 Armenian and 16,000 Jewish houses, and carried the inhabitants into captivity; it was also devastated by the Tatars in the thirteenth century. Nahitchevan was celebrated among the people in the East for its waters, which were the most cosmetic of all the towns of Iran. The bath of Zal Pasha was 'a soul-delighting bath, owing to its fine water and excellent attendance: the walls are faced with porcelain, and the floor paved with jasper, marble, and granite of various hues. In the large basin, ten feet square, which is underneath the cupola, the young people swim like angels of the sea; the bath-keeper every day pours into the basin a basket of rose-leaves, which attaching themselves to the bodies of the bathers, forms a kind of veil which is very becoming; thus they sport and play like peacocks and doves, their nakedness being covered by rose-leaves; in short, this bath is so delightful, that such poets as Hassan and Selman could not sufficiently praise it; how then could it be possible for me, poor Evliya, to succeed!'[2]

The return journey to Tiflis may be performed in the summer season by passing through Etchmiadzin and Mastara to Alexan-

---

[1] Joseph, *Antiq. of the Jews* I. iii. 5. Saint Martin, *Mém. sur l'Arménie*, i. p. 267.
[2] Evliya Effendi, *Travels*, &c., ii. p. 128.

dropol the principal Russian fortress and arsenal in the Caucasus, whence two roads, the one by Amamly and Karaklyss to Delyjann, the other through Beydeban, the Lorghys steppe and Sarvann, lead into the Erivan-Tiflis post-road. A new road from Alexandropol to Akstafa has lately been constructed.

Between Mastara and Alexandropol, but on Turkish territory, are the ruins of Ani, one of the most ancient capitals of the kingdom of Armenia and a royal residence from 961 until 1045, in which year King Kahig II. succumbed to the Emperor Constantine Monomachus who appointed a governor; at that period, the city consisted of 100,000 houses and 1,000 churches, when the usual form of administering an oath was to swear by the 'thousand and one churches.' Ani became the patriarchal seat from 993 until 1064, when it was taken by the Turks, who however permitted the head of the Armenian Church to return in 1082, his successors continuing to reside there until 1113. An Armenian chronicler thus quaintly describes the scene after the Mongols had destroyed Ani and slaughtered the inhabitants : 'Parents and their children lay over each other like heaps of stones ; priests and the ministers of the holy altars were stretched out here and there about the plain, where the earth was deluged with blood and the fat substance of the wounded ; delicate forms habitually washed with soap, had become livid and swollen. They who had never gone beyond the gates of the city were dragged into slavery shoeless and on foot, and the faithful who had partaken of the sacred body and blood of the Son of God, fed off the flesh of impure animals, and drank the milk of unclean mares...'[1]

In 1837 an English traveller 'found the area within the walls

---

[1] Kiracos de Gantzac, p. 127.

RUINS OF ANI.

of Ani covered with the prostrate remains of houses, the forms of some of which could be traced among the ruins, as also the outline of some of the streets. He was struck with the solid and beautiful masonry of what remained of the walls and palace, which seemed capable of resisting the wear of time for centuries if undisturbed by earthquake and the destroying hand of the Turk. Several apartments of the latter were entire with the exception of the roof, and on the former were many long Armenian inscriptions in excellent preservation."[1]

[1] *Notes of a Tour in Armenia in* 1837, by K. E. Abbott, Esq. H.M's. Consul at Teheran, published by the Royal Geographical Society, vol. xii. p. 214. 1841.

ARMS OF THE CHRISTIAN KINGS OF ARMENIA.

CHAPTER XXIV.

THIRTY-THIRD TO THIRTY-FIFTH DAY.

The Sardar's summer residence—Yousouf and Mariam—The last of Abdoullah—The Lesghians—Departure from Erivan—*Essáatyn*—Intractable *tchapars*—Insects—The Marie Canals—The Karayass steppe—Arrival at Tiflis—'The Merchant of Venice'—The Armenians enthusiastic—Defaulters in high places.

IT was the wrong time of year to select any route other than that by which I had already travelled, for my return journey to Tiflis; I therefore engaged the *calèche* which had conveyed the Governor from the capital, and fixed upon one o'clock as the hour of departure. In the course of the forenoon we went to the summer-palace of the Sardars, in a large garden or rather poplar plantation, on the right bank of the Zenga. The pavilion is an insignificant building gaudily painted throughout in poor imitations of the Persian style of decoration. As we crossed the bridge, we were reminded of the story of Yousouf who had posted himself on it to watch that part of the palace which contained the Sardar's women; and looking upwards at the apartments in the fortress, it is easy to picture to oneself the lattice of the window at which Mariam appeared when the amorous Georgian saw her lean forward, retreat, lean forward again, then more and more, until, by a sudden effort, he beheld her fair form in the air, falling down the giddy height.[1]

[1] Hajji Baba, II. c. xii.

The offer of a seat in the carriage was accepted by an Armenian gentleman, who was desirous of proceeding to Tiflis. He spoke Russian, French, and Turkish, and was, under the circumstances, a very desirable travelling companion. I took warm leave of their Excellencies, and by half-past one we were ascending the outskirts of the town over the horribly rough road already described.

As His Excellency waved a last adieu just before we started, Abdoullah, whose zeal was equal to that displayed on the first day of our meeting, busied himself stowing away some well-filled hampers kindly prepared with the usual forethought of my hosts. The Lesghian had been more than attentive to me during my stay at the residence, for he was ever at hand when I required him, but he unfortunately also persisted in his officiousness when I felt that I could have dispensed with his presence, and I found every attempt to control him quite hopeless; indeed, it was only by appearing displeased and offended that I was enabled to enjoy a little privacy. Abdoullah, who was a loyal and good servant, had accompanied his master from his native country, where the General had held a command. He was always attired in his national dress, which consists of a black gold-braided *tchekmett*, 'tunic,' with the *k'hazyr*, 'cartridge sockets,' on the breasts; trousers that tighten below the knees and at the ankles, where they meet a pair of sharp-pointed shoes with the toes slightly turned up; and a leathern belt with silver clasps and bosses, to which a *kynjàl*, a long single-barrelled pistol, and a sabre are suspended. He wore the *koudy*, and a *bourka* over the shoulders, a *bashlyk* being twisted around the neck. When Abdoullah rode out he carried a rifle at his back. Farewell, Abdoullah! thou hast shown how a Lesghian may be faithful and honest, as he is reputed to be brave, for the Lesghians are brave and hardy mountaineers.

Shortly after the annexation of Georgia to Russia, the Lesghians made a descent into Kakhety, and Prince Tzytzyanoff having despatched a force to punish them, they made their submission to Russia. In 1846 they attacked overwhelming numbers of their neighbours the wild Tchentchen, but were repulsed with heavy loss; the latter in their savage exultation fell upon the wounded, and, reverting to an ancient custom, cut off the hands of their enemies and nailed them to the doors of their dwellings. The Lesghians under Schamyl contributed greatly towards the subjugation of the Tchertchen, for the prophet knew how to avail himself of their religious fanaticism.

Although I was no longer travelling under the ægis of a Governor, I got over the ground at fair speed with the aid of some papers obtained at Erivan. The favourite and very unsatisfactory reply of Russians of every class and at all times is *scy-tchass*, 'this very hour'; it is significative of instant attention, but more frequently implies execution indefinitely deferred. The Armenians have an equivalent to the Russian words *scy-tchass*, which they employ in the same reassuring tone, and at the same valuation. *Essáatyn* is the invariable reply in these parts, and substitutes the provoking *scy-tchass*.

On reaching the boundary of the government of Erivan I began to experience greater difficulty in being attended to. At Delyjann, for instance, the *tchapars* positively refused to provide an escort notwithstanding the order I produced, so we drove to the quarters of the *palkovnyck*, 'colonel' in command of the garrison, and while my companion was preferring our complaint to that officer, the *tchapars* galloped up and took their position, one on each side of the carriage; *honores mutant mores!* The colonel, who was very civil, said he had no control over the *tchapars*, but would send forthwith to make the necessary inquiries. We were, however, spared further delay by the appearance of the escort, and proceeded after thanking the *palkovnyck* for his attention.

I passed one weary night at Elénovka, and another at Salaogly, at both of which places the usual tormentors must have been

THE RED BRIDGE.

in myriads, for, besides being teased by them, I felt them darting like flies at the close of summer. I envied the sound sleep my companion enjoyed on both nights, as if the voracious pests were a pleasant incentive, and his couch the most comfortable of beds instead of a hard board with his *bourka* only to wrap himself up in.

Abreast of Novo Alghetka, the third station from Tiflis, are seen to the right the Karayass plantations irrigated from the Kour. The canals, named Marie after the Empress, were constructed in 1865-67 by an English engineer[1] on the property of 'The Society for the Restoration of Christianity in the Caucasus.' The antelope *subgutterosa* is seen in droves at Karayass, where good shooting is to be had.

We arrived at Tiflis at 4 P.M.

In the evening we went to the theatre[2] at the Tamamshoff Karavansaraï; it has a pretty interior in the Moresque style. The bill for the evening was tempting, inasmuch as the first and last acts of the 'Merchant of Venice' were to be given by Armenian performers. The house was full and the audience seemed well pleased with the acting, for thunders of applause greeted the discomfiture of the Jew by Portia, a comely black-eyed Armenian; and when, towards the close of the first scene, Gratiano, a character that was well sustained, added exultingly—

> In christening thou shalt have two godfathers;
> Had I been judge, thou should'st have had ten more,
> To bring thee to the gallows, not the font—

the Armenians, usually so grave, showed their delight in noisy enthusiasm.

Performances by amateurs in Russian and in Georgian are also given at this theatre, and an Italian company is usually engaged; the good people of Tiflis, however, have been deprived the luxury of the Opera for two winters, a great disappointment to a musical people, forced to submit to the privation through no fault of their own. The directors, who are in the service of the State, contrived

---

[1] Mr. E. Legh Harris.
[2] This theatre has lately been destroyed by fire.

to squander in one season the Government subsidy for three years, amounting to a total of 90,000 roubles! The matter has never been cleared up, and although the delinquent officials in high places were removed from the management, they have been *appointed to still higher offices!*

GEORGIAN NOBLE.

CHAPTER XXV.

THIRTY-SIXTH AND THIRTY-SEVENTH DAYS.

Arrangements for crossing the great range—Outskirts of Tiflis—The 'Devil's knee'—First-class post-stations—Time service—A bad night—Ananour—Broad-tailed sheep—Siberian exiles—The Emperor's solicitude—Pasanaour—The Hefsours—The Ph'tchavy—Osset villages—M'lety—Ascent of the great range—Goudaour—The mountain spirit—Limits of vegetation—Tinted snow—Koby—Crystals and pyrites—A speculative *stóroj*—Kasbeck.

To perform the journey over the great range a carriage should be hired at the *Bureau des équipages de la Poste*, to be engaged by the week or for the trip to Vladykavkaz, and return if desired. In making the agreement at the *bureau* for a carriage and four post-horses, it should be stipulated that for the ascents from M'lety to Goudaour, and from Lars to Kasbeck on the journey up, and from Koby to Goudaour on the return journey, six horses shall be provided; this is essential, to avoid otherwise tedious and laborious climbing. No extra charge should be submitted to, for on proceeding on the descent, in reversing the order of stations just named, two horses only are attached to the carriage, thus making pre-payment correct for value to be received. The road between Tiflis and Vladykavkaz is so extensively travelled upon that horses are in continual demand; a courier might therefore be of service when working against time, escorts not being needed, nor are they to be obtained. Preferring not to overload the carriage, we dispensed with the courier, and having been favoured with a *kazyónnaya padarójnaya*[1] by one of the authorities, our way was considerably smoothed throughout.

A sufficient supply of provisions, to include bread, tea, sugar and wine, must not be forgotten, and the carriage should be ordered a full hour before the time fixed upon for starting.

We left Tiflis at 2 P.M., in a north-west direction above the right bank of the Kour, passing at the outskirts a monument of porphyry surmounted by a cross, which marks the spot where the Emperor Nicholas was thrown out of his carriage, in October 1837, when upon his return to Russia. A mile beyond is the Gastýnnytza slyoss, 'Inn of Tears,' a roadside hostel, where Georgians who are proceeding abroad—for some still consider Russia a foreign country—take leave of the friends who have accompanied them thus far. Hence the road lies between a range of low hills and the river, the summit of Kasbeck becoming the *point de vue*. Crossing a small stream, the Vera, we entered the Dygomy valley, and then came to a defile formed by lofty cliffs, those on our left being pierced with numerous crypts which are quite inaccessible.

Before reaching a sharp bend in the river, called by the Georgians, Namouh'lya, 'Devil's knee,' we passed the remains of an ancient bridge said to have been constructed by Pompey. After the Roman general had traversed Iberia and routed the Albanians on the banks of the Cyrnus he re-crossed the river, but met with great resistance, for the barbarians had fenced it on their side with palisades. Notwithstanding their opposition, Pompey marched

---

[1] 'Crown padarójnaya,' an official order for horses, for the use of all persons travelling on special service, and which takes precedence of the ordinary *padarójnaya*. It usually entitles the bearer to the luxury of occupying a 'general's room,' exempts him from detention at tollgates, and secures to him every attention on the part of the station-master.

into their country, seized upon Aramazt, the acropolis[1] (*temp.* Artaces, King of Karthly 81–66 B.C.), and crossed the river. The fortress of Aramazt[2] was within a short distance of the ruins of the bridge.

From M'zhett, the first station, a perfectly straight road bisects the fertile plain of Tzylkann. When Prince Bariátinsky was Governor-General, well-built post-houses were erected on the new road and furnished with every comfort for travellers, the first-class stations being at Tzylkann, M'lety, and Kasbeck; all are now in a dirty and discreditable condition, with no attendance but that of a *stóroj*, invariably drunk and incapable. 'Who is responsible for the direction of these post-stations? Is there no *maître de poste*?' I asked a colonel who was travelling on the road. 'Mais, mon Dieu! certainement; il fait sa visite une fois, deux fois, par an, mais on sait toujours d'avance le jour de son arrivée, et on lui prépare tout, de manière qu'il est persuadé qu'il n'y a pas de quoi se plaindre.'

'But your governors of provinces and other great people?'

'Toujours la même chose—on leur fait arrêter les chevaux et préparer leurs appartements.'

'And other officials, and ladies and gentlemen?'

'Eh! hé! chez nous en Russie on ne fait pas grande attention à ces choses-là, et si même on voulait se plaindre, à qui s'adresserait-on? Croyez-vous, monsieur, qu'on ajusterait les choses? Non, chez nous on vit d'un jour à l'autre. D'ailleurs, si la parole est l'argent, le silence est le seul bien-être!'

This is a sentiment frequently uttered by men of education who feel their utter helplessness and the hopelessness of seeing any social improvements under the present baneful system of

---

[1] *Plutarch's Lives*, Langhorne. Dion. Cass. xxxvi., xxxviii. [2] See page 176.

ANANOUR.

centralisation so universal throughout the empire; 'a principle which secures the momentary strength, but ever ends in the abrupt destruction, of states'—an evil that generates such parasites as by servility understand zeal, and by time service duty.

On leaving Tzylkann we entered the valley of Araby spyr, 'Arab's mouth,' and turned up a winding ascent to the left, reaching an upland named Bygmys Myndory, on which is the lake Bazalet. We stopped for the night at the station, a mile or two from the town of Doushett which was the favourite residence of King Vakhtang Heraclius.

Vermin, and the commotion caused by the frequent arrival and departure of travellers, disturbed our rest throughout the night, and we were only too glad to leave the unpleasant post-house with the first relay of horses we could get in the morning. Our *jemstchyck* was a Malakan, who entertained us on the road by recounting wonderful stories of the fortress of Ananour, for which place we were bound.

On approaching Ananour, attention is at once drawn to the picturesque castellated walls and watch-towers on an elevation above the village. Within the old stronghold are two churches that were erected in 1704 by George, *erystav* of Aragva, who came to a tragic end in 1737, when a certain Tchantchy was the chief of a neighbouring *erystvat* called Ksan. A lengthened state of feud between these two chieftains, culminated in the *erystav* of Aragva carrying off by force the wife of one Jesé, brother of the *erystav* of Ksan, and making her over to the Persians. Tchantchy determined upon revenge, and accordingly placed himself at the head of a body of Lesghians whose alliance he had secured, and laid siege to Ananour where George resided with his family; the place was carried by assault, and all the defenders put to death. The residence of the *crystav* is to the right on entering the fortification at the square tower, and the burial-place of the unfortunate George and of his children is pointed out inside the small church. The larger church has many sculptured ornamentations on the exterior, the most striking being a large cross—a representation of St. Nina's cross of vine-stems; it is supported by two chained lions, and strangely enough the grapes are being devoured by demons.

From Ananour the road lies by the banks of the Aragva through the valley of the same name, where large flocks of sheep and goats were grazing; the rams and goats were fine longhorned animals, and among the sheep was a species with very broad tails, but that member had scarcely attained in any instance the 'full cubit's breadth' of the Arabian sheep described by Herodotus.[1] Unlike the shepherd on the Karayass steppe, who is armed to the teeth, here his sole weapon is the crook.

At this part of our journey the *yemstchyck* pointing ahead, cried out *Kátorjnye! Kátorjnye!* 'convicts, convicts'! and in a few moments we approached five men in fetters and under a strong escort: they were resting by the roadside and having a meal. 'Where are you going to?' we asked a soldier. 'To Vladykavkaz.' 'And where are they going to?' we again inquired, pointing to the prisoners. 'To Siberia,' was the ominous reply. One of the unhappy men was a fine-looking fellow, apparently of birth and education; he may have been a political offender, for there was no fraud or murder on his handsome and open countenance.

It seemed hard that these men should be travelling on foot. So far back as the year 1867, Baron Viliot (for some time

---

[1] Hero l. iii.

Governor of Odessa) obtained from the Minister of the Interior his approval of a plan by which exiles to Siberia were for the future to be spared from journeying on foot in winter, but should be conveyed to their destination by rail, river, or road, according to circumstances. This improvement in the treatment of prisoners had been preceded by a slight amelioration in their condition due to the provisions made by a committee which sat in 1861, and which led to the consideration of fresh reforms. In former days the unfortunate creatures had to walk in all weathers, so that many sank on the way, while others contracted sores which caused much suffering and frequently resulted in permanent injury.

It was in 1858 that, at the command of the Emperor, exiles and prisoners under sentence of transportation to Siberia were for the first time sent from St. Petersburg to Moscow by rail, early evidence of the humanity of the beneficent Alexander, then only in the third year of his reign. In olden times prisoners were sent from all parts of the Empire to Moscow, Nijni Novgorod, and Kharkoff as the great centres, and from those cities they were forwarded to Kasan the chief head-quarters, whence they were distributed among the towns of Perm, Yekaterynbourg, Tumen, and Tomsk across the river Irtisch. Stations at which to rest for the night were erected at a distance apart of 20 *versts*, and they still exist except where transport by river and rail is available; they may be noticed in the Caucasus and in the Crimea.

At the narrowest part of the valley of the Aragva are the Tchertaly and Vanselop'pe, two old Georgian forts which guarded the pass, and a few *versts* beyond is the post-station of Pasanaour. 3,621 Here has lately been erected a church gaudily painted in questionable style, after the manner of many sacred edifices at Moscow, and by no means producing the pleasing contrast to the huts and *doukanns* in the village, that was probably aimed at in its external decoration.

At Pasanaour horses may be obtained to ride to the Hefsour villages in the hills. The nearest is ten miles up the Bakourheby rivulet, but the largest, named Ah'ho, distant thirty-three miles, can be reached in summer only, for the Hefsours are completely snowed up in winter. The Hefsours or Khevsours,[1] anciently called the Ph'khovel, seldom quit their impregnable homes, and are therefore reproached by their neighbours with being wanting in warlike qualities. Although nominally Christians, they reject the use of churches and the service of priests; St. George is their god of war, but they have other saints, and elect a *kadah'h* 'elder' when they meet for prayer. The Hefsours claim descent from some Crusaders, who they say halted in Kakhety on their return from the Holy Land. When dressed in his best, the Hefsour wears a shirt of mail over a gold-braided garment dotted with small crosses; from his *tchaktchaoun*, 'helmet,' falls a net of steel; he has knee-pieces over short tight trousers, and carries a buckler. The females wear a petticoat with tunic, and bind up their heads in a black kerchief. The Hefsours are a rude tribe, proud and supercilious, settling their differences by hand-to-hand combats, a wound received in a duel being indicated by a piece of red cloth sewn to the garment over the hurt. They are a dirty people, and somewhat inimical to Russia, terming the soldiers of the Tzar, *bahahè*, 'frogs,' from the colour of their uniforms.

To the east of the Hefsours are the Ph'tchavy, another rude tribe of puzzling religious tendencies, and very superstitious.[2]

Beyond Pasanaour, we observed about the heights numerous

---

[1] The Hefsours number about 5,000.
[2] Brosset, *Hist. de la Géor.* i. p. 126.

small settlements consisting of flat-roofed cottages and trapezoid towers peculiar to the Ossets, not readily noticed at a distance from being built of the same dark-grey stone as the rocky ground on which they stand; they overlook the luxuriant valley of Kvyshety, irrigated by the Goud that falls into the Aragva. It was a pretty sight to see the banks of the rivulet profusely covered with snowdrops, crocusses, and forget-me-nots.

M'lety, which station we reached at one o'clock, is the rendezvous of the caravans about to ascend or that have descended the pass. Whilst essaying to obtain admission into the small village church, said to be charged with many ancient and interesting relics, two men—one an Osset, the other a Georgian—advised us to ride over the hills; in the one case to visit an Osset village at half a day's journey, called Lomyss-kyshell, promising we should see grand ruins and strange tombs; the Osset probably meant Lomysa, where was the ancient Church of St. George, at one time rich in golden and silver vessels.[1] The Georgian on his part proudly claimed Saksann-kyshell as being superior in interest.

The post-house was in a condition filthy beyond description, and the officious and offensively tipsy *stòroj* was only got rid of after some trouble. We had a hasty lunch in our anxiety to get away from such unpleasant quarters, and proceeded the instant fresh horses were ready. An excellent bridge spans the Aragva, from the left bank of which we commenced the ascent of the great range on one of the most remarkable of mountain roads, along a succession of cliffs that have necessitated short zigzags and sharp turnings until the summit is gained. A slab let into the rock at the steepest part of the road records the completion of the superb work during the Governorship-General of Prince

4,961

---

[1] Brosset, *Des. Géog.* p. 223.

Bariátinsky.[1] As we toiled upwards and looked over the brink into the Tchórtova Dalýna, at the bottom of which courses the Aragva, we got an occasional glimpse of the old road completed in the reign of Alexander I., with here and there a hospice. Lermontoff, who knew this country well, asserts that the word is from *tcherta*, 'line,' and not *tchort*, 'devil,' because the *dalýna*, 'valley,' marked the ancient frontier of Georgia.[2]

It took us two hours and twenty-one minutes to get over the ten miles from M'lety to the next station of Goudaour, where the thermometer in the observatory marked 30°. We were in a region completely covered with snow, with not a speck of colour to be seen in any direction over the vast expanse of white that reached to the mountains of Galabdour and Shebysat. The Krestóvaya 7,977 gará, 'mountain of the cross,' a little way beyond the station of Goudaour which it overlooks, is the highest point over which the road is constructed; the cross on a granite basement was erected in 1834 by General Yermóloff, on the site of a cross said to have been placed there by Queen Thamar.

8,175(a) Kouroush (*a*) in Daghestan, Kalota (*b*) in Ossety, and Goudaour,
7,746(b) are the three highest inhabited points on the mountains of the Caucasus. Goudaour, a corruption of Goud-aoul,[3] is in the district of Ossety, and the home of a mountain spirit.

The following is the legend of the mountain spirit, Goud : —

'There lived in the *aoul* a poor family blessed by the Lord with a daughter, for the Lord is merciful to the poor; there was no finer child in Ossety than Nina, who was the admiration of all people, and the merchants as they went by in caravans, made her presents of fine and bright-coloured stuffs. The spirit of the

---

[1] The cost of the great military road into Georgia amounted to nearly 4,000,000*l.*
[2] Lermontoff, *Gheroy nashevo vremeny*. *Byela*, ii., p. 264.   [3] *Aoul*, village.

mountain whose name is Goud, had never in his long life beheld such a beauty, and like everybody else he fell in love with her and adored her with all the passion of youth. When Nina scrambled up the mountain, Goud was sure to make the way easy for her; and when she went in search of flowers, he put the sweetest and prettiest within her reach. Nina's father had five rams, but none ever went astray, nor were any devoured by wolves; in fact Nina became like a queen in Goud's kingdom, for the old man was very, very fond of her. In this manner fifteen years passed away, and the child grew to be a beautiful girl, old Goud's love increasing with her growth. He wondered whether from being a mighty spirit, he might not become a simple mortal, even a poor Osset; but the maiden never noticed his love, for she was too much taken up with her neighbour young Sasyko, a handsome and nimble youth who never missed a shot with his gun; he could dance the Ossety dance, and was quite accomplished in the *lezghynka*. Old Goud became so jealous that when Sasyko went out shooting he made him lose his way by spreading a thick fog before him, or by having him caught in a blinding snowstorm.

'At last winter set in and old Goud was not able to see his love as often as before, but Sasyko and Nina met daily. Goud was aware of this, so that he stormed and raged until he was beside himself. It happened, however, that one day when Sasyko and Nina were alone in the *saklya*,[1] Goud blew a great avalanche over them; far from being alarmed, the lovers were quite pleased at the chance which would leave them undisturbed, so they made a nice fire, and went on talking together. After some hours spent in this way, they began to feel that although their hearts were full their stomachs were quite empty; but finding a

[1] Hut.

couple of cakes and some cheese, they appeased their hunger for a time. The following day, however, the *saklya* resounded with cries of despair, for they no longer thought of their love, being tormented with hunger. A third day passed away, and on the fourth, death seemed inevitable. Sasyko moved restlessly from corner to corner, until of a sudden he turned and fixed his sunken eyes on Nina, and seizing her firmly, buried his teeth in her shoulder. Nina screamed and fell to the ground. At that moment noises were heard and the door flew open. Nina and Sasyko rushed to their deliverers; but they loved each other no longer, for their love had turned to loathing. Old Goud was so delighted at this termination to Nina's attachment that he laughed, and laughed quite loud, until he shook a great shower of stones into the valley, where they have remained to this day. This is the way our mighty Goud laughs.'[1]

The highest snow-line on the mountains of the range is at an altitude of 9,600 feet to 12,200 feet above the level of the Black Sea, there being a difference of upwards of 1,000 feet between the southern and northern slopes, while the limits of vegetation are from 9,854 feet to 11,000 feet.

Limit at which the beech-tree will grow				8,300 feet
,,	,,	barley	,,	8,100 ,,
,,	,,	corn	,,	7,906 ,,
,,	,,	wheat	,,	7,400 ,,
,,	,,	the vine	,,	3,570 ,,[2]

Beyond Goudaour a party of soldiers and labourers were employed shovelling the snow off the road and piling it up at the sides, where it formed great walls; their eyes were well pro-

---

[1] *Ystorya vayny y vladytchestva Reussyh' na Kavkazye.* Doubrovine, St. Petersburg, 1871, i. p. 324 326.

[2] From reports made at the Observatory, Tiflis.

tected against snow blindness, but they were badly provided with feet covering. The Ossets, whose homes are in these mountains are bound to assist in keeping the public ways clear for traffic during the winter months, and on this condition they are exempt from paying taxes, a boon to a people living on barren and unproductive soil; for the Ossets in these parts are indigent in the extreme, and depend upon the plains for their supplies. We thought of the poor exiles we saw in the morning, and of their hard fate in having to trudge over so much bleak and cheerless ground, covered with snow two and three feet deep.

I do not know whether it was an optical illusion, but it appeared to us more than once that there was a pale rose-coloured tint about the snow. It did not show on the surface, but rather on the side of the road facing the east, under a gloomy and wintry sky, after the sun had dipped behind the mountains to the west.

We descended rapidly to the valley of the Terek, feeling the cold more keenly than we did at Goudaour. The road, like the river, winds in great curves until it reaches the station at Koby, a 6,500 short distance from the picturesque church and tower of the village. Some pretty specimens of crystal and pyrite were offered for sale by the tipsy *störoj*, who buys of the mountaineers and speculates with travellers. Collectors would do well to ask for ores at all the stations from Koby to Vladykavkaz.

We had purposed visiting the troglodyte caves occupied by some Tchentchen at a distance of two miles from this station; but the approach is by a somewhat difficult path, and the late hour obliged us to give up the idea.

At a couple of miles beyond Koby we obtained our first good view of Kasbeck. It was quite dark when we drove through the valley of Zion and crossed the Tchórnaya retchka to the Kasbeck station, which we reached at eight o'clock. The *stóroj* was a smart youth of eighteen with an eye to business, for he pressed us very hard, on the shortest possible acquaintance, to buy his crystals, pyrites, and horns of the tour; and then after a generous allowance of *sey-tchass*, served us with a very creditable steak, a pleasant change from the cold meat diet of the last twenty-four hours.

It was a glorious night, of which we took full advantage, for we never tired of looking at the bell-topped Kasbeck towering towards the star-lit sky in its chilly covering, not mightily, scarcely majestically, but with a proud individuality most interesting to behold.

10.30 P.M. ther. 37°. (March.)

A DOUKANN.

CHAPTER XXVI.

THIRTY-EIGHTH DAY.

Legends of Kasbeck—The cross—Superstition—The Capra ibex—Osset respect for the dead—The Kysty—Their pagan altar—The river Terek—Pass of Darial—Russian fort—Queen Dary'ya—Dar-i-alan, described by authors—Lars—Tribes of the Ossets—Balta—Arrival at Vladykavkaz—Visit to the Governor—The Club—Emancipation of Russian ladies—Inns and private houses—Russian character—District of Ossety—The Ossets—Their history—The Ossets and the Alains.

WITH the aid of a liberal allowance of *persydsky parashok*,[1] we contrived to pass a tolerably good night in the 'apartments for generals,' kept in fair order at this station. We were also fortunate in the weather, which being bright and clear enabled us to enjoy a perfect view of the great mountain.

Kasbeck is called M'kynvary, 'ice mountain,' by the Georgians; 16,546 Ourz-K'hoh, 'white mountain,' by the Ossets, Tcherysty tchoub, 'mountain of Christ,' and Bett-le-hem by the Christian Ossets, and Beshlem-K'hoh, 'mountain of Bethlehem,' by the Christian Tchentchen, for the belief exists that, high up Kasbeck, amid the perpetual snows, is the tent of Abraham, in which are placed for security many treasures, including the holy manger brought from Bethlehem.

About one hundred years ago, an aged priest in the odour of sanctity ascended the mountain accompanied by his son, for the

[1] Insect powder.

purpose of recovering the sacred relics; the old man succumbed to fatigue, but the son returned bringing with him a piece of the manger, which was presented to the king, Heraclius II.

The ascent to Kasbeck from the village and post-station lies through Gvelety, four miles beyond the post-house, and Gherghety, the village seen from the station. The path leads

KASBECK FROM THE POST-STATION.

thence to the right of the cliff on which are the ruins of the Monastery of Sameba, 'the Holy Trinity,' a sanctuary in which at one time were deposited the treasures of the Church of Mtzkhetha and the cross of St. Nina.[1] The ascent is thence continued in a westerly direction towards the glacier of Orzvery to the south-east

[1] Brosset. *Desc. Géog.* p. 227.

of the summit. Two other formidable glaciers are the Devdoraky to the north-east and the Abanot.[1]   9,050   7,600

Between the glaciers Abanot and Orzvery there is a stone cross, 5 feet in height; near it are several crypts in the rock, in one of which the Virgin Mary passed a night when on her way from Egypt into Ossety! An Armenian gentleman, whose route on his partial ascent of Mount Kasbeck has just been described, related to us that when he desired to go to the cross and crypts, the mountaineers refused to accompany him; for they said that if a mortal should presume to approach the cross he would die, and his death would be followed by a deluge. He finally prevailed upon one man to go with him, and as they were traversing the glacier and nearing the sacred symbol, the terrified creature knelt at every half-dozen steps he took and crossed himself. When it was known upon the gentleman's return to the village that the cross had actually been reached, the people murmured, and matters looked worse when a slight shower passed over their heads. Notwithstanding, however, the misgivings of the guides, the night was passed in the village without any molestation, and as the morning was fine the natives gathered around the stranger, the Christians to cross themselves, the rest, who were pagans, to look on with perfect indifference.

At 9 A.M. we left the station, crossing the Kouron, or Ara-don, 'mad river,' a torrent so named from the impetuosity of its waters. Four miles beyond, the Terek is forded at the path that conducts

---

[1] Kasbeck was ascended for the first time in 1868 by Messrs. D. W. Freshfield, A. W. Moore, and C. C. Tucker. Freshfield, *Travels in the Central Caucasus, &c.*

Mr. P. M. informed me at Tiflis that the statement made by these gentlemen to the effect that they had attained the summit of this mountain was generally doubted, until he himself had reached the top by following their route. I observed to the Russian gentleman that the character of these Englishmen needed no justification.

to Gvelety, a village where guides are obtained for ascending to the glaciers, or for stalking and tracking the wild goat *Capra ibex*, called also *Capra Caucasica*, but best known as the tour,[1] and the chamois, *Rubri capra*, both to be found on Mount Kourou, and in the Amgatchy mountains to the east of the Terek.

A chief of Gvelety named Tzogol, a noted huntsman we saw at Kasbeck, promised to have some large game ready for us by the time we returned from Vladykavkaz, but when we stopped at Kasbeck a few days later we were disappointed in not finding any. A death had occurred in the village of Kasbeck, and Tzogol said that it was the custom among the Ossets (who here belong to the Dygorty tribe) not to fire so long as a corpse lay unburied; his people respected the customs of their neighbours, and he was therefore unable to have any sport. In connection with this usage, Poushkin relates having visited an Osset *aoul* near Vladykavkaz at a moment that preparations were being made for a funeral. He found a crowd in front of the *saklya* and an *araba* with two oxen in the court; the relatives and friends of the dead man were continually entering the *saklya*, beating their foreheads with their fists, shrieking and crying until the corpse was carried out, in the Russian poet's own words, wrapped in a *bourka*

> . . . like a warrior taking his rest,
> With his martial cloak around him,

and placed in the *araba*; one of the men then took the gun of the deceased, shook out the charge, and laid it by his side.[2]

There is a village on the mountain not far from Gvelety, called Goslett, where the Kysty have an altar—a cairn of stones upon

---
[1] Dubois, iv. p. 279. The Ossetian name of the tour is *dsaäouter*.
[2] *Sotchynenya Poushkyna*, v. p. 63.

which are piled the horns of the tour for the worship of Da-ba, a Supreme Being of whom they can give no account; but they also worship St. Matthew, after whom they have named a mountain, and sacrifice to the Virgin Mary at childbirth. The Kysty are a tribe of the Tchentchen who live to the east of Darial.

In the valley of the Terek, the road winds with the rushing and impetuous river, the bed of which is on an incline of one foot in sixty. We entered a gorge of lofty rocks of basalt, granite and porphyry, several hundred feet in height, with huge masses on either side above us looking as if they must fall, and destroy the road or turn aside the river's course. As we neared the actual pass of Darial the naked rocks rose higher towards the heavens, threatening in some parts to exclude their light; and when the precipitous summits closed with each other, presenting themselves before us at every turning we took in the road, we almost felt as if we had been led by enchantment into the depths of some vast chasm. There is nothing to relieve the interminable nudity but a little wood that shows itself from time to time up the narrow side glens, or through the topmost fissures on the heights, for

> Ev'n cold Caucasian rocks with trees are spread,
> And wear green forests on their chilly head.

We had come prepared for some little excitement which we imagined the difficult and perhaps dangerous nature of a drive through this famous defile would occasion, but the road is excellent, and constructed almost parallel to the Terek. At the narrowest part on a level with the river is the Russian fort of Darial, and 4,122 abreast of it one of the toll-bars where travellers with the ordinary *padarójnaya* are stopped and put to delay and inconvenience, owing to the sluggish manner in which those papers are usually examined by the soldiers on duty; but as we held our order aloft, pointing to the additional black stamp, the bar was instantly raised, and we passed on without molestation.

Half-way up the cliff on an escarpment above the river's left bank are the remains of the old fortress of Darghalan or Darialan, the *pas d'armes* of many a king of Georgia. The first mention made of this fortress in the annals is in the reign of Azouc or Armazd, 87-103 A.D.[1] A Georgian legend thus ascribes to this ancient stronghold the name of Darial.

Once upon a time there lived a great queen renowned for her beauty and powers of fascination, whose name was Dary'ya. She was in the habit of occasionally inviting the neighbouring lords to her castle, that she might make the choice of one for a lover. But Dary'ya was as fickle as she was beautiful, cruel as she was engaging, and soon getting tired of the husband she had chosen, threw him over the parapet into the river. She would then select another lover by a similar stratagem, and destroy him in the same manner; and so the castle has been named after the great queen Dary'ya.

The defile of Darial is described by Strabo as a road by the side of the river Aragus, of such narrow dimensions as to admit of one man only passing at a time.[2] Pliny is more explicit, for he takes care to distinguish the *portæ Caucasiæ* from the *portæ Caspiæ* at Derbent; the former he says is a great work of nature, *ingens naturæ opus*, which divides the great mountain chain, and the castle was known as that of Cumania.[3] The Georgians anciently called this the defile of the Aragva because the river of that name flowed

---

[1] Brosset, *Hist. de la Géor.* i. p. 70. In the reign of Mervan I. 162-112 B.C. appears the name Daroubal, *l.c.* i. p. 46, which Dubois believes to apply equally to the gate of Darial.

[2] Strabo, XI. iii. 5.   [3] Pliny, VI. xii.

to the south of it; they called the Terek also the Aragva, imagining them to be one and the same river.

Ali-Abou-Hassan Maçoudi, an Arabian who travelled over the Mahomedan provinces between the years 930–940, wrote of the fortress which was five days' journey from Tiflis, that it was constructed by Isfendiar, king of Persia, the son of Joustasp, for the purpose of resisting the Alains in their irruptions on the mountains of the Caucasus; he describes the fort as being on a steep rock and seeming to be suspended in the air.[1] The eastern geographer Emaddeddin Aboulfeda, 1271–1331, wrote that the principal fortress of the Alains, Bab-al-Alan, 'gate of the Alains,' was one of the strongest places in the world, being 'covered with clouds as if with a turban ...,' and situated on a mountain that stretched towards the iron gate,[2] meaning Derbent.

The origin of the name Darial is doubtful; according to Saint Martin, the Ossets pronounced the word Daïran, and the Georgians called the defile Khevys-kary, 'gate of the valley.'[3]

Dar-yol signifies in Turkish 'narrow road,' or 'path.'

Professor Brosset believes the name to be derived from the Persian, Dar-i-alan, 'gate of the Alains,' and asserts the existence of the word Darialan in a MS. of the tenth or eleventh century, but it does not appear where the MS. was consulted.[4]

At one part of the defile the *yemstchyck* pointed to the position of a spring, at this time of the year covered with snow, whence he said issued warm water, smelling strongly of sulphur and disagreeable to the taste, but of which people drank when they were

---

[1] Maçoudi, *Les prairies*, & c., p. 42.
[2] *Géographie d'Aboulfeda*, trans. Reinaud, 1848, ii. p. 287.
[3] Saint Martin, *Mém. sur l'Arménie*, ii. p. 193.
[4] Brosset, *Rev. Archéo.* Rapp. i. p. 96.

ill. Might not this be the stream of an 'abominable odour' which Pliny says was below the gates?[1]

3,682 At Lars, the next station at which we changed horses, we found a couple of Russians smoking lustily, and swallowing *vodka* in marvellous style. Being smartly attended upon, we were soon covering ground at a fast rate in the valley, which widens considerably at Djerahoffsky, a Russian fortification garrisoned in summer for the purpose of military exercises.

The numerous old towers on the heights would produce a far more picturesque effect, but for the general nakedness of the hills and the almost entire absence of anything like forest land. It was only by mercilessly felling the trees, that the Russians were able to overcome the stubborn resistance of the mountain tribes and put an end to their guerilla style of warfare; they levelled whole forests, brought up their artillery, and formed intrenched camps. When it was announced to Schamyl that his enemies were cutting down the trees and advancing, he exclaimed, 'Now that the Russians are clearing away the woods, I perceive that Woronzoff has discovered the secret of my strength.'

Allusion has been made to the Dygorty Ossets; we were now among another tribe, the Tagaour, the supposed descendants of a fugitive king of Armenia, whose name they have inherited. There are two other tribes of Ossets: the Kourtalyn, who are the neighbours of the Tagaours, and the Alaghyrs, in the valley of the river
2,754 Ardonn. The Dygorty are reputed the bravest.

As we approached the last station on our journey, Balta, we left the steep slopes behind and entered the plain. At one o'clock we crossed the Terek over a handsome iron bridge, and entering
2,429 the town of Vladykavkaz alighted at the post-station.

[1] Pliny, VI. xii.

SOCIAL EVILS.

We lost no time in calling with an introduction upon his Excellency the Governor,[1] who received us very courteously, and promised any assistance we might need.

In the same building with the post-station is the club-house, a large suite of apartments handsomely furnished. It was a guest night, but as dancing, the usual way of spending it, is forbidden during Lent, these Sunday evenings are set apart for the reception of married ladies only, a large gathering of whom we found distributed at eight or ten card-tables, where they were engaged at whist or *impérial* with the assiduity of ancient dowagers, while a military band was playing some lively airs in the gallery of the ball-room. None of these ladies could have been over thirty. With the exception of three or four smart-looking young officers who were making a decided set at as many flowers, all the gentlemen were in the *buffet*, a stifling and reeky apartment with every window and door closed, smoking zealously, drinking, and making great noises; and in this sociable way the time was spent until one in the morning. *Vive la bagatelle!*

The blowing of the *zourná*, and the beating of the *nahará*, attracted our attention at a very late hour, and with a feeling of curiosity, we turned into the side street whence the sounds proceeded, to find a crowded procession, led by the musicians and people carrying lanterns, in which several men were each bearing on their heads an enormous tray, piled with apparel and other

---

[1] General Loris Melikoff is one of the few Armenians who have risen to distinction and honours in the Russian service. At nine-and-twenty he attained the rank of colonel and held the responsible post of commandant at Kars, when that fortress was restored to Turkey at the close of the late war. Still in the prime of life, he is aide-de-camp to the Emperor, governor of one of the most important provinces in the Caucasus, and commander-in-chief over the imposing force of 40,000 men.

There are 501,483 souls in the province of the Terek. (Census 1873.)

VOL. I.   U

effects. They constituted the trousseau and wedding gifts that were being removed after the consummation of the marriage, from the house of her parents to the bride's new home, a Georgian custom, now prevalent among the Christian populations throughout the Caucasus.

Vladykavkaz, from *viadyett*, 'to hold,' *Kavkazom*, 'the Caucasus,' was founded in 1785 by Potyómkyn over the site of the Osset village Zaloutch, called by the mountaineers Terek Kaleh, and Kapou Kaya, 'gate to the rocks,' at a time that it was of considerable importance to the Russians as a post of defence against the mountain tribes; it is now a fair specimen of a Russian provincial town, with its fine broad streets, either very dusty or very muddy, laid out at right angles, and planted with trees between rows of houses irregular in their size, a few being of stone, some of brick but more of wood. There is the conspicuous residence for the Governor, numerous whitewashed churches with green roofs and domes, the practical fire-brigade watch-tower, a *gastynny dvor*, 'bazaar,' a boulevard, and a large untidily kept garden for the recreation of the public; whilst the numerous uniforms, civil and military, testify to the predominating influence of absolute power.

The population of Vladykavkaz amounts to 15,000 souls;[1] it was raised to an *oblastny gorod*, 'provincial town,' in 1861, and has for many years been the point of transit for goods passing into the Caucasus, and the halting-place of travellers. That the thousands of Russians who pass through the town annually, are content to put up with the discomfort attending the limited and distasteful accommodation available in it, is a significant fact. There is nothing at Vladykavkaz with the least pretension to

---

[1] In 1862, when the population was 3,558, the revenue of the town amounted to 19.532 roubles; in 1874 it attained the sum of 40,953 roubles.

being a hotel, the best inn being bad, and that the uncomfortable and unclean post-house; the same may be said of other towns in Russia.[1] At St. Petersburg, Moscow, Kieff, and Odessa, the hotels are quite as good as will be found in most Continental states, but they have been introduced to meet the requirements of the many foreigners who are continually passing through those cities. That the progress of civilisation in the country is sluggish is evinced by the noxious condition of inns and post-houses, which swarm with all manner of insects, and where, as well as at railway stations and in numerous private houses, the absolute indispensability of a human habitation either does not exist at all, or is allowed to remain in a filthy and disgusting state, landlords and tenants alike scarcely caring to remedy the evil. To this should be added the swinish condition in which the better classes compel their dependants to live, for on the premises of some of the first people in the land even, the sleeping apartments allotted to domestics are usually such, that an English farmer would reasonably hesitate before he sheltered his cows in one of them for a night. The fact is undeniable that propriety is far from being understood in Russia as it is in England; and this is probably owing to the slothful temperament of its people, for the *vis inertiæ* of a Russian is proverbial; the necessity for the least exertion becomes a nauseous and laborious task to him, and he is content to put up with any discomfort, however unseemly and uncommendable, rather than suffer his indolent spirit to be disturbed. The truth is that Russians at home are Oriental in their habits, yet there are many who feel, that 'man should have many wants, for wants are not only the sources of enjoyment, they are the sources of improvement; and that nation will be the most

[1] The inns at Vladykavkaz are the Ivanoff and Hector.

enlightened among whose populace they are found the most numerous.'

Vladykavkaz is at the frontier of the country known as Ossety, which is bounded on the north by the Kabardines, on the east by the Tchentchen, on the south by the Georgians, and on the west by the Swanny. It is impossible to recapitulate here the opinions that have been enunciated by various authors on the history of so interesting a people as the Ossets; many are agreed that the Ossets and the Iron are the same, and have maintained that the Iron or the Ossets and the Alains or Alans, were identical, while others have undertaken to prove that the Alains or Alans, the As, Osses, were entirely distinct from the Iron or Ossets. There is at any rate a remarkable concurrence of evidence which leads to the inference, that the Ossets of our times are descended from and still inhabit the same parts as were peopled anciently by the Alains or Alans.

About the earliest mention of the Alans is made by Josephus, who tells us that they dwelt on the shores of the Lake Mæotis, whence, passing through the 'iron gates,' they fell upon the Medes and plundered their country, and having entered Armenia, lay all waste before them.[1] A similar account is given in the history of Armenia, where we read that in the reign of Artaces III., 72–120 A.D., the Alains,[2] who lived to the north of the Caucasus, passed through the defile of that mountain, and having conquered Iberia, entered Armenia. Artaces defeated them, and they were compelled to retire across the Cyrus.[3]

The irruptions of the Alains into Asia Minor are mentioned by

[1] Joseph., *Wars. &c.*, VII., vii. 4.
[2] In the annals of Georgia they are styled Osses.
[3] Saint Martin, *Mém. sur l'Arménie*, i. p. 300.

Arrian, whose duty it was, as Prefect of Cappadocia, to defend the eastern provinces of the Roman Empire against those barbarians.[1] The historian of the fourth century[2] calls the Alains, Messagetæ, who peopled Scythia east of the Tanaïs ; they were said to be a fine race, of goodly stature, and with fair hair ; they delighted in the dangers attending warlike expeditions, and those among them were reputed great who chanced to fall by the hand of an enemy—a manner of meeting death that up to the latest times was considered the most glorious among the Ossets. According to Herodotus, the Messagetæ inhabited Mount Caucasus and made war upon Cyrus whom they slew.[3]

In the fifth century the Osses invaded Georgia, when they were repulsed by Vakhtang, *Gourgasal*.

Procopius distinctly refers to the Alans as holding the territory between Mount Caucasus and the Caspian gates, and for their better identification, makes mention of a people called the Brouhy as being between the Alans and Abhases.[4]

The conversion to Christianity of the Alans or Osses was effected in the reign of Justinian, but they afterwards abjured their new faith, dismissing their bishops and priests. The kingdom of the Alans at that time was next to Serir,[5] the chief town of which was Houmradj, possibly the Hemry of to-day on the river Hemry-ouzỹn in Daghestan. After the accession of Queen Thamar to the throne, Christianity was for the second time introduced into Ossety, the people again relapsing into paganism and Mahomedanism.

[1] *Handbuch der alten Geographie*, Forbiger, Leipsic, 1842, i. p. 424.
[2] Amm. Marcell. xxxiii., xxxi.
[3] Herod. I.   [4] Procop. *De bell. Goth.* iv. 3, 4
[5] By Serir the Arabs meant the country of Thrun, which was situated on the north-west of Derbend. *Derbend nameh*, translated from a select Turkish version, with notes, &c., Mirza A. Kazem Beg. St. Petersburg, 1851, p. 200.

We are next reminded that Sviatoslaff, the conqueror of Tmoutorakan (Taman), subdued the Kassogues and the Yasses in 966; in the former we recognise the Tcherkess or Cossacks, and in the latter the As, Osses, or Alains; and when in 1116, Yaropolk the third son of Vladimir Monomachus, made war against the Polovtsy on the banks of the Don and took three of their cities, there were many Yasses among his captives; to one of whom, a female of exquisite beauty, he himself became wedded.[1]

According to Edrissi, the Arabian geographer, 1099-1165, the Alains had a fortified town named Aksinia (?) at a distance of 150 miles from Roussia (Taman?), twenty miles from Aksala (?) which was near the coast, and twenty miles from Istiberia (?) a busy and well-built seaport town.[2]

Some Alains were met at Kerim (Esky-Crim), the chief city in Crim Tartary, by the ambassadors of the sultan Bioars, 1260-77,[3] and we read of there still being in that peninsula *Gothic et aliqui Alani*, circa 1333, as reported by the Venetian traveller Marino Sanutor.[4]

Giovanni dal Piano di Carpine, a Franciscan monk who was the bearer in 1245 of a conciliatory letter from Innocent IV. to Batou the Khan of the Great Horde, makes mention in the interesting relation of his mission, of the Alans or Assy and of the Circassians, as being neighbours;[5] and Rubruquis[6] a few years later, describes the habitations of the Cherkis (Tcherkess) and of the Alani or Aas, as being on the slopes of the great mountains in the Caucasus; beyond them were the Lesgi, and next to the Lesgi

[1] Karamsin, i. p. 214, ii. p. 191.
[2] *Géog. d'Edrisi*, trans. Jaubert, 1836, ii. p. 399.
[3] Quatremère by Makrisi, 1845, i. 213, 218.
[4] M. S. Kunstman, 105.
[5] *Recueil, &c.*, iv. vii. 2; ix. 1.
[6] *Recueil, &c.*, iv. p. 243, 246 *et seq.*

the 'iron gates,'[1] which, through misapprehension, he attributes to Alexander of Macedon, who raised them for the purpose of excluding the barbarians from Persia. The monk further records having met at Scacatay some Alans, or Aas as they were called by the Tatars, who were Christians of the Greek Church, with whom he offered up prayers for the dead. When Rubruquis was among the Alans in their own mountains, he found many that were armourers, who wrought excellent weapons, a quality inherited by the Ossets—the makers of most of the arms with which the people in the Caucasus are provided.

At about this period the Alans or Yasses secured the alliance of the Kiptchaks, and sought to arrest the Mongols in their onward march of conquest and devastation, but they were defeated,

[1] A Russian traveller makes the following observations in reference to the great wall of Derbent in which were the 'iron gates,' of which so few details are possessed : ' The great wall of Derbent, so far as it is known to Russian topographers, extends to the mountain of Koushan-dagh in the district of Kasy-koumouh' in the province of Daghestan. The farther from the city, the better is its preservation, and its extraordinary windings are consequent upon the formation of the mountains. There are forty-three fortifications over a distance of 80 *versts*, and it was to one of these defences that Kazy mullah * purposed withdrawing, but was deterred from so doing by the difficulty of obtaining water. Trees have grown to a great size on some parts of the wall, and rent it asunder ; in other places villages have risen over the ruins ; no inscriptions have been found, but it is said that an ancient gate remains in perfect preservation near the village of Lydjyly, 36 *versts* from Derbent. Mahomedan writers have maintained that the great wall was erected by Nashervan † the Just, a statement that cannot be questioned, for such a gigantic work could only have been undertaken by a powerful monarch. Writers of antiquity do not mention this wall, and its construction must therefore belong to a more recent period ; that the Arabians found it completed is further evidence that it was constructed by the Sassanides, and the appellation of the wall of Alexander, like the Yadjudge and Madjudge, must have reference to the eastern shores of the Caspian.

' According to Oriental chroniclers, forts were erected along the wall at short distances from each other ; they had iron gates and were filled with soldiers ; if it be true that the

* Kazy mullah, the companion and firm friend of Schamyl, was the first imaum of the *mourshids*, fanatic 'disciples' in Daghestan ; he fell at Goumry when that fastness was attacked by the Russians under General the Baron Rosen.

† Chosroes.

losing their city Dediakoff to the Khan Mangou, who had compelled the Russians to unite their forces to his own in an expedition against that people in 1276. The As who, according to Aboulfeda, occupied Kyrkyer (Tchyfout Kaleh), were in all probability the countrymen of the As met by Piano di Carpine and Rubruquis in North Caucasus, and identical with the Yasses, rather than the descendants of the Alans who had established themselves in the Tauric peninsula before the great immigration of the Germanic races.

The Ossets are a remarkable people in the history of nations. Isolated as they are in the centre of the mountains of the Caucasus, in the midst of populations with whom they have no affinity, they appear to be the only connecting link between the Indo-Persian branch and the European branch of the great Indo-Germanic race.[1]

The natives of this district call themselves Assett, rather than Osset, and their country Assety, rather than Ossety. The latter wall is 400 *versts* (266 miles) in length, as stated by the natives, its termination may be placed near the river Alazan.* The people of Derbent say that the hour of prayer used to be communicated along this wall.'

The fortress of Derbent was taken by General Zoboff after ten days' bombardment, on May 10, 1796.

See *Derbend-Nameh*, p. 196, for the wall of Derbent. 'After Iscander (Alexander) it was Anushirvan who conquered this mountain, took possession of it, and fortified it all with numerous warriors, and it was he who built over the gates or a. the fronts of the difficult passages of the *mountain of victory*,† three hundred and sixty seats (or fortifications) bordering on the dominions of the Khozars.'

[1] For a historical and ethnological account of the Ossets, see *Tableau historique de l'Asie*, Paris 1824, pp. 48, 176, and *Note sur l'identité des Ossètes avec les Allains*, by M. Klaproth, in *Voyages, etc.* : du Comte J. Potocki, 1829, ii. p. 328 ; also Dubois, iv. pp. 320-407.

* The river Alazan courses through Kakhety, and unites with the Kour in the government of Elyzavetopol.

† Name given to the mountains bordering on the territory of the Khozars, for the possession of them gave dominion over the Persians, Turks, and Arabs.

terms have been employed as being in sufficiently close affinity, and because they are the more familiar.

The population of Ossety is estimated at 65,000, of which number 50,000 are said to be Christians.

WOMEN OF OSSETY.

www.ingramcontent.com/pod-product-compliance
Lightning Source LLC
Chambersburg PA
CBHW021203230426
43667CB00006B/528